H. Richard Niebuhr

H. RICHARD NIEBUHR

Theology, History, and Culture:
Major Unpublished Writings

Edited by William Stacy Johnson

Foreword by Richard R. Niebuhr

YALE UNIVERSITY PRESS   NEW HAVEN AND LONDON

Designed by Sally Harris/Summer Hill Books.
Set in Baskerville type by
Rainsford Type, Danbury, Connecticut.
Printed in the United States of America by BookCrafters,
Inc., Chelsea, Michigan.

Library of Congress Cataloging-in-Publication Data

Niebuhr, H. Richard (Helmut Richard), 1894–1962.
Theology, history, and culture:major unpublished writings / H. Richard Niebuhr;
edited by William Stacy Johnson; foreword by Richard R. Niebuhr.
p. cm.
Includes bibliographical references and index.
ISBN 0-300-06370-9 (cloth : alk. paper)
0-300-07437-9 (pbk. : alk. paper)
1. Theology. I. Johnson, William Stacy. II. Title.
BR85.N615 1996
230—dc20   95-22557   CIP

A catalogue record for this book is available from the British Library.

The paper in this book meets the guidelines for
permanence and durability of the Committee on
Production Guidelines for Book Longevity of the
Council on Library Resources.

10 9 8 7 6 5 4 3 2

Contents

v

CONTENTS

PART III. CULTURE

5. Religion and the Democratic Tradition

6. Sermons

Foreword

This volume presents eighteen previously unpublished essays and lectures by H. Richard Niebuhr. Since HRN was not only a teacher and author but also minister to various congregations in his lifetime and preached regularly in Yale Divinity School's Marquand Chapel as well as at various commencements and ordinations, it also offers the complete texts of three of his sermons, which are representative both of his personal faith and of his preaching style. (The greater number of his extant sermons are in annotated outline form only.) Selecting the particular writings to be included in this book has been an exacting task, requiring much time, much deliberation, and consultations spanning several years. This book would not, in fact, have come to be at all, were it not for the initiative, dedication, discipline, and discerning intelligence of its editor, Professor William Stacy Johnson of Austin Presbyterian Theological Seminary. I owe to Stacy Johnson an inestimable debt.

In his introduction, Stacy Johnson has carefully located each of the chosen pieces in the immediate context of its composition and/or presentation as well as in the larger context of HRN's working life at Yale Divinity School. Hence, these selections require no further comment from me. One or two of my personal recollections and several recorded remarks by the author himself may be of interest to readers. The earliest in time of our selections, "Theology in a Time of Disillusionment," dates, as Johnson explains, from the author's first year of teaching at Yale. Only a little while before, our family had traveled in its old Chevrolet the narrow highways from St. Louis eastward and crossed the Great Smoky Mountains on twisting roads of endless hairpin curves to visit my grandmother Lydia Hosto Niebuhr at Black Mountain, east of Asheville, North Carolina. After that visit, we swung northward to New Haven, Connecticut, and Yale. In the ensuing years we made frequent automobile trips back to the Midwest. Evidences of the devastating Great Depression were then everywhere recognizable. Most conspicuous were the homeless men trudging along the roadsides, asking for whatever food and milk we might spare from the midday picnic meals we spread along the verge of the asphalt roads. In 1931, Yale's Divinity School was still located on Elm Street, bordering New Haven's beautiful green. The school sat more or less diagonally across from the old freshmen campus. The university's nearby undergraduate residential colleges, with their imposing Gothic architecture, and its cathedral-like Sterling Library made an oasis of almost medieval grandeur in a setting otherwise considerably more prosaic save for the magnificent elm trees arching over many of the city's broad avenues. Those trees have, of course, long since disappeared.

In those early years of the 1930s, I sensed though scarcely comprehended my father's increasing apprehension at what he described as the "class crucifixion" (not "a class struggle as Marx believed," he noted, "but . . . a class crucifixion, as Christ demonstrated")[1] then taking place in our unhappy country and at the growing social and political turmoil he had personally witnessed in Germany as well as at the ominous significance of the Japanese army's occupation of Manchuria. In the immediately succeeding years, as the Second World War drew nearer and American isolationism grew stronger, he pondered the nature of American democracy, especially the writings of the Federalists, and the relations between Christianity and democracy. At least two of the essays in this volume are the issue of such reflections. He filled his shelves with volumes on the Civil War and read deeply in the histories of Lincoln and Lee and Grant and of the causes of the conflict between North and South, which he, like so many others, perceived as a defining moment in the life of this nation. His Taylor Lectures, published in 1941 as *The Meaning of Revelation,* directly allude to that defining event.

Another enduring focus of his thought was the manifest tension—sometimes marked by acrimony—between the so-called liberal theologians and the so-called neo-orthodox. It is not uncommon even today to find his name ranked among the latter. But while his essay "The Idea of Original Sin in American Culture" exhibits his realism about the fact that human beings have always and will always abuse whatever power they may acquire, it also shows how uncomfortable he was with the theological tendency, then so pronounced, to make the doctrine of original sin into the first article of orthodox Protestantism's creed. Now I know, as I did not before, that even well before arriving at Yale he had grown weary of the contentiousness of theological parties and expressed his distaste for it. "The great political game of 'Power, power, who gets the power?' is attracting Christians now as it has done before. Capitalists, fascists, proletarians, agriculturalists, industrialists, intelligentsia all have their ambitions and delusions. The Christian revolutionary intelligentsia are among the worst. They are persuaded of their own disinterestedness and how they would love to wield power for the sake of their brothers. But how can they believe that they will be uncontaminated by the exercise of power when they look at the past[?]" HRN could align himself neither with those who defended what he then called "religion within the bounds of pure divinity" nor with those who espoused "religion within the bounds of pure humanity." The one, he noted, exhibits "mysticism without ethics"; the other, "ethics without mysticism."

In the mid-1930s he was also engaged in thinking through his own idea of theology and in laying the foundations of what he would later publish. He jotted down several propositions partly summarizing the "main motifs" of his theological thinking. Among these are (1) "Confessionalism is the proper method in theology. We must report what happened to us and not pretend to have a system that starts at rock-bottom." To this he added, (2) "God is pure act. He is living, creating, judging, redeeming now"; (3) "Life is togetherness. Being with something & somebody. Rationalism, idealism, realism are abstractions. Life & mind are interchange"; and (4) "Christian life is constant response to God." To these maxims he then appended the following musings: "These seem the main ideas. But how can I get them together, in one system? What is the starting point? It must be God as pure act, but in that case how [to] bring in the rest?"

It will not surprise some readers that a constant companion for HRN throughout the thirties, forties, and fifties was Jonathan Edwards. Unlike many of this century's so-called neo-orthodox, Edwards did not make original sin nor the infinite qualitative difference between creator and creature the operative first article of his creed, though certainly he took the doctrine of sin as seriously as any theologian has. The first article, for Edwards, was that the glory of God is the ultimate end of creation, and he was as capable as any theologian of describing its beauty as a mirror of God's beauty, while also remaining realistic about human nature. To be sure, HRN disagreed with Edwards on many points, one of them being the latter's "purchase" theory of atonement. But as witness to their underlying affinity, we have what HRN wrote about Edwards in his 1937 book, *The Kingdom of God in America*, and, there are some lines he wrote to me in March 1958. "Today I'm working on an address to be given at the Jonathan Edwards bicentennial at Northampton tomorrow. I'm enjoying working on the job, but also frustrated. One would need to believe in God with the wholehearted-ness, the absolute surrender of JE himself to speak rightly about him in the right context. I am a petty believer alongside him and an undisciplined one. But I feel nearer to him as theologian than to any others except for Luther & Calvin & maybe Augustine. Except for the problem of demythologizing his hell I can take him almost straight."

At some point not far from the end of his life, HRN wrote out a conviction that in fact runs throughout much of what he said publicly; it is a fitting thought for the conclusion of this foreword. "Sometimes every one who has taught through spoken and written words needs to look back on his activity with the question, What has been the intention of my work? Not, What did I intend? I always intended something very specific—to gain clarity or give some clarity about this point or that—to satisfy my curiosity about some puzzle—to understand some relationship. I have had and have intentions but what does all the work taken together intend? This is Kierkegaard's question in *Point of View for my Work as an Author*.... What was the intention behind all my intentions, the fundamental intention which I represented rather than willed, the thing to which I was committed rather than committed myself? In unbelief I call that intention fate—what was I fated to do—in confidence I call it divine governance."

My last word here is one of deep gratitude to L. Charles Willard, Librarian of the Andover-Harvard Theological Library and member of the Faculty of Divinity of Harvard University, for his generous, scrupulous, and imaginative care of the papers of H. Richard Niebuhr that lie in the archives of the Divinity School.

Richard R. Niebuhr

Introduction

The influence of H. Richard Niebuhr on twentieth-century theology has been long-lasting and profound. This may surprise those who have come to think of theology as primarily a matter of "doctrine." In the narrow sense of creedal formulas, doctrine was never the primary focus for H. Richard Niebuhr. Niebuhr fits much more readily into Karl Barth's category of the "irregular" or "occasional" theologians, that vast majority of theologians for whom what matters most is not the system-building of dogmatic treatises but the application of theological insight to the pressing problems of the day, whose highest work is not creating a *summa* for all time but speaking an intelligible word for *this* time. For this reason, in his first major address at Yale Divinity School in 1931, Niebuhr called upon his colleagues to pursue a "theology of the present moment." By this he meant not a theology cognizant of the latest fads, but one that looks expectantly for the activity of God in all the ambiguous circumstances of the present day. Theology was to be a ceaseless dialogue, a pilgrimage with neither resting place nor end. It was to be a "permanent revolution" of heart and mind, a continual imperative to think of all of life in relation to the ultimate and to apply that vision to the transformation of life in all its aspects—to politics and economics as well as to church and academy. The doctrinal content of this vision is tested in the living. In this sense we may say of Niebuhr, as was said of his great eighteenth-century guide Jonathan Edwards, that his doctrine was all application and his application all doctrine.

This collection of Niebuhr's previously unpublished lectures, essays, sermons, and addresses gives evidence of this integration of theology and practical living and testifies to the author's broad-ranging interests. Many of these pieces were delivered at major universities before cross-disciplinary audiences. Others were prepared for presentation and discussion at professional groups or for circulation among the company of his colleagues. The themes are diverse, some referring to contemporaneous events, some to significant religious figures, some to important issues in theology, and some are, in effect, interpretations of American history and culture. As in his published writings, he here enlists into the task of theological reflection the disciplines of philosophical anthropology, symbol theory, value theory, and the philosophy of history and culture. Because of the breadth of issues addressed, this volume will serve both to enrich the understanding of those already familiar with Niebuhr's concerns and to recommend Niebuhr's reflections to those approaching his work for the first time.

Niebuhr's Life and Work

Helmut Richard Niebuhr was born the son of Gustav and Lydia Hosto Niebuhr in Wright City, Missouri, on September 3, 1894.[1] Gustav Niebuhr, a pastor of the German Evangelical Synod of North America, immigrated to the United States in 1878 at the age of seventeen. Lydia Hosto was American-born, the daughter of German immigrants, and her father was a pastor with whom Gustav had worked as a young man. Richard was the youngest of five children. Two of Niebuhr's older siblings were theologians and leaders of the church in their own right. Reinhold Niebuhr was doubtless the most famous American theologian of his generation, a distinguished pastor for thirteen years in Detroit and, from 1928 until his retirement in 1960, a professor of Christian ethics and applied Christianity at Union Theological Seminary in New York. Hulda Niebuhr was a church educator and, from 1946 until her death in 1959, a professor of Christian education at McCormick Theological Seminary in Chicago.

In 1908 at the age of fourteen, H. Richard Niebuhr entered Elmhurst College, an institution affiliated with the Evangelical Synod and located just outside Chicago. In those days Elmhurst was more a secondary school than a college. Niebuhr graduated in 1912 (though without the bachelor's degree, since Elmhurst at that time was unaccredited) and then studied for three years at his denomination's professional school, Eden Theological Seminary in St. Louis, graduating in 1915. A major influence at Eden was Professor Samuel D. Press, the first American-born professor to teach there. Press had been a student of Adolf von Harnack and Reinhold Seeberg in Germany. In 1913, while Niebuhr was still a nineteen-year-old at Eden, his father died suddenly at the age of fifty. From 1915 to 1916 he worked as a newspaper reporter for his brother Walter in Lincoln, Illinois, where his father had once been pastor and where his mother had returned after her husband's death.

In 1916, at the age of twenty-two, Niebuhr was ordained to the ministry at Walnut Park Evangelical Church in St. Louis, a congregation he served for two years. When the United States entered World War I in 1917, Niebuhr enlisted as an army chaplain and underwent training; but before he could be sent overseas, the war ended.

In 1919, Niebuhr was called by his former teacher, Samuel Press, who was by then Eden's president, to join the faculty and teach theology and ethics. He held this position for three years, during which time, in June 1920, he married Florence Marie Mittendorf, whom he had met some years earlier in the Lincoln, Illinois, parish.

As a young man, Niebuhr pursued his education at every available turn. While serving the Walnut Park congregation, he began attending Washington University in St. Louis and, in June 1917, earned an M.A. in German, philosophy, and psychology. He wrote a master's thesis entitled "The Problem of the Individual in Richard Dehmel." Dehmel was a nineteenth-century German poet. In spring 1919, Niebuhr enrolled at Union Theological Seminary and at Columbia University in New York, but that educational opportunity was cut short by the welcome call to come to Eden.[2] While at Eden, he enrolled in summer courses first at the University of Michigan and later at the University of Chicago. In 1922, the desire for learning still strong within him, Niebuhr decided to pursue graduate work in earnest—this time, at Yale Divinity School. There, he was influenced by the religious empiricist and value theorist D.C. Macintosh and the New Testament professor Frank Porter. While also serving as a minister in Clinton, Connecticut, he earned a B.D. and a Ph.D. His dissertation, directed by Macintosh, was entitled "Ernst Troeltsch's Philosophy of Religion." The intellectual influence of Troeltsch was to remain pervasive in much of Niebuhr's writing.[3]

Upon leaving Yale in 1924, at the age of thirty, Niebuhr was invited to become the president of Elmhurst. He served for three years, during which time the college increased its endowment and advanced toward accreditation. In 1927 he was asked to return to Eden as its academic dean. Niebuhr's second tenure at Eden lasted four years and culminated in his first book, *The Social Sources of Denominationalism* (1929). Employing Ernst Troeltsch's typology of "church" and "sect," he traced the career of the denominations in America and concluded that denominational affinities are driven more by socioeconomic considerations than by genuine theological differences.[4] During spring and summer 1930, he was awarded an eight-month sabbatical to study in Germany. Richard and his family spent most of their time in Tübingen and Frankfurt. They were joined by Reinhold Niebuhr, and toward the end of their stay the brothers left Berlin for Russia, on a two-week excursion sponsored by Sherwood Eddy, a wealthy church leader and a longtime colleague of Reinhold's. During this trip, Richard Niebuhr published a number of reports on life in Germany and in Russia.[5]

Upon his return from Europe, there awaited Niebuhr an invitation to join the faculty at Yale Divinity School. Though somewhat reluctant to leave Eden, he finally accepted and began as an associate professor of Christian ethics in the fall semester of 1931. He became a full professor in 1938 and later occupied the prestigious Sterling Chair of Theology and Christian Ethics. During his thirty years at Yale, he was a revered and influential teacher. Along with Roland Bainton, Robert L. Calhoun, and Albert Outler, Niebuhr made Yale Divinity School a formidable intellectual and religious center.

In the early years at Yale, Niebuhr soon became identified with the so-called neo-orthodox or new-Reformation theological movement.[6] In contrast to the liberalism of the nineteenth century, which had emphasized autonomy, progress, and accommodation to culture, the neo-orthodox theologians seized upon the sovereignty and mystery of God, the pervasiveness of human sin, the elemental need for conversion and grace, and, concomitantly, the necessity for a radical criticism of the pretensions of Western culture. As early as 1929, Niebuhr had expressed a guarded appreciation for these neo-orthodox convictions. The 1935 book he and co-authors Wilhelm Pauck and F. P. Miller wrote, *The Church Against the World*, with its call for "the liberation of the church from its bondage to a corrupt civilization," was seen by many as a clear endorsement of neo-orthodoxy.[7] Indeed, early on he had read the bellwether of this new movement, Karl Barth, with particular fascination. The second edition of Barth's *Römerbrief* had gained its author fame throughout Europe. Niebuhr's own German edition of the *Römerbrief* was well worn and generously marked.[8] Moreover, in 1962, just before his death, Niebuhr would list Barth's Romans commentary as one of the ten most important books in shaping his own intellectual outlook.[9] Still, from the very beginning Niebuhr maintained a critical distance from neo-orthodoxy, and especially from its Barthian forms, which Niebuhr saw as reducing theology to the dogmatic assertion of biblical revelation.

Although he had been stimulated by Barth's voice, Niebuhr in the early 1930s was inspired even more by Paul Tillich's "belief-ful realism." He had heard Tillich lecture during his time in Frankfurt. In 1932 he published a translation of Tillich's *Die religiöse Lage der Gegenwart* (1926); the title was *The Religious Situation*.[10] Tillich later credited Niebuhr's translation with making possible Tillich's move to the United States in 1933.[11] Niebuhr was echoing Tillich when he concluded his 1931 Yale Alumni Lecture, "Theology in a Time of Disillusionment" (published here for the first time), by calling upon theologians to focus on the act of God in the present moment. "What is God doing in the world?" would become the guiding question for Niebuhr. As he later stated in *The Responsible Self* (posthumously published in 1963): "God is acting in all actions upon you. So respond to all actions upon you as to respond to [God's] action."[12] Thus, his admonitions in the 1930s about the need for a strategic withdrawal or disengagement from culture—whether theologically, as in *The Church Against the World*, or politically, as in his call for nonintervention during the Manchurian crisis in 1932—were made not for sectarian reasons of world-denial but for the sake of an ever more serious engagement with the world. What Niebuhr in the 1930s called "radical faith," or in the 1950s "radical monotheism," was the belief that selves encounter God in all events, and that reality should be interpreted and transformed according to the purposes of God.

In the 1930s, Niebuhr also became engrossed in the important texts of the American theological tradition. In 1937 he published *The Kingdom of God in America*, a work that exhibited with stunning clarity the sweep of his reading during these years.[13] *The Kingdom of God in America* was destined to become a classic in American historiography. It spanned three centuries of American religious history—its revivalisms, its millennialisms, its establishment figures, and its dissenters—interpreting mainstream religious faith in America, or what Niebuhr called "constructive Protestantism," as keyed to a radical faith in the dynamic reign of God. The central irony was that because of the dynamism it espoused, and because of its focus on the need for continual reformation, "constructive Protestantism" led inevitably in directions it could neither predict nor control. Although this dynamic openendedness was altogether fitting, it had also helped create in Niebuhr's own day the dilemma of mainline religion: By succumbing to a moribund liberalism in the nineteenth century, it had lost all vitality. Under liberalism, "a God without wrath brought men without sin into a kingdom without judgment through the ministrations of a Christ without a cross."[14]

In 1941, Niebuhr published another classic text, his best if not his best known, *The Meaning of Revelation*. In this book, which comprised the 1940 Nathaniel W. Taylor Lectures at Yale, he saw himself combining the critical perspectives of Ernst Troeltsch with the constructive designs of Karl Barth.[15] If historical study is beset by relativism, as Troeltsch had insisted, then how can a revelation of the divine be said to occur in history? Niebuhr's answer was to convert the supposed vice of relativism into a virtue. The historical relativity championed by Troeltsch leads not to theology's demise, as some charged, but to its fresh beginnings. A proper appreciation of relativity legitimates, even necessitates a theological beginning that is resolutely confessional and non-defensive, a beginning launched from the only place one *can* begin: from the historical point of view of one's own religious heritage. So far this sounds very similar to Troeltsch, but there is more. Like Barth, Niebuhr believes that divine revelation is a disclosure of God's own self (rather than mere information about God), a disclosure that calls religion itself into question. He is also aware of the transforming power of revelation in shaping Christian identity anew in the present moment. Christian identity comes from appropriating afresh the biblical narrative as the dynamic, revelatory story of one's own life. Revelation, therefore, is always performing the role of an occasionally luminous sentence in an otherwise obscure or difficult book. Through it, one gradually gains a new understanding of the whole, so that revelation functions as the "intelligible event which makes all other events intelligible."[16]

This definition of revelation holds in tension two impulses that run throughout Niebuhr's writings and the writings of his students. On the one hand, the revelatory story is "irreplaceable and untranslatable," meaning that there is a certain "givenness" to the "internal history" of one's own tradition. On the other hand, the story demands what Niebuhr termed the "permanent revolution of heart and mind," meaning that the "givenness" of tradition is never beyond challenge. It is challenged from without, from the "external history" of observers, by those with at least one foot outside the tradition. In the process of appropriating the realities of internal and external history, one comes to have one's own parochial vision enlarged, until finally one sees one's own place in "internal" history only in relation to the universal history of all people. In short, Niebuhr's vision expresses a longing for the ongoing transformation of life, both in one's perspective and in one's way of living.

The transformation Niebuhr envisioned within the church was meant to extend into the public sphere. Permanent revolution in theology implied permanent revolution politically as well. For some time Niebuhr was a member of the Socialist Party and even ran once, unsuccessfully, for a school-board position. Along with Reinhold Niebuhr, he was active in the Fellowship of Socialist Christians, whose purpose was to express social Christianity in ways independent of pacifism and Marxism. He eventually resigned from the Socialist Party in 1936 and supported Franklin Roosevelt. But he never simply accepted the "givenness" of the reigning social and economic structure in America. The American attitude toward the war during the years 1939 to 1945, for instance, was of particular concern to Niebuhr. In a war that involved obliteration bombing and other atrocities, Niebuhr was critical of pacifists and just-war theorists alike, for neither seemed to him sufficiently attentive to the ambivalence and the nightmare of war. If the Allied cause was to be endorsed in World War II, it was only reluctantly, as a compromise, and not on the pretentious basis of a so-called just war. So severe were the war years for Niebuhr that in October 1944, shortly after his fiftieth birthday, he checked himself into a hospital for treatment of depression, and he stayed for two months. When the war ended and some were hoping for a "just and durable peace," Niebuhr once commented, "The best we can hope for is a *just endurable* peace."[17]

In the postwar years, Niebuhr continued to develop his stance that all culture must be transformed. In 1949 he delivered a series of lectures at Austin Presbyterian Theological Seminary; they were published in 1951 as *Christ and Culture.*[18] In this his most familiar book, he significantly reinterpreted Ernst Troeltsch's typology of "church" and "sect," expanding it into a pattern of five types. Over against the "sect" type that withdraws from the world and situates itself "against culture," he proposed an opposite, "of culture" type that completely accommodates culture. Troeltsch's "church" type he then divided into the three forms of the "church of the center": the "above culture" types or "synthesists" (Thomas Aquinas and Roman Catholicism), the "paradox" types or "dualists" (Martin Luther and Reinhold Niebuhr), and the "transformationists" (Augustine, John Calvin, and F. D. Maurice). It was the transformationist perspective to which Niebuhr himself aspired.

From 1952 to 1957 he continued to work on the question of faith and culture, construing faith through "confidence" and "loyalty." With the McCarthy hearings—and their loyalty tests—the Cold War, and the Korean War as a background, Niebuhr argued that the more active side of faith, loyalty, can be sustained only if there also exists a framework of support to nourish the more receptive and passive side of faith, confidence. Here again, theological convictions and political commitments must converge. To have faith in God, one must believe that God is powerful enough to engender confidence and good enough to merit loyalty.[19] Similarly, without the interaction of loyalty and confidence, a democratic society cannot long endure.

Niebuhr intended to publish these reflections in a book to be titled "Faith on Earth: Essays on Human Confidence and Loyalty." In the end, only a portion of the overall project was published during his life, the Montgomery Lectures on Contemporary Civilization, which he gave in 1957 at the University of Nebraska. Published in 1960 as *Radical Monotheism and Western Culture,* these lectures challenged "polytheism" (many gods) and "henotheism" (a nationalistic god). They advocated instead "radical monotheism," which calls all forms of cultural life to accountability and faithfulness before the one, true God.[20] The remaining segments, those pertaining to the meaning of faith, were published only posthumously.[21]

From 1954 to 1956, Niebuhr assumed the leadership, in collaboration with Daniel Day Williams and James M. Gustafson, of an intensive study of theological education in North America. This study resulted in three books: *The Purpose of the Church and Its Ministry*, by Niebuhr alone; *The Ministry in Historical Perspectives*, a book of essays edited by Niebuhr and Williams; and *The Advancement of Theological Education*, by all three men.[22] The insights coming out of this work continue to influence theological education.

Throughout the 1950s, Niebuhr was engaged in serious reflections on the changes he believed were needed in theology. These reflections culminated in the lecture series entitled "Next Steps in Theology," presented as the Cole Lectures at Vanderbilt University in 1961. The Cole Lectures are published in the present volume for the first time. In the early sixties, Niebuhr was planning a comprehensive work on Christian ethics, a project he had postponed until after retirement. Death intervened, and the work that would have crowned his lifetime of labor as an ethicist was never completed.[23] In pursuit of that goal, however, Niebuhr did write significantly about moral selfhood. In spring 1960, Niebuhr delivered the Robertson Lectures at the University of Glasgow (the series was entitled "The Responsible Self"), abbreviated versions of which were repeated at Cambridge University and at the University of Bonn.[24] He presented similar materials in 1962 as the Earl Lectures at the Pacific School of Religion.

On July 5, 1962, Niebuhr died suddenly of a heart attack at his summer home in Rowe, Massachusetts, at the age of sixty-seven. The Robertson Lectures and portions of the Earl Lectures were published as *The Responsible Self* in 1963. Niebuhr's manuscripts on faith, which required much more extensive editing, were published by Yale University Press in 1989 as *Faith on Earth: An Inquiry into the Structure of Human Faith*. Both books were edited by his son, Richard R. Niebuhr. The remaining unpublished papers have for some time now been housed in the Archives of the Andover-Harvard Theological Library at Harvard Divinity School. The library at Yale Divinity School has a few duplicate documents on file. These unpublished manuscripts have long been available to scholars, and some occasional pieces from among them have been published in journals.[25] Shortly after his death, a projected volume of Niebuhr's essays, sermons, and other writings was promised by Richard R. Niebuhr. Now, with the publication of the present volume, that promise is fulfilled.

Niebuhr's Unpublished Manuscripts

This volume presents the best of H. Richard Niebuhr's unpublished addresses, essays, and sermons.[26] Part I focuses on theology. It includes three of the 1961 Cole Lectures (on the nature of theological reflection) and two pieces, one of which was published in Niebuhr's lifetime, addressing the problem of the church's relation to the world especially in light of the modern ecumenical movement. The subject of Part II is the interpretation of history. Three of these selections approach their topic more or less theoretically; the other four are actual interpretations of pivotal figures or events. In Part III, the topic is the relation of religious faith to culture. Three of the essays contain remarks on religion and democratic society, including reflections on the nature of war. The book concludes with three sermons selected from among the many delivered at various times during Niebuhr's thirty-year career at Yale.

Part I. Theology

THE COLE LECTURES: "NEXT STEPS IN THEOLOGY" Towards the end of his career, Niebuhr complained that neo-orthodoxy had gone far enough. The neo-orthodox corrections to liberalism, having served their purpose, were turning into hyper-corrections. This concern prompted the question posed in the Cole Lectures, namely, what should be the next steps in theology?

The Cole Lectures were delivered at Vanderbilt University in April 1961.[27] The first three lectures are the opening selections in the present volume. Niebuhr thought of them as the "old man's" last bequest to a younger generation of theological students.

The opening lecture, "The Position of Theology Today," explores the need for striking a new theological balance, as illustrated through a discussion of three polar relations: past and present, self and other, and thought and action. First, in order to contest the neo-orthodox overemphasis on the past versus the present, Niebuhr felt the time was ripe to make two countermoves: to reevaluate the heritage of Friedrich Schleiermacher, in hopes of avoiding a new repristination of Protestant orthodoxy; and to redirect theology's gaze toward the future, by means of a more eschatological focus. Both of these suggested countermoves have come to fruition in our day, as seen in the resurgence of nineteenth-century studies in general and Schleiermacher studies in particular, and in the emergence of the eschatological theology of hope, though the latter's ambiguous view of creation would have given Niebuhr some pause.[28] Second, in considering the imbalance caused by neo-orthodoxy's one-sided focus on the objective revelation of God—an instance of the polarity of self and other—Niebuhr thought that human experience should receive a renewed emphasis. Third, the neo-orthodox passion for knowing God—representing one side of the polarity of thought and action—should not be allowed to obscure the equally pressing need for moral obedience. The neo-orthodox revitalization of theology, that is to say, should not occur at the expense of liberalism's traditional concentration on ethics. Through these three polar relationships, then, Niebuhr sought to demonstrate that theological balance was a perpetual necessity.

Something more was needed, however, than a mere rebalancing of priorities. The second Cole Lecture challenges theologians to move toward new symbols. What is one to do, asks the author, when traditional religious symbols lose their vitality? This loss may occur in two ways. Symbols either replace the reality to which they refer—for example, the stigmatization of racism or the reduction of everything in life to a dollar value—or else become worn-out or monotonous. What is needed then is a "resymbolization." In *The Meaning of Revelation* he had spoken of interpreting one's world through the images, parables, and analogies drawn from revelatory experience. In the 1950s, Niebuhr considered the consequences of a religion that was no longer good enough.[29] Similarly in the Cole Lectures he asks how to go about reinhabiting a religious symbolism gone vacant.

In addition to a resymbolization of religious faith, Niebuhr also called for a reinvigoration of the religious affections. The third Cole Lecture, "Toward the Recovery of Feeling," contends that the needed symbolic reconstruction of theology is a concern not of the intellect alone but of the emotions. Symbols express and elicit emotions, which validate and invigorate symbols. Feeling is parsed symbolically, and symbol is mediated through feeling. Western society, argues Niebuhr, tends to denigrate the affective dimension of life as subjective, purely private and unverifiable. He himself in earlier writings had questioned a one-sidedly anthropocentric emphasis upon feeling.[30] In the Cole Lectures, however, he describes feeling as itself a kind of knowing, putting human beings in touch with something reliable, something real. He therefore calls upon theology to rethink its neglect of the religious affections, to validate the realm of feeling, and to map its uncharted terrain. Significantly, he praises Jonathan Edwards—that great American thinker who lives in the background of so much that Niebuhr wrote—as an exemplar in this enterprise. Were Niebuhr at the beginning rather than at the end of his theological career, he would "follow in Edwards's footsteps more."

The fourth Cole Lecture, which survives in a form too rough for publication, was entitled "Toward the Service of Christendom." In it, Niebuhr recognized that the West could no longer be viewed as a predominantly Christian society. Instead it had become a "post-Christian" world. The paradigm of "Christendom," regnant in the West since the days of Constantine in the fourth century C.E., had to be abandoned. Still, Jesus Christ is present in the post-Christian world, if only in memory. For both cultural and theological reasons, a simple division between church and world will not do. Niebuhr thought that a church proclaiming itself history's ultimate goal was a strange church indeed. Theology must situate its intellectual endeavor on that imprecise boundary of church and world, where the line "runs through every soul not between souls."[31] This sort of broad-mindedness caused him to seek a vision of God in relation to all of life.

AN ECUMENICAL VISION Niebuhr's faith in the one God led him to hope for the unity of the Christian church and of all people. While he was dean at Eden Theological Seminary, for example, he had conducted negotiations that eventually brought about the union of the Evangelical Synod and the German Reformed church. He contributed papers, moreover, at both the formation of the World Council of Churches in Amsterdam in 1948 and at its subsequent meeting in 1954 in Evanston, Illinois.[32] Niebuhr's concern as a theologian of ecumenical vision is revealed in the next two essays in the present volume.

"The Doctrine of the Trinity and the Unity of the Church" was first published in 1946 in *Theology Today*, a journal of Princeton Theological Seminary. It is reproduced here because of the important light it sheds on Niebuhr's thought and because it complements the previously unpublished piece that follows it, "The Church Defines Itself in the World." The trinitarian lens through which Niebuhr viewed the question of the church's life in the world was visible throughout his career. It was present in *The Kingdom of God in America* (1937), which had interpreted America's religious history as a succession of three one-sided but nevertheless essential ways of viewing the work of God in history: the sovereignty of God, the kingdom of Christ, and the coming of the kingdom. The trinitarian perspective also set the interpretive framework for *Christ and Culture* (1951), in which the central predicament of Christianity is the ethical task of relating Jesus Christ to its cultural environs and the theological problem of conceiving Jesus Christ in a unity-in-difference with God the Creator and God the Redeemer. The Trinity essay elaborates upon this persistent Niebuhrian (and classically orthodox) theme: the God who creates, who reconciles, and who sanctifies human life is one God. Niebuhr identifies three "unitarian" distortions of this radically monotheistic conviction, that is, deism, the Jesus cult, and spiritualism, each of which threatens the integrity of holistic Christian witness and of an integrated ecclesial life.

Niebuhr's relationship to the ecumenical movements of his day was both critical and constructive.[33] He believed ecumenism had its limits. The church is an emergent, eschatological reality, incapable of full attainment in this life. It is not to be identified with any visible institutional embodiment. The church's growth into community is subject to limits imposed by its character as institution.

An essay from the 1950s, "The Church Defines Itself in the World," ostensibly on the nature of theological definition, has as its context the search for church unity. Niebuhr observes that ecumenical movements tend to become overly preoccupied with the church's parochial concerns. As always, his perspective is theocentric in focus and trinitarian in shape. Against those who would urge the church simply to be the church, Niebuhr countered that the church must first determine to let God be God. Karl Barth's assessment—one cannot say God by saying "man" or "human being" in a loud voice—had Niebuhr's wholehearted agreement. He would have added, however, that neither can one say God by saying "church" in a loud voice.

Part II. History

THE MEANING OF HISTORY   Although H. Richard Niebuhr never considered himself a "guild" historian, the problem of how to interpret history was present in everything he wrote. Three of his books, *The Social Sources of Denominationalism*, *The Kingdom of God in America*, and *Christ and Culture*, are classics of historical interpretation. A fourth book, *The Meaning of Revelation*, is a classic of another type, demonstrating how the religious community engages in intelligible historical interpretation through faith. Niebuhr considered the problem of history in relation to theology so important that he offered a course at Yale entitled "The Christian Interpretation of History."[34] It is not surprising, then, that he left a number of essays on the nature of historical interpretation and on pivotal figures or movements.

What Niebuhr wrote in the preface to *The Kingdom of God in America* about the relation of history to theology is equally true of his own life's work: "The theology has grown out of the history as much as the history has grown out of the theology."[35] As a theologian, he sought to respond to God's presence in history: "God . . . is always in history; he is the structure of things, the source of all meaning, the 'I am that I am,' that which is that it is. He is the rock against which we beat in vain, that which bruises and overwhelms us when we seek to impose our wishes, contrary to his, upon him."[36] God is the ground that structures human possibilities and limits. In keeping with this conviction, one of the guideposts in Niebuhr's historiography was the Augustinian axiom "Whatever is, is good," though this of course did not mean "Whatever is, is right."[37] His perspective was not simply that of a stoic assenting to fate. He was not content to focus solely on the world as it is, as he sometimes accused his brother Reinhold of doing, but he looked for the world as it should be, the world reconstructed in the light of God's reign.

Niebuhr distinguished two ways of approaching history: the first focuses upon the realism of events; the second attends to the interpreter of events, especially the interpreter's place in a community of inquiry and the cultural patterns by which the interpreter comprehends history. As might be expected from one seeking a theology of the present moment, he thought of himself as an interpreter of history, in the manner of Wilhelm Dilthey or R. G. Collingwood, rather than a historian of the events themselves, in the manner of Karl Marx or Arnold

Toynbee. Nevertheless, his rock-solid belief in the reality of God and God's reign, together with his sensitivity to the subject-object situation in history, meant that his approach was never reducible to a simple either/or. He always held "critical realism" and "critical idealism" in a sophisticated balance.[38] For him, history was an idealistic, active, and imaginative participation of *selves* in the present moment, as well as a participation in the *reality* of a living past.[39]

"A Theologian's Approach to History," the first selection in Part II, was prepared as an address to the American History Association in Washington, D.C., on December 30, 1955. Niebuhr begins with brief remarks about the inseparability of the human subject from its object and about the relationship between the engaged approach of the humanistic disciplines and the detached mode of inquiry in the sciences—distinctions that echo the dichotomy of "internal" and "external" history in *The Meaning of Revelation*.[40] He presents the theologian as one who seeks a unitive pattern for interpreting past and present in universal history. His emphasis upon unity should not be misunderstood, however, as an effort to foreclose meaning or impose a premature settlement upon dissent. Historical study is a critical effort that leads to a sifting of all biases and parochialisms and to the continual enlargement of dialogue.

"Reflections on the Christian Theory of History" is one of three papers in this volume that Niebuhr presented originally to a group of roughly twenty-five colleagues known as the "Theological Discussion Group."[41] The group included such notable figures as Roland Bainton, John C. Bennett, Robert L. Calhoun, Georgia Harkness, Francis P. Miller, Reinhold Niebuhr, Wilhelm Pauck, Paul Tillich, Henry P. Van Dusen, and Gregory Vlastos. The group was convened twice a year starting in 1931 by Van Dusen, a colleague of Reinhold Niebuhr at Union Theological Seminary. Papers were circulated among the participants in advance, and these served to focus two days of discussion on selected topics.[42] The essay "Reflections on the Christian Theory of History" proposes a more modest goal for Christian philosophy of history than, say, the grand sweep of Augustine's *City of God*. The theologian does not need to map out the "whole strategy of the divine campaign" but only so much "as is discernible and as is necessary in order that the ethics of faith in God may have some guidance in understanding what is required of man in the immediate situation." Negatively, when seen in relation to God and God's reign, history requires a relativizing of the meaning of temporal existence. Positively, a Christian philosophy of history seeks to discern a meaningful pattern for human history, in the present day and throughout the ages, a pattern centered in the life, death, and resurrection of Jesus Christ. Theology must hold this denial and this affirmation together as the dynamic of permanent revolution runs its course, and theology must not fall into either a naturalistic or spiritualistic reductionism, or into dualism or paradox.[43] Dualism or reductionism separates God's redemptive work from some sphere of reality, thus denying that God is the God of the whole of life, a God at work in the present moment.

Whenever H. Richard Niebuhr criticized "dualism," he usually had Reinhold in mind. To Richard's way of thinking, Reinhold's dualistic appeals to moral and historical "paradox" inevitably brought acquiescence to and compromise with the world. Reinhold approached history with "ideals" that were only imperfectly realized, whereas Richard proceeded with an ethics of responsibility and the conviction that God is acting everywhere. Richard looked for God's activity in history in the present moment; Reinhold thought of God more as a principle of transcendence in light of which history is judged. Central to the differences between them were their respective views of history.

"Reinhold Niebuhr's Interpretation of History," another paper prepared by H. Richard Niebuhr for the "Theological Discussion Group," was occasioned by the publication of *Faith and History* (1949).[44] The essay reflects the amiable but earnest disagreements the brothers had carried on privately over the years. One of these disagreements, which was aired in print during the brothers' lifetime, resulted from the Manchurian crisis in 1931 and 1932. The crisis was a precursor to the hostilities in the Pacific theater during World War II. In September 1931, the Japanese army invaded Manchuria, posing a direct threat to the Chinese government in Peiping and creating instability in the entire region. The options facing Western leaders, the president of the United States among them, were to intervene or support intervention militarily, adopt economic sanctions, or do nothing.[45] In a *Christian Century* article, H. Richard Niebuhr had counseled patient restraint rather than economic embargo or boycott as some pacifists, then including Reinhold, were advocating. "China is being crucified (though the term is very inaccurate)," wrote Richard, yet the only viable Western response was, he said, repentance and forgiveness under God.[46] More than anything else H. Richard Niebuhr wrote, this article contributed to the mistaken view that his was a quietistic stance toward history. This implication is clear in Reinhold Niebuhr's response, "Must We Do Nothing?"[47] In a rebuttal, the younger brother noted that the crux of their disagreement was not activity or inactivity but was *which* activity and, more to the point, which view of *history* one should adopt.[48]

In the later essay presented to the "Theological Discussion Group," the contours of this disagreement over history are explored. In "Reinhold Niebuhr's Interpretation of History," the principal difference turns on the issue of the *goodness* of God in history. According to Richard, who saw his own task as the interpretation of all things in relation to the divine goodness, Reinhold's view of history tended to appropriate the divine goodness negatively, by claiming that nothing in history is good in itself. Although Richard did agree with this judgment up to a point, his complaint was that Reinhold failed to give the *present*, redemptive power of resurrection full sway in history. History is not only a divine judgment; it also reflects a divine transformation and forgiveness.

HISTORICAL INTERPRETATION   The next four essays provide glimpses into Niebuhr's assessment of movements or figures that were important to his own intellectual development and also to that of many theologians of his generation. "Theology in a Time of Disillusionment" was the Yale Divinity School Alumni Lecture in 1931. The young scholar had just returned from his extended trip to Germany and was settling in to his first year as a faculty member at Yale. In Germany, he had witnessed Hitler-sponsored rallies and had also conferred with leading German theologians; in the United States, the Great Depression held sway. Niebuhr remained convinced that theologians must abandon the liberal "religion of humanity" in favor of a more sober and postliberal "religion of God."[49] Surveying the pessimism about modern civilization that novelists, psychologists, and biographers displayed, Niebuhr revealed his deep awareness of the crisis into which the Western world was plunging. Both here and in the later Cole Lectures, Niebuhr exhibits some tentative attempts to think his way clear to a new direction for theology in a postliberal age. Niebuhr envisioned future theological work unfolding "in three spheres, all interdependent—in continued wrestling with the problem of Jesus and the historical meaning of the revelation of God in history, in continued realistic analysis of religious experience and the search for divine reality in actual religious life, and in ever more urgent effort to realize the eternal will of God, as we must see it from the relative point of view of the present moment, in some form of social and personal justice which will carry within it, as immanent, a revelation of the God who yet remains transcendent, which will be adequate to our own situation but which will contain the absolute demand." These compact remarks contain some of the major lines along which his own future work would advance.

As was so often the case, Niebuhr expresses in his lecture an appreciation for Karl Barth while also assessing Barth's theology as socially irresponsible. Niebuhr's critical appraisal and partial appropriation of Barth, together with his perception of his own work as poised "between Barth and Schleiermacher," is visible at several points in this volume and especially in the following essay.[50]

"The Kingdom of God and Eschatology in the Social Gospel and in Barthianism" was another contribution to the "Theological Study Group."[51] Though not as tightly written as the published articles, it nevertheless offers some important modifications of Niebuhr's earlier published works on both the Social Gospel and on Barthianism.[52] From the beginning, he was concerned that hope for God's reign should become neither so "this-worldly" as to eviscerate the heart of religion nor so "other-worldly" as to be irrelevant for social action. Significantly, he did not equate the "Social Gospel" with the sort of moribund "Liberalism" he believed had become theologically disastrous. Preserving the goals of the Social Gospel meant pursuing them with more deliberate theological integrity.[53] Bringing the Social Gospel and Barthianism into collaboration might provide just such a way forward. Early on, Niebuhr believed that Karl Barth's theology emphasized the transcendence of God too much to carry on the "revolutionary strategy" for advancing the Social Gospel legacy.[54] Later, after he had read Barth's reflections on theological ethics in *Die Kirchliche Dogmatik*, he somewhat revised this estimate.[55] Accordingly, the present essay "The Kingdom of God and Eschatology" demonstrates greater appreciation for the theology of Barth in its social and political implications.

"The Anachronism of Jonathan Edwards" is a meditation on the figure who, perhaps more than any other, provided the compass by which Niebuhr oriented his theological work.[56] He began reading Edwards in earnest during his early years of teaching at Yale in the 1930s. The emerging importance of Edwards soon became clear with the publication of *The Kingdom of God in America*, in which the author's excitement about Edwards is palpable. He would later include Edwards' *The Nature of True Virtue* in the list of the ten most influential books he had read.[57] The whole of Niebuhr's theological vision, including his view of divine sovereignty and human agency, his relational theory of value, and his interest in the religious affections, to name a few, derives significant strength from Edwards' writings. Niebuhr served on the original editorial board for the Yale edition of *The Works of Jonathan Edwards*, and had he not died prematurely, he was to have edited Edwards' ethical writings, a job eventually assumed by Paul Ramsey.[58]

He delivered "The Anachronism of Jonathan Edwards" on March 9, 1958, in the church that Edwards served as pastor in Northampton, Massachusetts, at an event commemorating the bicentennial of Edwards' death. The description of Edwards as "anachronism" he had borrowed from Vernon Louis Parrington, who said that though Edwards was destined for intellectual eminence, he had remained, alas, a Calvinist. In contrast to Parrington, who saw in Edwards a great tragedy of brilliance turned to backwardness, Niebuhr suggests that Edwards' vision of divine sovereignty, human bondage, and the fragility of life had become, in an age of death camps and other looming holocausts, no longer as anachronistic as an earlier age had believed. This essay delivers its message with a rhetorical power as compelling as anything Niebuhr ever wrote.

The final essay in this group, "Address on Martin Buber's Eightieth Birthday," was presented on April 17 1958, in New York at an event sponsored by the American Friends of Hebrew University to honor Buber, who had turned eighty on February 8. Buber's most famous work, *Ich und Du*, was published in 1923 (the English version, *I and Thou*, in 1958), and it profoundly influenced the theology of Niebuhr's generation.[59] In addition to praise of Buber's achievement, the essay contains Niebuhr's own reflections on the anonymity of selfhood in an increasingly impersonal and technological age.

Part III. Culture

RELIGION AND THE DEMOCRATIC TRADITION   Niebuhr sometimes thought of himself more as a reformer of the Christian church than as a reformer of the wider culture, which was the way he saw his brother Reinhold.[60] This comparison is only partially accurate, however, for H.

Richard Niebuhr himself sought to understand religious faith in meaningful connection to contemporaneous public issues. It is more true to say of H. Richard Niebuhr, as I mentioned earlier, that he situated his own intellectual endeavor on those imprecise boundaries between church and world. He believed that although his first responsibility was to his own immediate community, his wider obligation was to the community of all the faithful. Not unlike his brother Reinhold, but from a different theological perspective, H. Richard Niebuhr thought deeply about the momentous social and political issues of his day.

In Niebuhr's construal of religion and culture, loyalty to God must supersede and call into question every narrow loyalty to a merely parochial cause. Nowhere did Niebuhr stress this principle more forcefully than in relation to the state. The first three essays in Part III discuss the state from Niebuhr's radically monotheistic perspective.[61] According to radical monotheism, cultural commitments must be rightly ordered in keeping with their relation to God. In Niebuhr's view, a person's commitment to any given political society was subordinate to his or her membership in the universal commonwealth, which transcends the state and is answerable to God alone. The pervasive problem in modern Western societies, as he saw it, was that nationalistic loyalties tended to subvert monotheistic religion and deify those various lesser loyalties.

During the war years in the 1940s he found himself at theological odds with partisans from the whole spectrum of political opinion—pacifists, isolationists, interventionists, nationalists, and internationalists—all of whom, he thought, too quickly identified Christian faith with democracy and the American way of life.[62] The war called not only democracy's opponents but democracy itself to judgment.

Thus, in "The Relation of Christianity and Democracy," the 1940 Earl Lecture at Berkeley Divinity School, the first point he made was that Christianity and democracy need not necessarily be entwined. Christianity had perdured for centuries in non-democratic contexts, and a democratic state was entirely possible in non-Christian contexts. Rather than presuppose an intrinsic connection between them, he sought to reframe the question and examine whether a high view of the sovereignty of God in theology must guide one's politics to a firm commitment to popular sovereignty. To the question thus framed, the answer is yes. Christianity can flourish, to be sure, in any political environment. Nevertheless, belief in the sovereignty of God challenges all political totalitarianisms, and commitment to God's cause leads to democratic empowerment. Democracy as it arose in America, he argued, presupposed both a divine power that challenges humanity and a realistic view of human sin that inexorably entailed limits upon all human power.[63] Totalitarianism, by contrast, arrogates all power to itself and leads to tyranny and its hideous fruits: the crucifixion of the innocent. And in the present volume, the next two essays focus on the problems of war and sinfulness.

To interpret the theological meaning of war, Niebuhr turned to the metaphor of crucifixion. Like the Christian symbol of crucifixion, the event of war is a horrible tragedy the burden of which falls most heavily on the innocent; but, like crucifixion, war is a reality in which the redemptive work of God is visible in the midst of unfathomable suffering. The second document in Part III, entitled "A Christian Interpretation of War," constitutes Niebuhr's most comprehensive written reflections on the character of war. The various war writings are important: aside from his unpublished classroom lectures on Christian ethics at Yale, they constitute the best extant guide to the way his theological vision applies to practical moral problems.[64]

In addition to the two war articles previously mentioned, arising out of the Manchurian controversy in the 1930s, Niebuhr published three other articles on war in the *Christian Century* in the early 1940s.[65] These articles were distinctive in their emphasis upon God as the primary actor in time of war and upon the metaphor of "crucifixion" as the most useful one by which war should be interpreted. Niebuhr wrote: "Interpreted through the cross of Jesus Christ the suffering of the innocent is seen not as the suffering of temporal men but of the eternal victim 'slain before the foundations of the world.' If the Son of God is being crucified in this war along with the malefactors—and he is being crucified on many an obscure hill—then the graciousness of God, the self-giving love, is more manifest here than in all the years of peace."[66]

"A Christian Interpretation of War" was composed as an in-house study for the Calhoun Commission, of the Federal Council of the Churches of Christ in America, chaired by Niebuhr's Yale colleague, Robert Lowry Calhoun. The commission's charge in 1944 was to report on the church and faith during wartime.[67] Niebuhr was appointed to prepare a paper on the theological dimensions of the question. Although illness in 1944 prevented him from commenting extensively upon or editing the final draft, the report was based in part on the material he contributed, and the commission's final version displays his unique influence.[68] This is especially evident in the emphasis upon the "objectivity" of God's sovereign, creative activity, upon war as the corrective judgment of God and as a "crucifixion," and upon God as war's ultimate victim. There were differences as well. The commission, made up of twenty-six scholars, which somehow had to accommodate the views of both pacifists and just-war theorists, tended to speak of God's "relation to" war rather than God's "action in" it; of God's "redemptive" rather than God's "corrective" justice in war; and of war as crucifixion in an illustrative sense only.[69]

The third essay in this group, "The Idea of Original Sin in American Culture," was delivered February 24, 1949, for participants in the Program of Studies in American Civilization at Princeton University. This important and revealing essay compares the political and cultural implications of the liberal "religion of humanity," which Niebuhr and his generation had found wanting, and the postliberal "religion of God." What puzzled Niebuhr was the stereotype assumed by twentieth-century historiography: the liberal religion of humanity supports a liberal democratic politics; the religion of human sin and divine sovereignty bequeaths a reactionary politics of repression. He sought to refute this stereotype on psychological, logical, and historical grounds, since it was the result of both theological and cultural misconceptions. First, the theology of original sin is not so much about human "depravity" as about human "corruption," which presupposes the original goodness of creation. Sin, as a deterioration of basic goodness, is universal in scope, and it is total in extent, but not in degree. Hence humanity remains capable of the good. Further, the presupposition of human sin and divine sovereignty leads, he argues, to an egalitarian politics. To use the doctrine of sin to support conservative politics is simply to apply it defensively rather than critically and morally. Second, the cultural requisites of a free society have nothing to do with contract theory. Rather, the covenantal view, of human beings as relational and interdependent, can provide a basis for a truly humanistic polity. Thus he insists, both here and in a 1954 essay on this idea, that the Protestant conviction about covenant contributed significantly to the shaping of American democracy.[70] Contractual political arrangements freely entered into for political advantage can just as easily and freely be abandoned; covenantal politics presupposes commitment and a bond among human beings for the sake of which all political advantage must be subordinated.

SERMONS   If one asks where theology and culture come together for H. Richard Niebuhr, a sure response is, in his prayers and sermons. Having grown up in a parsonage and having been a pastor himself, he knew the preacher's craft, and he savored it. Once in a letter to Reinhold in 1937, he confided, "I remain a preacher more than anything else."[71] It is fitting to end this volume with three sermons drawn from the riches of H. Richard Niebuhr's thirty years of preaching at Yale.

Niebuhr was sought after to preach at baccalaureates and ordinations, as well as at worship services of local congregations. His sermons were intellectually and spiritually demanding, often compressing years of reflection into a single phrase. Full of thoughtfulness and using anecdotes or illustrations only sparingly, the sermons required work on the part of the hearer. One is reminded of Reinhold Niebuhr's early vow to choose meaning over elocution and never to be a "pretty" preacher.[72] As to style, Richard's sermons were usually more thematic and reflective than expository, though biblical allusions were frequent. Usually the sermon retrieved a single nugget from a biblical text and then used it to raise a theological query. The persistent themes were the priority of God's work and God's agenda, the demands of the human pilgrimage, and the continual necessity of repentance. The same themes pervaded his prayers. As a professor, he opened his classes with prayer, usually a collect he had composed; he read from a small card or scrap of paper pulled from his pocket. Many were preserved by his students and treasured:

Almighty God, we know thee but dimly and know ourselves and our neighbors as in a glass darkly. But thou knowest us through and through and with that we would be content, knowing also that thou wilt guide us to the fuller knowledge of thee and one another which is needful for us.

Our God, Father, who hast sent us on this journey of life so that we are pilgrims and strangers, we thank Thee for Thy companionship with us and our fellow travelers, though it be in a cloud rather than a pillar of fire that we are most often aware of Thee. Head us safely to our promised land where we shall be free and at home with one another and Thee.

Deliver us, O Lord, from presumptuousness, and from moral laziness, from presuming to a knowledge of Thee and of ourselves that we do not possess, and from the despair which tempts us to give up because we know so little.

Niebuhr was meticulous in writing and rewriting the lines of these prayers. The sermons, too, were often revised, Niebuhr paying careful attention to language and to turn of phrase.

The three sermons reproduced here exemplify Niebuhr's style and his theological concerns. He was often asked to preach at special observances. "Our Reverent Doubt and the Authority of Christ" was one such sermon, preached June 6, 1948, to mark the 126th anniversary of Yale Divinity School. "The Logic of the Cross" is a powerful sermon, communicating a critical theme from his last years. The cross calls into question the basis of all wisdom, confounding the pervasive "ethics of survival" and replacing them with an ethics of trust in God.[73] Finally, "Man's Work and God's," the most expository of the three, is a moving reflection on Psalm 90. It focuses on the transience of all human endeavors and urges reliance on God to establish the work of human hands. It expresses the hope that the value of what each person does in the present moment will be impressed into the permanent structure of God's work, which alone endures.

Preparation of the Text

A brief word should be said about the nature of the manuscripts collected here, about the basis for their selection, and about the editorial method employed in preparing them for publication. The editor was acutely aware of the responsibility involved in bringing before the public eye material that the author himself had never sought to publish. Niebuhr's papers include such things as class lectures, sketches of ideas, rough drafts of manuscripts, and other fragments deemed unsuitable for publication, though they remain available to scholars in the Andover-Harvard collection. The pieces chosen for inclusion, by contrast, were brought by the author himself before a public or quasi-public audience.

Some of the pieces included here are the equal of anything the author published during his life—for example, "The Idea of Original Sin in American Culture," "The Anachronism of Jonathan Edwards," and "The Logic of the Cross." Others, though understandably rough and reflecting the freer style of a lecture, are interesting for the light they shed on his overall corpus. This is especially true of the three essays on the interpretation of history and the paper on war he submitted to the Calhoun Commission during World War II. Perhaps most interesting of all, the Cole Lectures show us glimpses of where Niebuhr's mature writings might have led but for his untimely death.

Much thought was given to whether the materials would lend themselves to a single organizing theme or rubric. Because the subjects range so widely, though, no single theme emerged. Still, the present thematic organization of the volume—theology, history, and culture— reflects some of the pivotal concerns the author addressed throughout his career and provides coherence to an otherwise disparate collection.

The overall editorial goal was to remain as true as possible to the original texts while also making the emendations necessary to render the materials publishable. Orthography, punctuation, and syntax were altered where necessary to conform with customary English usage or to make the volume consistent. Only rarely were changes made in the author's style, and these were limited to the sort that ordinarily occurs in editing a manuscript for publication. No effort was made to render these papers into gender-inclusive language, which was not the convention in their day, though Niebuhr would likely have found the issue a congenial one.

The hands-on editing itself included making transcriptions from the author's handwriting or, in the case of the Cole Lectures, from voice recordings. A few of the extant manuscripts were themselves transcriptions of oral presentations made during the author's life. Sometimes this sort of material had to be modified in ways appropriate to the conversion of an oral address into published form.

A special word needs to be said about the Cole Lectures, which survive in two different forms. First, there are voice recordings of all four lectures transcribed at the time of delivery at Vanderbilt University. Second, there are surviving typescripts for the first two lectures prepared by Niebuhr in advance of delivering them. No such manuscripts have survived for the last two. From time to time as he delivered the lectures, Niebuhr would change the wording, elaborate, or offer asides to his audience, and these were preserved in the voice recording. In the process of editing the first two lectures, the original typescripts were allowed to control, except where Niebuhr's oral emendations were judged to be improvements. Passing comments that did not seem to reflect considered judgments were for the most part excluded.

Since the author never brought the manuscripts into finished form, it was necessary to supply formal academic citations and references that may have been familiar to Niebuhr's contemporaries but are less so today. Given the breadth of Niebuhr's reading, the job of locating references in some cases required a great deal of detective work. In some cases he left marginalia indicating the sources upon which he drew; in other cases it was clear from the context that he was drawing upon or alluding to a particular source, and these references have been provided. Quite often the notes supplied here refer to the actual editions available to the author; but in other cases, where the specific edition he used is a matter of conjecture or has since been superseded, it seemed more helpful to cite the most recent, critical edition.

The editor first had occasion to study the unpublished corpus during the summer of 1990. Within a year a project design was in place, and by 1992 the major editorial work had commenced. The final editorial decisions were made within a few days of the centennial of Niebuhr's birth in September 1994.

An endeavor such as this one incurs many debts. The Lilly Endowment provided a grant during the 1992 academic year to support the editorial work at Harvard. The Lilly Endowment has been a significant contributor to theological research and education ever since its early involvement with H. Richard Niebuhr in the 1950s. I am especially indebted to Ronald F. Thiemann, dean of Harvard Divinity School, for his many invaluable ways of supporting this project and to Charles Grench, editor-in-chief of Yale University Press, for shepherding it through to completion. John C. Bennett and James M. Gustafson were good enough to offer suggestions and support. An anonymous reader selected by Yale University Press offered comments that prompted refinements in the text. Thomas W. Gillespie, president of Princeton Theological Seminary, graciously granted permission to reproduce "The Doctrine of the Trinity and the Unity of the Church." Charles E. Raynall III, pastor of Davidson College Presbyterian Church and adjunct professor of theology at Union Theological Seminary in Virginia, shared correspondence from Albert C. Outler pertaining to the Calhoun Commission in the 1940s. The staffs of Andover-Harvard Theological Library, Stitt Library of Austin Presbyterian Theological Seminary, and the Library of Eden Theological Seminary were most accommodating in locating sources.

The work on this volume was begun at Harvard and concluded at Austin Presbyterian Theological Seminary, an institution where H. Richard Niebuhr delivered the lectures published in *Christ and Culture* and where he was scheduled to return as a resident theologian in the 1962–63 academic year but for his untimely death. The president, Jack L. Stotts, a former doctoral student of Niebuhr's, together with the academic dean, Robert M. Shelton, were enthusiastic in their support and provided relief from certain academic responsibilities at critical junctures. My faculty colleagues were more than eager to render their aid when needed. Jeanne French faithfully and cheerfully typed and retyped the manuscript. Margaret Hill provided valuable assistance in bringing the manuscript to completion. Several students helped in locating sources and proofreading: Lydia Hernandez, Blake Hurst, Kristen Hamilton-Sutherland, Elizabeth Johnson-Miller, and Erin McGee. Dieter Heinzl helped with the index.

Above all, I wish to express my deep gratitude to Richard R. Niebuhr for his generous encouragement and support.

William Stacy Johnson

I
THEOLOGY

1

The Cole Lectures
"Next Steps in Theology"

The Position of Theology Today

"Theology," said P. T. Forsyth in a series of lectures delivered to young theologians fifty years ago, "simply means thinking in centuries. Religion tells on the present, but theology tells on the religion of the future."[1] It is a part of the duty of the church in certain sections and on certain occasions to be less concerned about the effects of the Gospel on the individual immediately or on the present time and to look ahead to certain changes in the future. Forsyth's statement is doubtless directly contradictory to many of the experiences most of us have had many times in the study of theology. It has not looked ahead so much as backward. If there is truth in the statement—witness the theologian Luther, the theologian Wesley, the theologian Edwards—certainly there is challenge in P. T. Forsyth's understanding of the task of theology. When he delivered his forward-looking lectures on *The Work of Christ* in 1910 he was concerned about a danger he saw impending in the near future, roughly the danger of losing Christ in a vapid humanism. When we look forward now this is not (I think) the problem that concerns us, though in his day he was right about what lay ahead.

What is it then that we ought to prepare for insofar as theology can make preparations for the future? I believe that what concerns us most of all is not the question how to escape the dangers that may threaten

3

us in the future but how to meet the opportunities and needs that arise before us? And the great opportunity as I see it is the opportunity and need for a new awakening, a new revival, a new reformation of religion. I will not now undertake to fortify my judgment that we must prepare for this by citing to you the evidence which is the evidence of the widespread hunger, religious hunger, metaphysical hunger of our day, the evidence of the increasing sense of emptiness in modern man's life, a sense of emptiness that will be assuaged. And certainly I do not believe that theology by its own efforts can bring about the new awakening, the new revival, the new reformation. I shall only want to ask in these lectures whether there are any steps we can take now as theological pastors and theological teachers and students of theology to prepare the way for such an awakening in our future.

But before we undertake to think about such steps it seems necessary to assess our present situation. Where do we stand in theology today? At what longitude and latitude have we arrived in our time? First of all of course we must say that in view of the pluralism of our churches and of their schools we stand at no one place, we have arrived at no one precise point. The great divisions between the theologies of Roman Catholicism and Protestantism and of Orthodoxy; and within Protestantism the differences between the theologies of the sixteenth century Reformation and the eighteenth century revival and then again of conservative and liberal groups—these all remain. Yet none of these various schools and tendencies of thought is static. Each of them participates in the common spirit of a time and it is possible, I think, to speak at least roughly and in outline of a theological climate or of a preoccupation of all the theologies with certain general problems. There is such a thing as a movement in one general direction of all the various parts and components of our theological enterprises in church and school. In this sense let us try to speak of our general position.

I

In such a world as the one in which we carry on our inquiries it is impossible to speak about the position of theology by having as our reference point something in our culture since that culture is itself so full of changes. I think, however, that we can gain some insight into our situation if we orient ourselves by reference to our relations to some of the great polarities that characterize our human existence. For theology like all movements in human thought does seem to move inevitably between these universal poles, such as those of past and future, of subject and object, of contemplative and practical reasoning.

The first of these is given to us with our existence as selves who are always in the present moment, so that to be an "I" is to be in a "now"; yet in a "now," a present moment, that has a past behind it and a future before it. The present moment is often defined as lying between the "no longer" and the "not yet." Yet past and future are effective in us as selves as memory and as expectation. They are not really the "no longer" and the "not yet"; they rather mean what is still with us and what is already before us. There is no way of avoiding the pull of these two poles in any part of our human existence; even though with certain men of the present and of the past we make an effort to live and think only in the moment, in the immediate present. The theologians of the moment also tend toward one of the two poles, either the open future of a Bultmann or the contemporaneousness with Jesus Christ of a Kierkegaard. We are always oriented to a past out of which we come and which we carry in us, which we conserve and reject in its various parts, and we are always oriented in expectation, hope and anxiety toward the future. However, we rarely if ever live and think on an exact equator between these poles. In our various historical presents as well as in our various individual attitudes we are more inclined in the one direction or in the other. What we call conservatism is more past-minded on the whole, more intent on carrying the past into the future, more concerned with the reconstruction of the present by the principles and habits of the past than it is intent on the future reconstruction of our present *and* of our past. Whatever else liberalism in its manifold forms may mean, it is characterized by a tendency to turn from the past and to move toward what is anticipated more than toward what is remembered. To be sure, neither the conservatism that desires to recover and establish some past nor the liberalism that wants to forget what lies behind and to press on toward the things that lie before can ever exist either in the individual or in society without its polar counterpart. Yet in every present moment we are moving more in one direction than in the other. The dynamic present is never a dead-center between past and present. Christians who in recent days have been wont to speak of themselves as living "between the times" have never in their various present moments been equally oriented toward their remembered creation and their anticipated new creation, or toward

5

the recollected first coming of Christ and toward his expected second coming. We have always been either more retrospective or more prospective, more rabbinical, to use a term from the Jewish faith, or more eschatological.

Now I think it is clear to all of us that the dominant movement in theology during the past generation, in Europe let us say since 1919 and in America since 1933 or 1934, has been toward the remembrance of things past, toward conservation of the heritage, toward the recovery of ideas, convictions and habits that were effective in some earlier days of our history.[2] We note the evidence of this in all the different theologies of the last generation—in the neo-thomism and neo-scholasticism of the Roman Catholic schools, in the return to Reformation theology in Lutheran and Presbyterian scholarship, in the revival of something like Protestant scholasticism in the Barthian movement, perhaps above all in the return to what we call biblical theology and to the very strong emphasis on that word of God which was spoken and incarnated once and for all in the religious life of the past. This theological movement has had its counterpart in the religious life of the church—to a certain extent in a preaching that returned to the disciplines of the past, to a larger extent in the liturgies, in actions of adoration, supplication and intercession which used and continue to use to an unusual degree the forms hallowed by ancient usage.

This movement in theology is highly intelligible to us when we see it in its relations to what has gone before. One characteristic of the nineteenth century religious thought, especially as it had come to its development in the early years of our present century, was its anti-traditionalism, its tendency to reject the past. In Protestantism it had often reinterpreted the Reformation as an essentially medieval movement in spirit, and it had dismissed much of it along with that outmoded medievalism. It had reinterpreted the Scriptures so as to try to retain Jesus Christ without also retaining the christological doctrines and convictions of early, medieval and Reformation churches. This tendency had gone so far that Christianity was indeed in danger of losing its heritage. In this respect it was involved in the whole problem of Western civilization—of a Christendom which under the influence of repeated industrial, economic, scientific and political revolutions was in imminent danger of forgetting those fundamental principles, learned in its past and effective in its present, which had made those revolutions possible. Christendom faced—as it still does—the prospect of what has been called the "disinherited mind," that is, of a mind without capital with which to work, without fundamental established axioms on which to rely, a mind so impoverished that it must justify itself in each present moment by its works, its constant activity. In its own sector—which may well be the central sector in Christendom—the church experienced the situation with unusual acuteness. The traumatic experiences of the two great anti-Christian, anti-traditional revolutions, Communism and National Socialism, may have had a particular effect on the revival of religious conservatism. But long before these dramatic events emphasized the problem of the disinherited mind, sensitive spirits in theology as well as elsewhere had noted the presence of danger in the atmosphere prevailing in democratic, capitalistic, industrialized and urbanized Christendom and had turned toward the task of recovering the past. Karl Barth is for most of us the symbolic figure who represents that anticipation and that movement. What was at stake was the theoretical loss of the great convictions, the fundamental principles of Christianity—such principles as those of reliance on the Scripture, of the primacy of God's work and God's freedom over all human freedom and human work; the principles of sin and fall and redemption, of the life in Jesus Christ and many another element in the axioms and in the categorial scheme with the aid of which Christians had ordered their thoughts and guided their conduct. As in our political life, we were threatened with the loss of our inherited capital—for instance of our fundamental premises about a world of universal law and order, of human equality and of the primary value of liberty—so and more profoundly the anti-traditional movement in the religious depths of our existence seemed to lead to the abandonment of the faith of our fathers, of the basic principles we had inherited.

This movement toward the past, toward the recovery and reaffirmation of what was deepest in our memory was and remains clearly a most necessary one. Unless we remember what we were, what we committed ourselves to in the past, what we have encountered of the real in the decisive moments in our past, we remain ourselves. Precisely because we are going into a strange future, one wholly different from any periods of our past, we need to remind ourselves of what we are in consequence of all that we have been and of what we committed ourselves to be as a church in the world. So the question in theology today is not whether the correction of our former anti-traditional line of march remains necessary. The question is whether the correction is to be continued to the point where the movement toward the recovery of tradition becomes as extreme as the anti-traditional movement before it was.

Movement in theology as well as in every kind of thinking may be compared to the kind of balanced physical movement which we can observe in the case of a bicycle rider and which has its analogies, I believe, in all other physical movement, from those in walking to those in sailing ships and in jet airplanes.[3] The bicycle rider does not proceed in a straight line nor remain in a perfectly vertical position. His progress is marked by an almost infinite number of variations of the wheel to right and left and by a constant balancing of his body through small inconspicuous shiftings of weight. If the variations of the wheel or of his balance become extreme in one direction, they must be compensated for by extreme variations in the other direction and when the corrections become over-corrections there is catastrophe. So it is with the life and thought of men. There is no doubt that in the early years of our century the movement toward futurism, toward the coming kingdom, toward a new revelation, had become extreme. But now there is danger that in our correction of that movement we may shift our weight and direction so radically that correction becomes over-correction. When this occurs students of theology are likely to gain the impression that its history is one of violent pendulum swings, rather than one of balanced movement forward through the centuries. If we are to correct our movement now, we shall not do so effectively if we orient ourselves as completely toward the past in this part of the twentieth century as we oriented ourselves toward the future in the beginnings of our twentieth century.

There are some signs that we shall recover balance without going through that over-correction toward traditionalism which would invite another violent swing in the future. Among those signs I note the tendency to re-evaluate and reconsider the theology of the nineteenth century which the first reaction to anti-traditionalism had dismissed as altogether an erroneous movement, blaming a Schleiermacher for all the errors of which his successors were guilty. In that reassessment of the nineteenth century it is discovered that there was far more continuity in it with the past, far less of rejection of the great tradition than the early critics ascribed to it. Another sign lies in the fact that a Bultmann maintains his place as representative thinker alongside of Barth and that however strong our affirmation of the validity of the heritage is, there is an almost equally strong sense that it cannot be maintained unless it is reappropriated and in such reappropriation transformed. In wide circles of contemporary theology the feeling seems to prevail that the old doctrines are all true, yet unusable by men in the forms in which they have come to us from the past and that if we are to carry our heritage into the future we shall need to refashion it in reappropriating it. To us in this time the adage seems to apply with peculiar force: what you have inherited from your fathers you must earn again if you are really to possess it.

Movement between the polarity of the past and future has a wider and profounder meaning for theology than the one suggested by these references to traditionalism and anti-traditionalism in the last two hundred years. Christian faith—and Christian theology with it—moves, as I have suggested, between a past and a future coming of the Savior, between a revelation given and a revelation anticipated, between a redemption wrought and a redemption still hoped for, between a reconciliation accomplished and an atonement yet to be. Christian faith loses much of its dynamic when it is separated from hope and when the hope is understood in such vague fashion that it does not impinge on present existence. For many years now theology along with the Church tended to look backward only to revelation as a once-and-for-all event in our past, to redemption as accomplished by one sacrifice, to an atonement completed in fact though not in realization.[4] All the eschatological interpretations of the New Testament since Johannes Weiss and Albert Schweitzer have been accompanied by very non-eschatological theological concentration on what was done in a time past that was itself eschatological.[5] Millenarianism of every sort, as we know from our history, has its profound dangers, particularly when it confuses the Kingdom of God with some state of human culture which we have in prospect or with some Utopia we expect to achieve by our own efforts. But the answer to false millenarianism in theology and religion is not an equally false antiquarianism, though the dangers resident in the latter are always less conspicuous.

A theology today which has respect for the immediate future of man in our world will be concerned, as present-day theology rarely seems to be, with the reality and the meaning of Christian hope, of our future-directed existence. I shall not pursue this problem further at this time, though I will venture the prediction that Christians will come again to conceive a lively living hope and in that hope will be renewed. And I will venture also to give this counsel to young theologians of the present: that they reflect much on the role of hope and despair in our life and the nature of our Christian hope and that they give Agape and Eros a rest for a while while they look at Telos and Eschaton.

II

We can undertake to assess the present situation in theology in general by seeking to locate its position between two other constant poles of human life, the polarity which we designate in philosophy as subject and object or more generally as self and other. This, like the duality of past and future, is a genuine polarity in the sense that one element in this dyad is not definable without reference to the other. There are many kinds of dualities in our experience and many of them are not polar at all. When we make use of the principle of polarity we need to be on our guard against the temptation of interpreting all the appearances of two related sorts of things as polarities. In general we may say that if one partner of a dyad is thinkable without reference to the other, then we are not dealing with a polarity. God and Satan are not in polar relation, because we do not need to refer to Satan in order to define God. Life and death are not in polar relations, for life is knowable without reference to death, though death presupposes life. Being and non-being are not in polar relationship for the same reason, nor are good and evil, though there is a kind of goodness, namely virtue, which is polar to a certain kind of evil, namely vice. There are of course other sorts of dualities also not polar in character such as the rhythms with which we are daily concerned in light and darkness, strength and weakness, flow and ebb. But now subject-object, that is a true polarity. We cannot think the one without thinking the other. We cannot be objective without positing a subject, we cannot be subjective without thinking of the object the subject has before it.

In theology this polarity of subject and object appears in two familiar forms, the man-God and self-other forms. Let us content ourselves here with a brief circumscription of the first of these in order that we may then assess our present position with respect to our movement between these poles. Theology as theology is always concerned with God, yet only with God in relation to man or to ourselves as our creator and the creator of our world, as our ruler and the ruler of our world, as our savior and the savior of our values. A knowledge of the divine which is concerned with its relation to nature and natural powers abstracted from man is not theology. We usually call it metaphysics. A knowledge directed toward the ultimate ground of being in relation to all being simply considered as being, that is ontology. Though theology can have a fruitful dialogue with such metaphysics and such ontology, it will always resist equation with them for its own knowledge is directed to God before man, God related to ourselves. For it, a knowledge of the divine as the divine might be in itself apart from man, fearing, hating, and loving God, apart from ourselves as created, judged and redeemed by him, is not knowledge of God at all. Hence, for theology there is no knowledge of God which is not also a knowledge of ourselves before Him. All our religious language includes in statements about God references to man before God. It addresses itself to *my* God, to *our* Father, to the God and Father of Our Lord Jesus Christ, to the God of Abraham, Isaac and Jacob, to God in whom *we* live and move and have our being, to one who knows *us*, is merciful to *us*, in short to God with us, God before man. And so it never proceeds without a reference to the subjective pole, that is, to man. It is not, by the same token, concerned with man in relation to natural existences. The study of that subject is natural anthropology. Nor is it concerned with man in his relationship to fellow men only. That is the concern of sociology and social anthropology. The subject matter of theology is always man-before-God, man-related-to-God, so that the knowledge—or at least the acknowledgment of God—is implicit in all theological anthropology.

Here then is a polarity we cannot avoid. There is no way of our being concerned about God-before-man without our being concerned about man-before-God, nor is there any way of understanding this man except as we are drawn to the opposite pole. John Calvin in the opening sentences of the *Institutes of the Christian Religion* set forth the problem of theology in classical manner when he wrote, "True and substantial wisdom principally consists of two parts, the knowledge of God, and the knowledge of ourselves. But, while these two branches of knowledge are so intimately connected, which of them precedes and produces the other, is not easy to discover. For, in the first place, no man can take a survey of himself but he must immediately turn to the contemplation of God, in whom he 'lives and moves'; . . . since it is evident that . . . our very existence is nothing but a subsistence in God alone.'"[6] Schleiermacher [echoes][7] it with his feeling of absolute dependence: "To know myself is to know myself related to God." Calvin goes on to reflect then how "a sense of our ignorance, vanity, poverty, . . . depravity, and corruption leads us to perceive and acknowledge that in the Lord alone are to be found true wisdom, solid strength, perfect goodness and un-spotted righteousness; and so, by our imperfections, we are excited to a consideration of the perfections of God." And in summary, "the knowledge of ourselves . . . is not only an incitement to seek after God, but likewise a considerable assistance towards finding him." Yet it is equally clear "that no man can arrive at the true knowledge of himself, without having first contemplated the divine character, and then de-scended to the consideration of his own." For our pride is such, says Calvin, that we cannot know ourselves in our "unrighteousness, turpi-tude, folly and impurity,"—not to speak of our talents which overly delight us—"while we confine our attention to ourselves and regard not the Lord, who is the only standard by which this judgment about ourselves ought to be formed."[8] Calvin concluded his introductory chapter by saying that though the two kinds of knowledge are thus intimately connected, "the proper order of instruction requires" the theologian to treat first of the knowledge of God; and so he began at once to write not about God but about *man's knowledge* of him as given in creation and as extinguished or corrupted by ignorance and wick-edness.

The same polarity runs through the Bible with its movement from word-from-God-to-man to word-from-man-to-God. It runs through the christologies of the church in their movement from Christ the repre-sentative man, the great high priest, the head and king of the race, to Christ the representative of God, the one in whom the fullness of the Godhead dwells. It runs through our liturgies of course in their con-stant change of direction from preaching God's word-to-man to praying man's word-to-God.

Theology has shown its balance when it has moved between these poles without violent fluctuations in one direction or the other. Then it has turned from the effort to understand God-before-man to the inquiry into man-before-God and back again not, to be sure, without tension and strain, yet without catastrophe. The great classic ages in theology have, I believe, been periods of such balanced movements. You find balanced movement in Augustine, in Thomas, in Anselm, cer-tainly in Calvin as the quotation indicates, certainly in Wesley and in Edwards. These ages were not static for they sought greater knowledge of both God-before-man and of man-before-God just as they pressed toward fuller future knowledge without rejecting the past. But these ages have been interrupted by periods of violent fluctuations and we have recently come out of such a period and now one of our questions is whether we shall correct that movement by an equally violent swing toward the opposite pole.

It is now clear to us that the nineteenth century movement in theology was oriented toward the human pole and that the movement by the beginning of our twentieth century had led to a subjectivism in which the objective element had been largely lost to view. Theology tended in the generation of our fathers to become philosophy of religion, that is, an inquiry into man—before-his-God or his gods. That study was pursued in all the areas of theology with acumen and zeal. In the psychology of religion, religious emotions and states of mind were analyzed, the sense and experience of conscience were subjected to scrutiny; the differences between the states of mind of the once-born and the twice-born, as in William James, as well as the psychology of conversion were examined. In biblical studies the state of mind of early Christians with their eschatological expectations, their enthusiasms as spirit-filled subjects, their beliefs in the resurrection, or the relation of the great prophets to the ecstatic *nabis*, or the ideas of Semitic peoples were carefully explored. Christian ethics became the ethics of the Christian conscience or the Christian disposition (*Gesinnungsethik*). In every field the movement toward self-knowledge, that is, toward the understanding of man-before-God, was dominant. The object before the religious or Christian self could not be ignored but it was an object of study only as it was reflected in the mirror of the subject; it was there as the human *idea* of God or as the perception or the image which aroused the feeling of the holy or as the universal law presented to the conscience. The movement in christology was unmistakably directed toward the man Jesus, the Jesus of history, the Jesus whose moral consciousness or whose faith was normative for Christians or for men in general—but in every case the profoundly human Jesus. Under the guidance of a theology that moved primarily in that direction the religious life and the Christian Church were led close to shipwreck on the rocks of human self-worship, for now it almost seemed that the creator of all good things was the human consciousness, that religion itself was man's redeemer from destruction, and that the important thing in the religious life was not God in whom man trusted but trust itself; not God known, acknowledged, and chosen in faith but

13

rather faith. The tendency was not confined to *either* the conservative or the liberal schools in theology, for while the latter in their movements away from tradition concentrated on present man's subjective emotions and value judgments, the former tended to value most highly not the object of historical confessions of faith but those confessions themselves or more specifically the doctrines of the past. The question between them was not God or man as the point of emphasis but what man?—contemporary man before God or Reformation man before God, or Catholic man before God?

Now the correction has come. Objectivism in theology is the watchword of the day. Not man-before-God but God-before-man is the subject of theological inquiry. Philosophy of religion has turned into philosophical theology, i.e., into an inquiry which has as its object not religion in its various forms but the divine as present to philosophical thought. Systematic theology has dropped its affiliation with philosophy of religion in the former sense of the word and has returned to the endeavor to set forth the doctrine of God. Our christology has made a 180-degree turn from the crest of the historical and human Jesus to the christology of the Athanasian creed, affirming Him to be very God of very God, one substance with the Father, a Christ in whom the fullness of the Godhead dwells bodily, a Christ who is not so much in our history as the one who is the *Logos* who was with God in the beginning, by whom all things were made, the Word that is God. In much biblical theology the movement away from the emphasis upon or even concern for historical man-before-God has resulted in a new formulation of the understanding that Scripture in its wholeness is word of God and no longer word of man to God, at all. The doctrine of the church has moved from the conception of this body as the creation of faith to our understanding of it as the body of Christ himself.

In Karl Barth this whole movement has found its representative theologian just as an earlier generation found its representative in Albrecht Ritschl. For just as many men who moved in the direction which Ritschl took owed nothing to his leadership, so there are many today who are remote from Barth in the explicit content of their thinking yet move with him toward objectivism. For them there is no way from man to God but only a way from God to man. For them as with Barth "faith-knowledge is knowledge through revelation. And that simply means," in his words, "that it is a type of knowledge unconditionally bound to its object."[9] The position is similar to that of those sense-empiricists who in analyzing man's knowledge of nature describe the mind as a blank tablet on which the object inscribed its character. When theology moves in this objectivist direction today, it is not of course showing itself to be less closely affiliated with our culture than was that subjectivist theology which it tends to decry as the idealistic religious thought of culture Protestantism. The general movement in Western philosophy quite apart from religion has, as we are all aware, been toward objectivism and positivism. Apart, however, from all such questions which we may raise about the relations of the two theological movements, the subjectivist and the objectivist, the problem arises for us whether we are to follow the objectivistic correction to the point where it becomes an over-correction and where we will invite catastrophe not on the rocks of Charybdis but on those of Scylla. If we forget that the God with whom we are concerned is God-before-man, we open the way eventually to a new authoritarianism in theology and in religion in which we shall insist, as men have done before, that our particular knowledge of God—our theological knowledge, our Reformation knowledge, our Christian knowledge—is wholly derived from the object and hence authoritative for all other men. And so for universal subjectivism we shall really substitute not objectivism but our particular subjectivism. Unconditional objectivism tends to lead always to some doctrine of an infallible truth which is the supposed possession of those men who claim to have a knowledge derived only from the object. If the tendency continues without correction in Protestantism, then Barth's or the Barthians' attempted correction of the reformers can result in the cancellation of some of the effects of the Reformation.

Will the movement toward objectivism—toward that attention to God-before-man which virtually excludes attention to man-before-God—be allowed to go so far that the balance will once more be destroyed and violent reaction be necessary? That is a question, I believe, with which all theologians must be concerned who are not slaves to the intellectual fashions of the day but try to move faithfully into the future, steering their course by the stars in the theological heavens instead of by allowing themselves to move with the prevailing winds and tides of the moment.

There is a third polarity which seems to be given to us with our human nature and which we cannot escape in religion and theology any more than in any other sphere. This is the polarity of thought and action or of the contemplative and the practical reason. As we move in our present with our past into our future, attending to ourselves in the presence of the not-ourselves and vice versa, we observe and we act, we think and we do, we conceive and we decide. This also is a true polarity for we cannot successfully abstract the one activity from the other nor reduce the one to the other. We cannot define human action without reference to human thought. Action without thought is not human but sub-human. Neither can we think without action, without decision, selection, choice. Thought without action is daydreaming or an activity of the unconscious mind. We do not exist, however, in some median state between thought and action, but constantly move with smaller or larger, more inconspicuous or more violent shifts in one direction or the other. Moving between these poles the desideratum would also seem to be balanced motion. This, of course, does not mean that in any society, and in the church particularly, there ought not to be the kind of *socially* balanced movement wherein certain groups—such as the theologians—devote themselves especially to one of these two interests, while other groups attend especially to the opposite focus.

If we think of the position of theology today from this point of view it may strike us that it is correcting a previous imbalance in the church in the direction toward action; that is, the previous direction was toward action. In the past generations, whose thought and action we are now reacting against, the emphasis lay on doing. One of its favorite biblical texts was, "If any man will do his will, he shall know of the doctrine, whether it be of God" (John 7:17, KJV). The pragmatic understanding of knowledge, according to which the test of truth lay with its consequences for action and according to which the beginning of knowledge itself lay in man's need for a guide to action, was deeply influential in all our theology. The question about the truth of theological propositions was largely the question about the results that they might have in action. What, for instance, it was asked, is the pragmatic meaning of the doctrine of the Trinity or the Chalcedonian christology? If they mean nothing for action, are they not really meaningless? Whatever could not be commended as having results for immediate action, though religious action was included, was suspected of being "mere" speculation. There were protests, of course, against this tendency but it was a dominant mood in most circles, and particularly in America.

The priority of action over contemplation appeared in theological education and the tendency to give precedence to practical subjects such as homiletics, education, and social ethics. In America we were particularly strongly oriented toward practice in education. It appeared also in the tendency to deal with theology primarily in the perspective of ethics, so that the basis of much theology was value judgment theory or the theory of the conscience.

Now in our time, or rather in these last thirty years, we have come almost full circle. Pragmatism is suspect in almost all places. We begin our study of the nature and the attributes of God not with a theory about good and evil, that is, of value judgments, but with reflections on the Lordship, on the power that is exercised upon us. With the tendency toward objectivism and positivism in the study of Scripture we combine a deep suspicion of all attempts to make these texts directly and immediately relevant to our practice in politics, economics, domestic life, and even in churchmanship. We no longer look to the Sermon on the Mount or other parts of the New and Old Testament for counsels or rules that will direct us in our buying and selling, our peace-making and war-making, even in our church organization.

The faith which we seek to understand in our theologizing is now for us in many circles, perhaps in most, a noetic faith, an acknowledging and a knowing. It is the human counterpart of revelation, of the disclosure of the mysterious other, of the unveiling of the hidden object. To confess our faith is no longer primarily to commit ourselves to a course of action but to affirm a teaching and a doctrine. Systematic theology has once more become doctrinal theology in very wide circles.

In these movements dangers are present of the kind of over-correction which sometimes in the past has led the church to define itself as a doctrinal community, a *Lehranstalt,* and which has made of theology a wholly speculative system, that is, a view of things as spectators see them. The danger of over-correction seems to me to be less great in our movement between these two poles than in our motion from future to past, or from subject to object. And this is true particularly again in America, where for a variety of reasons our orientation has been strongly in the direction of practical reasoning or of doing more than knowing. Hence, we need not be overly alarmed about the danger of soon becoming a purely doctrinal community in the church as once we tended to be a purely practical one. But in certain areas, in parts of European theology and in some areas of theological study even in America, the movement toward pure doctrine is evidently a movement toward pure reason, though to pure reason in a Christian form. Barth's *Church Dogmatics* seems for instance to many of us to be a speculative system, a kind of biblical Hegelianism, in which the movement toward pure doctrine, pure Christian reason, has gone so far toward the noetic pole that ethics becomes fundamentally an afterthought.

At all events, our theological movement needs to preserve balance in its movement between these poles no less than in the movement between past and future, subject and object. To recommend the principle of balance to you is something quite different from recommending the middle of the road. The middle of the road is the position which we take between antithetical, not between polar principles. It is the position we take between God and man, or between the service of the one God and the service of ourselves, between trusting in God and trusting in ourselves, between loving the world and loving God, between living in repentance and forgiveness and living by our self-justifying works. Of course theology also is tempted to live and think in the middle of the road. That is a constant temptation for all of us, theologians no less than non-theologians.

But when we think of the principle of balance, we do not think of the middle of the road but of that movement into the future which none of us can escape and which the church cannot escape. In the course of that movement, we are forever subject to the winds and tides which may carry us too far to the north or south, too far to the east or west, even though the winds and tides are in theology itself. Our problem then is that of steering a steady course, not in defiance of the winds of doctrine but in such a manner that we use their force to move us to our goal.

Of course the primary problem in theology today is not that of preserving our balance. I have dealt with this theme tonight only for the purpose of gaining for myself and perhaps for you some general orientation about the place where we now are. Our next steps must not only be balanced steps but forward steps carrying us into new territories. What some of these new territories are, in my view, I shall try to explain in succeeding lectures.

Toward New Symbols

We can approach one of the relatively new and urgent problems in theology by beginning today with a text. I take it from a book about Luther written by the Roman Catholic theologian Joseph Lortz.[1] Lortz is one of those non-defensive Roman Catholic scholars who understands that the Reformation was an event in the history of the whole church; that it remains an irreversible event; that it affected the Roman church no less than the new churches of the Reformation; and that because of it Catholicism today is very different from the Catholicism that Luther knew.

Lortz is more aware than is many a Protestant of the newness, the freshness that marked the Reformation. There is about that movement, when we look at it with his eyes, something that is akin to the clean, clear sweetness of air and earth and sky on a sunrise hour of a day in June. All things have become new. "The ultimate mystery of Luther's effectiveness," he writes, "was his own vitality." Life is present only there where there is something that has not been worn out, something new. But everything that belongs to the world of creatures must wither. And to this belongs even the form in which God's word proclaims to us God's never-aging revelation. In this situation the church must ever and again realize the word: "Behold, I make all things new."

Now there can be no doubt that the Christendom of late medievalism had become very old in this sense. Its formulae had been used in an unprecedented, unheard-of degree, and so had been used up. Or otherwise they were new but not derived from the word of God itself. They had, rather, been distilled out of other previously derived (excogitated) formulae and were strangely distant from the heart of the Bible and of the liturgy; they were strangely complicated, necessarily sterile. Luther sensed this in a measure beyond that of anyone around him. The secret of his success was that he broke through this sterile, antiquated, atomized conceptual language and forced his way to the source of a new proclamation. He made things new. He spoke a new language.[2]

Lortz's reflections on Luther and the Reformation direct our attention to a point that is basic to a whole set of problems of which we are becoming increasingly aware in religion and theology. We speak of the problem of making our preaching and teaching relevant to modern men. In ever new editions of revised and standardized translations we wrestle with the problem of reproducing the words of the prophets and the apostles in contemporary language. We engage in debates with philosophers about the meaning and the logic of religious language. We are concerned with Bultmann about the demythologizing and the remythologizing of the Gospel. We analyze the meanings of dramas and novels with the half-formed conviction that some of these are saying in their ways more effectively than we can what the Gospel says about man, though not about God. We consider whether the psychologists with their references to the primordial, or at least primitive symbols, with their use of myths from Greek rather than biblical antiquity are pointing us to depths of meaning even in our unconscious lives with which religion may be even more concerned than psychiatry and which theology ought to understand. In these and other ways church and theology are groping their way forward into an unmapped region that challenges penetration not only because of its mystery but because practical need requires them to abandon the overused, overcultivated land on which they have lived.

The time has not yet come when this region can be opened in its apparent wholeness, but as we contemplate our next steps in theology, both theoretical and practical, we are entitled to some reflections on the nature of the task that lies before us. As we do so we remind ourselves that, as in the case of every new physical region open to human experience and exploration, there have been predecessors. Every da Gama has been preceded by a Columbus, every Columbus by a Leif Erikson. In our own American theology Horace Bushnell with his essay on language and Jonathan Edwards before him with his reflections on the importance of images had this country of symbols in view, but they also had their predecessors all the way back to the prophets.[3]

I

Our problems, like those of Bushnell and Edwards, are ultimately practical. We are concerned with the apprehension and the communication of the real as we encounter, grasp and communicate reality in our own existence, in our life with God. But our preliminary steps toward understanding the nature of our problems must be somewhat theoretical. Otherwise we may be led to consider the practical problems at too superficial a level and devise only expedient and superficial measures for dealing with them, such as the superficial measures some theological students seem to have in mind when they ask how to translate the language of theology into homiletic discourse, as though theology somehow spoke an original language.

Our first step is to understand with the aid of such philosophers of language and symbolic forms as Ernst Cassirer, such students of anthropology as Benjamin Lee Whorf, such art historians as E. H. Gombrich, and with the psychologists of perception, how much our apprehension of things is dependent on the images, the symbols, the *schemata* with which we come to them.[4] The language we speak is not only a means of communication between speaker and hearer; it is also a means of communication between both and the objects about which they converse. We come to our early study of foreign languages with the simple notion that the common world is made up of a discrete number of things and processes for which different people have different names, and to a certain limited extent this is true. So that we can learn some rudiments of a strange tongue by pointing to objects and asking by gesture for the name of the thing: sun, *Sonne, sol, helios;* tree, *Baum, arbor, dendros,* etc.—interchangeable words apparently for the same thing. Interlanguage dictionaries are possible. Yet if we persist in our study of French and German and Japanese, Chinese, Russian, of Hebrew, Greek, Latin, we soon find ourselves in the presence of the untranslatable and discover also that many of the words we had translated have a somewhat different meaning in the context of the foreign tongue than the apparently parallel names have in ours. So we begin to wrestle with such questions as what the Hebrews meant by *amūnāh* and how what they meant is related to what the Greeks meant by *pístis* and to what the Latins meant by *fides* and to what early Anglo-Saxons meant by faith and to what modern Anglo-Saxons mean by faith and to what Luther in his time and then modern Germans mean by *Glaube,* etc. And then the understanding begins to dawn on us that language is not only a means men use for communication with each other about a common world but also a way they employ for constituting, articulating, apprehending such a world. With the aid of language on the symbolic and the symbols hidden in language, we organize this "blooming, buzzing confusion" of the sounds, the light waves, the forces that assail our sensitive spirits from without. There seems to be no perception of anything which does not contain an interpretation, and there is no interpretation which is not a function of our social communication as well as of our interaction with the objects. Communication is a three-way process in which an active questioning and answering, interpreting and correcting goes on not simply between speaker and hearer but between both of these and their common objects. Yet further, there are no really common objects except in a society in which the symbolic process goes on organizing, articulating, relating the sounds and sights that come from so-called objects.

We are trying to communicate right now, and you meet all these sounds that issue from my voice and from the microphone with expectations, with articulations, with symbolic forms. Otherwise there would be no communication, and we're talking about words and about symbols, the third thing in our minds, and we have to communicate with them if we are to talk with each other.

What inquiry into our verbal language suggests is reinforced by our experience with that other mode of expression and communication we call art. The poets, the men who make, the painters, the sculptors, we are inclined to say, use expressive language rather than informational speech. They body forth in images what they have seen, though the organ of their vision may be an inner, an intuitive or imaginative eye. Yet they also inform. What they seize upon and image becomes for those to whom they speak a form with which to apprehend the world about them. If their subject matter consists of natural beings, of trees and landscapes and faces, then their first task often seems to be that of freeing themselves as far as they can from tradition, from the stereotyped symbolic forms with which they and their society have always apprehended the surrounding world. Part of the story of modern art is this effort of the artist to break the stereotypes that are in our minds. Though they never achieve a complete innocence of eye, a perception of things bare of any interpretation, they do see with a certain freshness a world that is overfamiliar to their fellow men and which, because it is so familiar, is not really seen anymore. The result may be that those who are instructed by the artist come to apprehend the familiar freshly and with new vision. They no longer see the pictures in their own minds that were previously just triggered off by some impression on the senses, but they bring fresh schemes of interpretation to the common world. After Rembrandt has done his work, all who have looked upon his portraits see in the human faces round about them something of depth and tragedy and meaning that they could never have seen before when they had only been instructed by earlier artists with their portraits of the bland, otherworldly masklike faces of medieval vision. And this is true of landscapes also. The Constables and Turners, the Van Goghs and Cézannes have equipped the seeing eye with symbols of light and color and movement with which to perceive a world of nature not apprehended before. What had been seen before had been seen of course with the aid of other symbolic frames or *schemata* used in other types of art. This is not the place in which to deal with the differences between the various languages of art and science and so-called common sense. My point has nothing to do with these differences now but only with something they have in common, and what they have in common, I suggest, are these two things. First, they all use languages in which communication goes on not only between speakers and hearers, imagists and viewers, but also between both of these parties and their common world of objects. This is as true of science as it is of art. And secondly, the forms, the schemes, the images and concepts embodied in language and art and science shape and articulate the common world. The world we live in is always an interpreted world. The objects and the persons that surround us never photograph themselves directly on the sensitive films of previously unexposed minds. Every vision, every hearing that we have is something like a work of art in which we impose our interpretative images on what we see and hear and touch and smell and feel. We never deal with brute facts but only with artifacts. They are the product of the energies of what is given to us and what we give to it. All seeing and hearing is communication; it is a give and take. And in that communication the symbolic forms of our languages, of our arts and sciences play a determinative role. The argument I am making is not an argument for an idealism, for which the so-called real world is a projection of the spirit, whether of the individual spirit or of the group or of a world spirit. It is an argument—to speak in somewhat philosophical terms—for a critical realism, but for a critical realism of an historic sort. Such critical realism understands our communication with natural objects and with persons about us as a continuing movement in which correction is forever taking place and in which the process of interpretation never ceases.

II

If these first points will be granted at least provisionally, that we grasp reality with the aid of symbols mediated in our languages and that true communication is always a three-way conversation, we may then inquire how symbols lose their vitality and what the consequences of such loss of vitality are.

Loss of symbolic vitality may have many causes but I think it appears mainly in two interdependent ways. Symbols have lost vitality when they so merge with the realities to which they refer that communication between knower and known no longer takes place. Communication no longer takes place when there are no more questions and no more answers; when subject and object no longer have anything to say to each other, when all mystery has been banished. When my symbol for water, let us say, "H_2O" or the "thirst quencher," seems so wholly adequate that I no longer wonder about it, no longer ask whether the images of the poets and the concepts of the philosophers and the formulae of the scientists are helpful for understanding; when I no longer delight in St. Francis's naming of it as "sister water"; when it is just what the dictionary and my commonsense symbols say it is, a fluid, something that flows, something that cleanses; then the symbol and the thing have become so identified that communication between knower and known has stopped. This is the process of which we are aware in all these encounters with human individuals in which we substitute for that individual a symbol or image of the group to which he belongs. What happens in such stereotyping is this, that encounters with an individual who had a certain skin color or perhaps a certain facial conformation, simply aroused in the mind of the viewer the recollection of a stylized, stereotyped group portrait. And this is what he saw: the symbol by which he had learned to make his first hypothetical interpretation. He never saw the actual individual; he only saw roughly and in outline an image of a symbol. Everything looked alike to him, because he was not seeing what was before him but the symbol in his eye. The symbol or the scheme in such cases is no longer used in conversation as a hypothesis to be corrected but as a dogma to be implicitly believed. So there is no conversation with the object anymore. Knower and known live with each other as the somewhat fictitious old couples do who have nothing more to say to each other because they know each other so well and they know what is in the mind of the other, or so they think. The symbol has taken the place of the object, and with the symbol itself there can be no interaction; it is a tool. Such loss of symbolic vitality may be illustrated in all the realms of communication. It is present in science when a process or a thing is regarded as completely known by means of a current symbol. This seems to have been the case in the later days of Ptolemaean astronomy. Slight refinements, to be sure, could still be made in the adjustment of the scheme to the observed motions of the heavens. But the conversation between man and the stars was petering out until Kepler came along with fresh symbols and fresh questions.

The loss of symbolic vitality in the language of poetry is a well-known phenomenon. When all love is aflame and every beloved a red, red rose with lily white brows and rosy lips, what is left of the realities of love's encounters? Only the symbol remains and men begin to be in love with love, or better, with the symbolic images of love. Of course love is too strong a passion in human life to allow for any considerable time this substitution of the stereotype for the individual realities of persons and encounters. Hence, it may be that symbols of love on the whole do not succumb to the same kind of loss of vitality that we meet in such realms as those of patriotism and religion. Yet even in this case, as witness the dreary conventionalism of "realistic" love in contemporary novels, the loss of vitality can also take place.

In the realm of moral language and moral apprehension this kind of loss of symbolic vitality appears when we substitute for our encounters with the infinite world of delightful, useful, hateful, harmful, beautiful, sublime, wholesome, destructive beings—in their infinite relation to each other—some standard symbol of the good, for instance, the useful. Then we are no longer able to communicate with the world of values. We have only one question to ask of the things we meet, namely, what is it good for? How does it fit into the scheme of the useful? Even the marvelous richness of our natural world no longer excites us to conversation because we interpret it all by means of a utilitarian theory of evolution. And the argument here is not against evolution but against the nineteenth century version of utilitarian evolution. The oriole's and bluejay's magnificent colors, the cowbird's immorality, the strength of the oak and the rattlesnake's poison, the early coming of the crocus, are just so many examples of the survival of the fittest in the cold and hot wars of nature. And there are even simpler, meaner ways of reducing our encounters with the extravagant opulence of the world of good and evil to a kind of commercial transaction in which all that we have in mind is the mediocre symbol, such as that of monetary worth. A man may look upon a virgin forest of tall pines and see only so many million plank-feet of lumber.

25

In these and many ways our symbols may be so substituted for the real that communication with the world has ceased. The dreadful monotony of life among things which familiarity has led us to hold in contempt is monotony of life with our symbols. What is so familiar that we are contemptuous of it is nothing but our own symbolic interpretation of the real. The familiar is what we no longer see because we see only our symbolic pictures of it.

The loss of symbolic meaning may take place in another though related way. Symbols may cease to facilitate communication between men rather than between men and things. The symbol, the word or sentence conveying to you an image or a concept, may be so conventional, so agreed upon between us that there are no more questions to be asked, that there is nothing more that needs to be said, between us, nothing more that needs to be done. When symbols are used dogmatically among men there is no communication, but only impartation. If I have declared to you that the only correct symbol for a man's relation to his political society is that of patriotism, love of the fatherland, a relation like that of an obedient son to an admired father, and have required you on the ground of some authority, whether my own or that of the community, to use only that symbol in assessing and forming *your* relations to your society, then there is no room for further communication on the subject. No questions are permitted. No other symbols are allowed. Hereafter we shall use the word patriotism and the image conveyed by it without further definition and without further inquiry. We shall communicate with each other about this man's patriotism or that man's, but not about the character of proper and good relations on the part of men to their society. We shall *proclaim* patriotism only.

The dogmatic use of symbols which stops all communication about the thing symbolized and also all communication with the reality symbolized, usually results from less drastic procedures than those we have envisioned. It is the consequence of common usage rather than of fiat. It is established by prestiged persons rather than by those who have been formally appointed to authority or who have seized power. It is the outcome of our common tendency to regard as self-evident the symbols with which we almost unconsciously organize our world. Perhaps it is the outcome of that tendency which Karl Barth so magnificently described as a part of the human flaw, just sheer human sluggishness, laziness, torpor.

Yet as soon as symbols are used dogmatically, as soon as they are so identified in usage with the reality to which they refer that no other symbols are allowed, so soon real communication between the men who use them as well as with the realities to which they refer comes to a stop. They are no longer heuristic in character, instruments for the discovery of meanings in the other man's mind and meanings in the object; they become definitions, determinations, things to be proclaimed.

As a preliminary device for establishing a basis for communication, as in the case of young children, or in the case of our own learning of a foreign language, or a new science, the dogmatic method doubtless has a place in communication among men and between them and their common world. But when it is used primarily, it is no longer a way of communicating but simply of proclaiming. And its persistent use leads to loss of meaningfulness. Neither the symbol nor that which is to be understood by it can retain their meaning, since meaning is a function of relation; and what is identical is no longer related. It is significant, meaningful to say that the Bible is the word of God, when I and my hearer understand that "Word of God" is a symbol with the aid of which the Bible can be apprehended and understood. But when the two are identified so that word of God means Bible and Bible means word of God, nothing meaningful is being said anymore about the symbolized reality or about the symbol. When we say that the word of God is the Bible and the Bible is the word of God, we no longer communicate meanings to each other or communicate with the Bible. We simply affirm that we have decided to use two names for the same thing.

This illustration leads us then to the problem of the loss of vitality in the religious and specifically Christian symbolism in our time. The question arises for us whether we are not, in our Protestantism, at something like the point at which the medieval church found itself in the days before Luther and the Reformation. We also have used our formulae and our symbols to an unheard-of degree. Evangelistic and missionary preaching for hundreds of years now, sermons in millions of Protestant churches, avalanches of printed paper, Sunday School lessons, church papers, tracts, brochures, pamphlets, commentaries, popular and academic theological treatises—every minister's wastebasket and study table bears witness—have repeated and repeated and repeated the words and the symbols of our evangelical faith. The language is familiar. The symbols are worn. Are they worn out? The words

slide from our tongues and enter our eyes and ears without ever caus-
ing a shock, a shock of recognition of ourselves, a shock of encounter
with a reality that is different from all of our imaginings. They bring
us no surprises, whether by joy or sudden pain, whether by discovery
of the unknown or by revelation of a long-sought secret.

Let us consider how much this is the case with some of our formulae.
I have made reference to the designation of the Scriptures as the word
of God. That is a case in point. In the days of the Reformation when
the printing press was just beginning its work and few people could
read, when the world beyond life and death was nearer to men in their
whole symbolic relationship to reality than it is now, when the historical
consciousness was very different from that of our time, when the value
of words had not yet suffered from the great inflation that has gone
on through our highly vocal modern centuries, then this symbol for
the Scriptures and this symbol for the action by which God deals with
men had a meaningfulness we rarely recapture today, if ever. If we do
recapture it, if we do revitalize the symbol, this is done in other ways
than was the case in the sixteenth century. By and large the symbol is
no longer a means of communication with the Scriptures nor is it a
symbol of communication about the Scriptures between men. We tend
to substitute for it in our theological discourse derivative, secondary
formulae, dependent for instance on epistemological theories of revelation. In general we are in respect of this symbol in the situation in
which Lortz found medievalism. The "formulae had been used in an
unprecedented, unheard-of degree, and so had been used up. Or otherwise they were new [but] had been distilled out of other previously
derived formulae" and were "strangely complicated, necessarily sterile."

So it is with the great symbols of "justification by faith," and "faith"
itself, "conversion," "repentance," "sin," "grace," "sovereignty of
God," even "incarnation" and "atonement." We sense reality in the
powers and processes that we seek to apprehend and to communicate
with the aid of these symbolic words or verbal symbols. Yet the words
have so often taken the place of the actuality to which they once referred, they have been used dogmatically for so long a time, that this
reality comes barely into view and rarely comes into view in its strange
individuality. The scheme by which we apprehended the real has largely
taken the place of that which was once apprehended partly by its
means.

The problem which this situation raises for the preacher, the priest, the teacher, the theologian, and that myriad-minded so-called man in the pew is evident to most of us. There are, to be sure, those who tend to say that the language of Christian faith is of such a nature that it must use the conventional symbols and only these, that what is to be said must be said dogmatically, kerygmatically, by way of information, and only so. Preaching must be proclamation, not interpretation. Hence arises what seems to some of us to be one of the current great issues in theology: Is the language of our faith really primarily kerygmatic and dogmatic, stating what needs to be believed; or is it communicative, heuristic, interpretative language, the language of a dialogue in the three-way conversation of men with God and with one another in his presence? Without undertaking now to argue that question, taking the position that all dogmatic definitions are purely preliminary, and that our real concern in the church is with dialogue rather than with proclamation, I ask you to consider with me whether there are ways in which the symbolic system of our communication is being and can be refreshed, and in what directions we ought to look for its greater revitalization.

III

The first step in the direction of a revitalization of a symbolic system is taken I believe when men begin to understand that there is something wrong with the language they are using, when they become aware of the loss of meaning their symbolic system has suffered. A step of protest is made in consciousness of the fact that something is wrong, though what is wrong has not yet been determined. This sense of something wrong with our language and our symbolic system arises in the midst of our conversation with one another. I feel my lack of proper words and symbols when I am trying to communicate with a person who is present to me and indicating to me by gestures, for instance, that he needs to know something. I feel it also when I am trying to capture an idea, that is, to understand something of which I am aware but which I cannot know until I have a word and symbol for it. I do not really sense my lack of helpful words when I am trying to learn what is for me a dead language, that is a language for communication with folk who are no longer alive, and with realities no longer known by me with them. For some few people it may be that the question of religious language is the question of reviving a dead language. But most of us feel it is a problem of developing a living language, a language for the living. What we sense to be wrong is this, that there are many people around us who by their gestures, by their bearing, indicate their need of hearing something from us in the church but who shake their heads when we speak to them in our foreign tongue. And we have this uneasy sense as well, that we do not have the right words, the right ideas with which to capture and to bring into full consciousness the actuality of that Christ, that working of God, that sense of malaise in our life, that expectation of healing, which are all continuous, we believe, with what our fathers knew and are yet to be our own experiences, to be grasped by us with the aid of *our* symbols and *our* words and communicated by *us* in our living time.

All the speech about demythologizing and becoming relevant which goes on among us in church and theology, all the new translating of the Scriptures, are indicative of this sense of something wrong with our speech. Often while we are insisting that others should learn our language and that we fully know what we are talking about when we use our words, we yet remain unhappy for we sense that there is something provincial in our speech and something vague in our apprehension of the realities.

As in all other areas of life repentance, metanoia, sorrow for our failure, for our inadequacies, for our pride is a first step toward renewal and we may hope that we shall not in church and theology seek too quickly to assuage our bad consciences by blaming our companions for not learning our language, or by blaming the Gospel of God for being so mysterious and beyond apprehension. Metanoia is the first step, and we may need to stay for a long time in the situation in which our sorrow for our inadequacy places us. It is human to try to get rid of pain as quickly as possible, to find that fast-acting pain reliever which is quicker than anything else. But God does not heal us with the aid of such patent medicines. He often requires long periods of repentance.

We take another hesitant and microscopic step toward the renewal of our symbols or toward the discovery of new symbols when we recognize and fully accept both the necessity of symbol and the differences between symbol and reality. Skepticism about our symbols may of course turn into skepticism about the acts and powers to which they refer or which are grasped by means of them. But contrariwise such skepticism may be a function of faith itself. Just because a man becomes aware of God he may become skeptical about all the names for God he has heard and has used, and may refuse to commit himself to any one of them. Just because he has become aware in the depths of his personal existence of the power that Jesus Christ exercises, he may become skeptical of the adequacy of any and all the categories by which Christ and his work have been apprehended. Just because he has been made aware of the gift of a life that is not like this life, he may refuse to give absolute credence to the symbols of everlastingness or immortality or freedom or resurrection.

When we arrive at this point of making a distinction between symbol and actuality, we may be tempted to follow the way of negative theology and of mysticism in religion. And certain temptations to pursue this course arise for modern men out of the development of philosophy of language. But neither the need for communication with God through Christ in the Holy Spirit, nor the need for communication with our fellowmen from whom we need to learn and to whom we must give what we can, allows us to pursue the negative road. Where there is only silence there is no communication; there is no communication between men and there is no real communication in silence between ourselves and the other. We must accept then the necessity of symbols while denying to them ultimate validity.

The other way we can then choose in our awareness of the unity and the difference between symbol and reality, is the way of multiplying symbols so that not one of them will ever be accepted by ourselves or those with whom we communicate as adequate or as identical with the reality interpreted with its aid.

This is, it seems, the way of Scripture. Who is God? With what likeness will you compare him? He is the maker of heaven and earth. He is the cosmic poet who by his word brings forth what he has imaged in his mind. He is the King. He is the Judge. He is the Captain of the host of heaven. He is the one who will be there. He is Father. He is the one who hides himself. Every symbol that the Scripture uses is at once denied as to its adequacy by the introduction of another symbol. Consider the Lord's Prayer: "Our Father who art in heaven—thy kingdom come." So in the case of Jesus, he is the Anointed One, the Messiah, the Lord, the Spirit, the Great High Priest, the Savior, the Son of God, the Captain of salvation, the author and perfecter of faith. What is the newness like that which comes into human life when it relates itself to this God with the many names, in the company of this many-titled Christ? It is like turning around and having everything on the left hand that was previously on the right, that is being converted, turned. It is like being born again. It is like being killed and being raised again to life, being crucified and rising with Christ. It is like being a criminal before the bar and knowing that one is guilty and then having the judge set one free. It is like being reconciled and brought to peace with an enemy after a long war. It is these things, yet it is only like these things and not to be identified with any one of them.

We note further that the symbolism of the Scriptures is never static. In every age, among every new people, old symbols are refreshed by the addition of new ones. The God of the fathers is called the God of Sinai and the Creator and the one who does new things; the messiah becomes the *Kyrios*, The Spirit, the Great High Priest, the *Logos*, the Son. Each new symbol doubtless brings with it the danger of a new dogmatism and a new idolatry in which the category takes the place of the reality it was meant to interpret and not to replace. But the multiplication of symbols with the addition of new ones opens up communication with reality as conventionalism never does.

The addition of new symbols did not stop with biblical history. It has gone on through all the ages, particularly in the ages of revival. And we are adding some in our time, a few, such words and phrases as "alienation" and "encounter" and the meeting of "I and Thou" and "courage to be" and words we take over from psychology and sociology: "anxiety," "guilt feeling," "integration," and many more are not alien intruders into a language that ought to be kept pure at all costs. They are the rather hesitantly used symbols of a still living language which has not yet been fundamentally renewed.

Such new additions to our symbolic system are very modest contributions to its grand renewal. When may we expect that more radical renaissance which our religious need and the religious need of our fellowmen appear to require? Fundamentally I believe that we can expect it from no other kind of source than from the kind represented in Luther's experience. He made all things new in his day. He could translate the Gospel into the vulgar tongue of his day. He found freshly minted parables. He brought forth new symbols because he wrestled with, he encountered, he experienced, he heard, he searched out himself-before-God and God-before-himself. What he communicated was not the word of God in the Scriptures but the word that he had heard God speaking to him, Martin Luther, in the Scriptures. It was not the word that anyone could hear but which came to the ears of an agonized listener, of one who was fighting for his life, who was crying for help and heard the distant answer of the helper. Man's wrestling with God or with himself before God takes different forms, in different lives, and different times. Of this, however, I think we can be certain, that a new religious language and a new symbolism do not in the first place grow out of our need to communicate to our fellowmen something we already know but out of our encounter and communication with the actuality, with the reality of our own existence in, with, before God—in all of our searching out of what we do not yet know but experience in twilight, sense as present, recognize as inescapably there and still have no word for it.

To this I am inclined to add this final observation. On the side of theology taken by itself—though it never really can be taken by itself, apart from religion, from the church and all the work of the ministry— a next step toward the renewal of symbols or toward new symbols may be taken by accepting more seriously than we have yet done the meaningfulness of man's symbolic life. The symbol itself becomes a symbol with which to apprehend the reality with which we are dealing. The symbolic function of Jesus Christ in our life of interpretation is a subject for our exploration. The recognition of Jesus Christ as interpretative symbol of God and also of men does not need to lead us into the realm of mythology but may lead, I believe, in the direction of a better grasp in our day of who he is and of what he does. The symbolism of the symbolic has its own dangers, of course, but if we are always frightened by the dangers of heresy we shall eventually speak only a dead language.

Toward the Recovery of Feeling

The frontiers of religion and theology, like all borderlands which lie beyond the scene of cultivation, are vaguely defined areas. Reports and rumors about the unknown territory reach us, for there have always been earlier adventurers who have brought back their surmises as well as their observations. This is true of that region of symbols about which we spoke in the previous lecture, and into which our religion and theology are moving hesitantly, slowly with many a retreat before threatening dangers. Will the land on the border turn out to be a desert? Are the mountain ranges too high to be passed without disaster? Would it not be better to return to the cultivated land where custom and habits have given us security? If such thoughts assail us when we think of theology's task in the exploration of man's symbolic life, and of religion's work in bringing forth new symbols out of its encounters with the ultimate, they also arise perhaps even more acutely as we think of this other borderland, the land of man's emotions.

The emotions are deeply suspect in our time, and not least suspect are the religious emotions. That we are emotional creatures is all too evident to us. But that our feelings put us into touch with what is real, objective, powerful, abiding, this we greatly misdoubt. That we can rely upon them in any way so to guide us in our reactions to the environing powers as to bring forth good, this we scarcely dare to believe.

The climate of opinion, that is, the accepted presuppositions of our era, predispose us to value most highly our observing, our spectator reason and our technical intelligence. We no longer live, to be sure, in that age of rationalism which reached its zenith in the eighteenth century, yet we live in a successor time to that era. We are not so confident as our forebears two hundred years ago were that the world about us is a great rational structure, a machine operating according to implicit laws inscribed into it by a great designer, or that it is a great logical system in which consequences follow inexorably from premises according to the immanent laws of a cosmic mind. The world of nature around us and the social world with its history are for us more pluralistic and complicated. We suspect that there may be powers and movements in nature and in history which do not operate according to laws of mechanical causality or of logical development out of known premises. We also know ourselves to be less rational in our judgments about what is going on and in our decisions about what to do than did the rationalists of the eighteenth century.

Yet the more suspicious we have become of total, all-encompassing rationality in our world and in ourselves, the greater has grown our confidence that by means of cool understanding, disinterested, unemotional observation of the actions of things and of men, we shall be able to discover an inner rationale in specific things, and the greater has become our faith in the ability of our reasoning to outwit things.

There is a man in space this morning.[1] Technical, scientific reasoning has achieved its victory, if that is what it is.

The world may not be one great system with a single logic pervading all its parts, but we do believe the various elements in it have discoverable, predictable ways of behavior. We are confident that by observation and theory we can understand these ways and we can react accordingly so as to maintain and perhaps advance ourselves.

Ours is then an age of confidence in the sciences and in technical reasoning, as we are often reminded. It is an age of confidence in analytic more than in synthetic reason. We are less concerned with questions about the great constancies in nature and human history as wholes than with the constancies in manageable specific entities. Hence, we are suspicious of big questions, but we specialize in answering small inquiries. We do not think it worthwhile to ask, What is the cause of evil? But we do regard it as significant to inquire, What is the cause of cancer or of juvenile delinquency, of guilt feelings, of race prejudice? We do not ask what are the laws of nature or of human society, but what are the modes of behavior of streptococci, and what are the positive decisions of judges in our society.

Yet, even so, the question which is most important for us is the question which the observer asks about what is the case. So we remain in general in a period of rationalism, that is, in a period in which we regard as the most important element in our human makeup, our ability to understand objective actions in their quantitatively measurable characteristics.

We do not grant much importance to that other activity of ours which accompanies all our analysis of things, namely our loving, rejecting, hating, being attracted, being repelled—our valuing. On the contrary, the temper of the times is one which deeply suspects this element in our existence. We are suspicious of enthusiasm as the rationalists were in the eighteenth century. The emotions, the passions, the feelings are up to nothing good, we believe. They furnish us with no knowledge of what is the case. They are nonobjective for us almost by definition. They are not elicited, we believe, by objects. They rather project unreal objects before us. They do not discover value in what is present to them and what excites them; rather they attribute value to what has nothing of value in itself. Value and emotion are thought to go together, and the one partner in this partnership is as dubiously dependable as the other.

Emotions are not only subjective in our general view, giving us no knowledge of what is the case, they are also in this general estimate of our time private and personal. The emotional statements that something is good or bad, that there is loveliness, ugliness, fearsomeness, holiness around us are personal, individual statements expressing the attitudes of those who make them. They are not statements about what is really true, nor are they statements on the whole of a common spirit subject to corroboration by others who deal with the same objects.

Some exceptions, to be sure, must be made to this general judgment. It seems reasonable to some of our moral philosophers who find no rational—that is, objective—grounds for value judgments that we should nevertheless be guided by certain common emotional attitudes prevailing in our society. But the ultimate bases of such emotional attitudes they find hard to justify.

Three counts, then, interlock in the indictment of the emotions. They are subjective, so that they do not give us knowledge of what is really the case. They are essentially private, so that their findings are not subject to social verification. They present false objectives to us, objectives that can be neither relied upon nor verified.

Since for the most part the emotional objectives or values, good and evil, are the value characteristics of objects, the indictment of the emotions is also an indictment of the reality of the world of values. This dominant temper of the times is explicitly set forth in its most extreme fashion in the kind of logical positivism which dismisses ethics, religion, and poetry as speaking meaningless languages.[2] But this extreme statement is indicative of a general attitude. And I mean attitude, an emotional attitude upon the part of the decriers of emotion, which is less extremely expressed in all the preferences accorded to scientific and technical reasoning which alone is thought entitled to the praiseworthy adjective "objective." It is indicative of the attitude present in all the

implicit judgments we make that poetry and music belong to the lux-
uries of life, not to the necessities of our existence; that ethics, as a
concern for values, is really hopelessly subjective and must be reestablished on a scientific foundation; and that the emotional life of man
has its residence in the shadows of our unconscious.

This attitude in our time toward the emotions is not dissimilar to the
attitude which the Greeks, especially Plato, took toward the sensations
and the reports of sense experience. The sense realm was for them the
realm of mere opinion, of *doxa*, of the transitory, the unreliable, the
illusory. Reason needed, they were convinced, to turn resolutely away
from this world of things men saw and heard and touched to the contemplation and examination of the formal which alone was reliable and
abiding. After that suspicion had been established in the common
mind, it required a great revolution in thought before the senses could
be reestablished as one of man's main contacts with the real, the powerful, the reliable, the objective.

The suspicion of the emotions which is prevalent in our culture has
been communicated to theology. But the latter has grounds of its own
for dealing charily with feeling in the religious life. Among these are
the reasons which led the reformers to oppose the enthusiasts—i.e.,
the spirit-filled religious revolutionaries of the sixteenth century—almost as strongly as they challenged the established Roman church. Did
not reliance on feelings lead to anarchy, to the appearance of scores
of wild prophets, each claiming personal inspiration; to the confusion
of spiritual with physical hunger, of hatred against human enemies with
the hatred of Satan, sin, and death; to the confusion too of Eros and
Agape? More importantly, perhaps, especially in America, the so-called
excesses of emotionalism in the revival movements seemed to warn the
church and theology against putting reliance in men's religious feelings
of grief and joy, of being rejected or accepted by God, feelings of
having been saved or being damned, feelings of guilt and feelings of
release.

To these historic reactions against emotionalism I must add the continued and probably necessary tendency of institutional religion—and
institutional religion is necessary—to convert the personally experienced, the immediately grasped into something general, something
that can be conceptually communicated. The community that shares
in immediate sense experience, in visions of a given reality is always
changed for many reasons into a community of common beliefs about

37

that reality. The experience of those who saw a risen Lord must be mediated to new generations as a doctrine that the Lord is risen, and as the belief that he was directly known by apostles in the past to be risen. And so with the emotional experiences, in which confidence and trust are elicited, in which forgiveness is received, hope given, joy communicated—these also are encapsuled in doctrinal forms and the religion is then transmitted as a set of beliefs shared by minds more than communicated in a society of feeling, loving, grieving, hating, fearing, anxious, adoring selves.

When now we add to such historic and perennial reasons for our theological suspicion of religious emotions the influences of the modern climate of opinion, then we need not be puzzled by the very sober and respectable character of religious life in our time. Nor need we be astounded that while our theology seeks contact and dialogue with philosophy and science, it tends to be ashamed if it is found in the company of the poets. When our fate is called poetry, as it is by some, theologians tend to accept the statement as it is meant, to be an indictment, and they rush to defend man's relation to God against the charge that it is an affair of images more than concepts and that religious man is more concerned with the feeling [of] apprehension, of the goodness and the badness, [of] the glory and the shame of his world than with disinterested analysis of sober facts by means of coolly conceived theories.

There is protest of course against all this deprecation and suspicion of the emotions. Man being what he is, there must always be protest. In that eighteenth century age of reason which was the precursor of our own, the emotions of men found their spokesmen at last in the romantic poets and the romantic philosophers. The age of reason had to yield, for a while at least, to the age of feeling. In religion the supernaturalism and super-rationalism of an orthodoxy that was the counterpart of naturalism and rationalism in secular society were overwhelmed by the passionate ardor of Methodism, evangelicalism, pietism, the Awakening. The revival of religion manifested itself as a revival of religious emotions. The Great Awakening was an arousing of the religious affections.

The protest of the emotions in our time, a time of another sort of rationalism, has not appeared in such dramatic form. Some of our poets indeed are moved to protest, but characteristically it is not so much in their poetry as in their prose analysis of what is wrong with man today that this protest is voiced. Archibald MacLeish in his book *Poetry and Experience* has said that the great crisis in history today is not the crisis of the Cold War but fundamentally this: knowledge of the fact has somehow or other come loose from the feel of the fact, and it is now possible for the first time in human history to know as a mind what you cannot comprehend as a man. "To feel emotion," he goes on to say, "is at least to feel. The crime against life, the worst of all crimes, is *not* to feel. And there was never, perhaps, a civilization in which that crime, the crime of torpor, of lethargy, of apathy, the snake-like sin of coldness-at-the-heart was commoner than in our technological civilization."[3]

For the rest, what protest there is, appears in our day in the confused expressions of an emotional life which will not be denied, which is powerful within us, and which when it is banned to the irrational underground will there carry on its furtive activities. Perhaps the least harmful and also the least useful protest of the emotions appears in contemporary man's passion for amusement. R. G. Collingwood in his *Principles of Art* has offered an intriguing and largely persuasive analysis of amusement.[4] In amusement, he points out, emotions are aroused for no other purpose than to be immediately discharged. This is the opposite of the emotions aroused in rite. In rite, emotions are aroused for the sake of being put to work later on, as in the rites of patriotism and in the rites of religion. But in amusement they are aroused for the sake of being immediately discharged. The electricity of love and hate is generated for the sake of producing an immediately grounded spark, not a current to be used in work. We watch our baseball games and have our aggressive feelings kindled, our hopes of victory inflamed, and having killed the umpire in words and realized the great eschaton of the ninth inning with rejoicing, or accepted the grief of defeat, we go away and that is that. So we read the whodunits and view the TV shows—spectators by and large—with spectators' vicarious and immediately discharged emotions. So also we tend to make a game even of human love, man's most perennial occasion for the emotional involvement of being with being but now so often reduced to an amusement that is supposed to have no consequences beyond the moment.

Religion too may become amusement religion, in which religious affections are cultivated for the moment then immediately discharged

in delicious tremors of the feeling of the Holy at eleven o'clock on
Sunday morning, in induced sorrows for sin, quickly assuaged by ab-
solution that must come at once.

When we reflect on the tendencies present in amusement we may
raise the question whether it is really so harmless after all. The emotions perhaps have been made harmless by their discharge in amusement, harmless to interfere with the serious business of technological
reason. But what harm has been done to the objects of the emotions
and to emotive man himself by this relegation of feeling to leisure-time
activity? If feelings are *not* nonobjective, or if those who feel them are
not merely creatures of the moment, then amusement may be more
serious business than we think.

We are aware of more tragic exhibitions of the protest of man's demeaned but irrepressible passions and ardors, fears, faiths, and hopes
in movements such as those of fearsome and brutal nationalism and in
such private searches for transport and for ecstasy—and we all desire
transport and ecstasy—as we find in the drug addictions and alcohol-
isms and in many other emotional confusions of individuals in our
time.

As we reflect on these aspects of our human situation we may arrive
at certain convictions about ourselves such as that our calculating, technical, analytical reasoning has been unable to give order, unity, and
nourishment to us in our irrepressibly emotional existence, and that in
the nature of the case this must be so. We may want to put this in
another way. The love of truth in [the] knowledge of things can never
drive out or supplant or make true our other love of true realities. We
may arrive at the belief with Mr. MacLeish that the wealthier we have
become in knowledge of facts the more impoverished we have become
in our apprehension of values, and that this impoverishment is directly
connected with our enslavement of the emotions, or with our banish-
ment of them from the world of respectable activities. If every age of
darkness has its own kind of light, then every time of enlightenment,
such as ours, has its own obscurantism. And there may grow upon us
in the third place the surmise, that what we suffer from in our religion
is not really the impoverishment of religious emotions only but rather
our failure to understand that religion is primarily an affair of emotion
and of all the emotions of man, and that—or perhaps—our religion
may be related to our total emotional life somewhat as conceptualizing

reason is related to that other way of experience in which we are also subject to so much confusion, namely the way of the senses.

Insofar as such ideas and surmises commend themselves to theologians today, they come to think that one of their next steps must be into the frontier lands of men's feelings. Of course it may not be theology which will take that next step, but practical religion itself in its activities of proclamation, interpretation, prayer, adoration, teaching, and confession. Insofar as theology is challenged to move toward the recovery of the feelings, or better toward the validation and disciplining of man's emotional life, it will find itself following in the footsteps of at least a few of its greatest exponents in the past. And it will not be out of harmony at all with its great guide toward the understanding of God-before-man and man-before-God, namely the Scriptures.

The Bible—which we study age after age, in order to understand the concepts with which the Israelites and early Christians interpreted their experience, or in order to know what theory about himself God communicated to man through his word and *logos*—is written largely in the language of the emotions. It is a book of images, eliciting and expressing emotions, more than a book of concepts, expressing the concerns of an epistemic or technical reason. It speaks of a God who is feared and hated and loved, who is known in fear and love and trust and hope, a God who is objective, but objective to man as emotional being. He is himself wrath and grace, loyalty, steadfastness. Fear of him is the beginning of wisdom [Psalm 111:10]. As a father pities his children he pities those that fear him [Psalm 103:13]. God is love. In thousands of variations the Scriptures play the music, sing the poetry, set forth the images in which love and fear, anger, grief, joy, hope, confidence, peace are expressed and elicited toward and by their proper objects.

The morality of [the] Scriptures is the morality of the rightly reorganized emotions of men, not of the suppressions of emotions by reason. Consider such summary statements of the good life as St. Paul's. "But I say, walk by the Spirit, and do not gratify the desires of the flesh. Now the works of the flesh are plain: immorality, impurity, licentiousness, idolatry, sorcery, enmity, strife, jealousy, anger, selfishness, dissension, party spirit, envy, drunkenness, carousing and the like. I warned you, as I warned you before, that those who do such things shall not inherit the kingdom of God. But the fruit of the Spirit is love, joy, peace, patience, kindness, goodness, gentleness, self-control; against such there is no law. And those who belong to Christ have crucified the flesh with its passions and desires" [Galatians 5:16, 19–24].⁵ What is noteworthy about such passages is that they contain no deprecation of man's emotions in favor of his reason. They rather present the disordered life as a life of disordered emotions, and the life in the Spirit as an emotional life redeemed, liberated, and ordered. In [the] Scriptures it is not reason which drives out fear, but love. The true God is not the object of the intellect—the logical reality calling forth an intellectual apprehension—but God is known, apprehended, loved with heart, soul, mind, and strength. He elicits by his manifestation of his great glory, the praise of all that is within us to bless his Holy name [Psalm 103:1]. God differs from idols, not as reason differs from emotion, but as true love, constant love differs from dissipated love. Because [the] Scriptures speak from feeling to feeling about the objects that elicit feeling and cannot be known without feeling, therefore their devotional use, that is, their use by men who are whole men and not abstracted intelligences has never been supplanted in the church by the conceptualized schemes we developed in our theologies.

Not many theologians, though many devout men, have followed the Scriptures in dealing with the knowledge of God and of man before him and of God's world of many creatures as an apprehension that involves the whole self, including the emotions. To be sure, none of them has been able or has desired to dismiss the contribution of the affections, but for the most part they have been almost as suspicious of feeling as the philosophers have been. They have located God's image in man in human reason, or in man being a subject, and have attended most of all to essences of the sort that concept-forming and idea-projecting reason can grasp. Look at the definitions of God in the creed, these "omni-" definitions: omnipresent, omniwise, and so forth. You never put a word like wrath into a creed, do you? Augustine with his understanding of man as a great deep, the creature of many loves, the Augustine who could set forth the meanings of his meetings with God only in the form of a confession full of expressions of feeling, is of course a great exception to the general rule. So are the reformers, especially in the early days of the Reformation, before the fear of enthusiasm and of social anarchy tempered their reflection. In those days—and later too—they knew that faith in God was fundamentally an affair of the personally trusting heart, much more than of the idea- and theory-accepting mind, that justification was an experience of trust by fearsome, guilt-ridden selves before it was a doctrine to be believed. A Protestant orthodoxy, more concerned with pure doctrine than with pure love and trust and hope, moved theology away from this dangerous area and directed religion to defend itself against the attacks of false ideas, more [than against the impulses][6] rising out of misinterpreted and misdirected emotions.

Pascal with his "reasons of the heart that the reason knows not of" spoke again, and as a theologian, to men in their total existence involved in their emotions. And then came the Awakening and the revival, pietism, the Methodist and evangelical movements; they produced great preachers, great leaders of the religious life such as Wesley, and a few great theologians. Most of these did their work after the wave of emotional religious life had subsided. But traces of its effectiveness showed in their work. Among them was Schleiermacher. Schleiermacher's theory of the feeling of absolute dependence does remind men fleetingly and abstractly of relations to their God and to Christ that lie at a deeper, more personal level than their explicit believings can express. But Schleiermacher did not venture far into the region of man's emotional apprehension of reality; the feeling of absolute dependence is really not an emotion. In Kierkegaard the aspects of man's involvement with himself and with God in anxiety and passion and guilt come to fuller exhibition and analysis. To be sure, moral and religious passion, as he understands them, seem to some of us to be rather dissociated from the fullness of human emotional experience. Kierkegaard enthusiasts and students doubtless find him to be a theologian of man's emotional relationship to God and neighbor. Yet for some of us, especially when we move from [the] Scriptures to him, he presents the picture of a man who was himself somewhat emotionally impoverished. Nevertheless, here are pioneers: Augustine, Luther, Pascal, Wesley, Schleiermacher, Kierkegaard, who have ventured into the land where God and self, neighbor, guilt and destiny, shame and glory are felt, and in that feeling known.

For us in America, the great pioneer who ventured most competently and lovingly into that country which theology in general seems to have avoided was Jonathan Edwards. The recent republication of his *Treatise Concerning the Religious Affections*, given the situation in which we find ourselves in a time of emotional impoverishment, has for us more than historical interest.[7] It was strictly addressed, to be sure, to the immediate problems raised by the great awakening of religion in colonial

America in the 1740s. But he set forth his examination of genuine and spurious manifestations of religious life within the framework of a general theory of religion as largely a matter of emotion and of the emotions as the moving element in human existence. Among the observations he offers are these. *First*, "God has indued the soul with two faculties: one is that by which it is capable of perception and speculation, or by which it discerns and views and judges things; which is called the understanding. The other faculty is that by which the soul does not merely perceive and view things, but is in some way inclined with respect to the things it views and considers; either is inclined to 'em or is disinclined, and averse from 'em; or is the faculty by which the soul does not behold things, as indifferent unaffected spectator, but either as liking or disliking, pleased or displeased, approving or rejecting"[96]. This faculty, Edwards points out, is sometimes called inclination, sometimes will, sometimes heart. He offers some very acute observations on the relations of this faculty to the body. He is a psychosomatic thinker who finds the body more affected by the approving and disapproving movements of the mind or heart than vice versa.

Edward's second great proposition is that "true religion, in great part, consists in the affections . . . in vigorous and lively actings of the inclinations and will of the soul, or the fervent exercises of the heart"[99]. True religion is not an affair of "weak, dull and lifeless wouldings." He invented that word. He had to get a symbol of his own: people who "would do things." True religion is not an affair of weak, dull, lifeless wouldings only little removed from indifference, but a matter of being fervent in spirit, serving the Lord, loving God with all thy heart and all thy soul and all thy might. Such affections, not the speculations of the understandings nor weak inclinations, not wills to believe, are the springs of action. The things of religion, he says, take hold of men's souls no further than they affect them. That is, no further, we would say, than they elicit and arouse emotion. For the support of this position Edwards appeals, as we have done in following him, to the validation of the Holy Scriptures which as he says "do everywhere place religion very much in the affections; such as fear, hope, love, hatred, desire, joy, sorrow, gratitude, compassion, and zeal"[102].

From these and other considerations, Edwards infers "how great their error is who are for discarding all religious affections, as having nothing solid or substantial in them"[119]. As there is no true religion where there is nothing else but affection, so there is no true religion where there is no religious affection[120]. We might paraphrase and translate Edwards's thought in this fashion. The problem of dealing with anarchy and wildness in man's emotional religion cannot be solved by trying to make religion more rational or more a matter of disinterested understanding. To attempt to do this after the manner of Kant on the one hand and the rationalists of doctrinal orthodoxy on the other is to get rid of religion itself. A bad affection can only be overcome by a good affection. Love of the low can only be conquered or sublimated by love of what is high. With these and many detailed observations on the religious affections, Edwards combined a theologian's reflection on the practices of preaching, the administration of the sacraments, and other means of communicating the Gospel. Any use of language, of symbolism and of imagery which did not have in view among other things the stimulation and the redirection of the affections, which was not emotionally true as well as conceptually true, was an inadequate use of language. Edwards worked at his sermons that their symbolism might be right, and had a symbolism and imagery which expressed and elicited the emotions. You may not like his Enfield sermon. He believed it was true, that sinners were in the hands of an angry God.[8] Think of all the images he used in order to speak to men, not to arouse false affection but true affection. He believed it. It was subjectively true for him. So Edwards in his time accepted the challenge of those who said that bad religion was emotional. Indeed, it is, he conceded; and so is good religion. The alternative to bad poetry is not prose, which may be equally bad, but good poetry. The alternative to a disordered world of values is not a reliance upon facts, which also may be disordered, but a world of true valuations. The alternative to lust is not cool reason but true love.

We face a different situation than Edwards faced in his time. The rationalism we encounter is not the rationalism of his day. Theology is not going about its tasks in a church that has been invigorated and also confused by strong reassertions of man's religious emotions. Our task may rather be to prepare for such an awakening than to deal with its purification and its defense. As we move into this area of religious affections, or of the religious ordering of the affections, we can, however, profit by the pioneering work that Edwards and other theologians have carried on. For the present, tentative steps into the emotional understanding of the realities with which we are concerned in religion and toward the understanding of the emotions themselves are being taken by those members of our theological community who are concerned with special problems more than with the general questions of the knowledge of God and the knowledge of ourselves. One thinks here of the pastoral counselor and the students of the place of religion in man's psyche, the psychologists of religion. To the former the questions about the human emotions bulk very large. They are often put in a difficult position, as men who must work with a theology that has no important place for the emotions and with a psychology that abstracts man mostly from his God-relations while it takes his domestic relations very seriously. Further they need to direct their attention very frequently to confused emotional relationships of men, to images of God and of themselves, self-images, that is, to the abnormal. Nevertheless, the concerns of pastoral theology today and the conversation of theologians with psychologists indicate one of the ways in which theology is taking preliminary steps toward the understanding of the importance and the dynamics of man's emotions, as a function not only of his natural but of his supernatural life.

The steps we take in liturgical theology are more hesitant. The increasing interest in liturgy and rite which leaders and laymen in the churches are manifesting seems indicative at times of the manner in which an emotionally starved time seeks to assuage its hunger. In liturgy and rite we do not talk about our loves and fears, our anxieties and hopes; we express them directly in interpersonal conversation. We do not analyze our relationships but manifest them. Liturgy and rite, being expressions of actual, existing, whole men in encounter with God, with Christ, in the Holy Spirit are as emotion-laden as all interpersonal meetings are. But the movement toward liturgical expression and enactment of our faith is often more an effort to reenact the meetings of our ancestors and to duplicate their emotions with the aid of their words than it is the living expression of our own fear and guilt and gratitude and joy in the presence of the Holy One. I know this is a problem with which the liturgical theologians are dealing. How to have this real, present, and not false, this interpersonal emotionally laden life of encounter? Sometimes, as I have noted, some liturgy almost verges on amusement religion, that is, on emotional realization and expression confined to the moment and to the particular circumstances of the institutionalized religious meeting. Nevertheless, despite all the difficulties it encounters, the theology of liturgy and rite, sacramental theology in general, is advancing toward the revival and validation of the religious affections.

The third movement in contemporary theology in this direction also remains largely unacknowledged by the guardians of pure liberal or pure orthodox or pure neo-orthodox doctrines. It enlists the interest of many adventurous younger spirits: it is the movement toward the rapprochement of religion and art. Since art in general in our society is suspect as unrevelatory of reality, as dealing with illusion, as expressive only of the private and subjective, as leisure-time activity for those who can afford such luxury, therefore all speech about art and religion is suspect among us as speech of men who are just playing with life. But then we are discovered as we discover, discovered by those artists who are more dead serious about our human existence than most of our philosophers seem to be, who are more aware of the actualities of our personal existence in despair and dread, in pain and fear and death and hope than our school theologians are with their ready answers to generalized problems that are not our personal dilemmas. And when we take note of this, when we are forced to give up the comfortable notion that art is concerned with the beautiful and only science with the true, then we reflect that though our colleagues who seek to understand man and God with the aid of the artist are venturing into areas where dangers lurk, they are beginning also to explore a realm of human experience of the real that may yield insights denied to those of us who deal only with or tend to deal only with ideas.

Finally among the movements in theological reflection that represent such advance into the borderland of the religious affections, there are the thinkers who enter into conversation with those philosophers who are concerned with the existing man's relations to his world and to himself. These existential phenomenologists who seek to probe our human way of being in the world, our life as life in care, in sympathy, in concrete individual coexistence with our fellows, in the historical present with our particular burden of our past and our particular closed or open future—these men have not turned their backs on science, and the theologians who converse with them do not turn their backs on history of doctrine or the development of systems of theology. But they do affirm that someone is here greater than all science and all knowledge: this living, feeling, dying, rising thou and I.

With all these hesitant steps of ours into the borderland where human affections meet the objects that only affections can meet, will all these become organized into a firm line of march? Will all these various companies of religious inquirers into man's life with his gods and with God find themselves ordered into one company, having a confident plan of attack? These are some of the questions that we raise as we stand on this frontier in theology. What seems to be required in addition to all these special movements is some unified, systematic inquiry, so that all the various approaches which theologians in different fields are making may be related to each other more effectively.

For myself, who am at the end rather than at the beginning of my work in theology, I can only say that were I at the beginning—and I am thinking of these lectures somewhat as the old man's bequest to the young theologians—I can only say that were I at the beginning I should want to follow in Edwards's footsteps more, and undertake an exploration of the land of the emotions with certain hypotheses almost amounting to convictions to be proved or disproved, refined or extended—the hypothesis that contrary to prevalent opinion about the emotions they put us into touch with what is reliable, firm, real, enduring in ways that are inaccessible to the conceptual and spectator reason.

The objectivity of emotional experience seems indubitable, though much discrimination is necessary in judging which objects are transitory and which are enduring, steadfast. Further, I believe that emotional relations to otherness, to objective being, are prior in meaningfulness to intellectual relations. Trust in parents or distrust of them is prior in time and probably personally prior to all identification of parents. So also it may be that love of God or enmity to God, hate of God, is prior to all articulation of our idea of who God is. And so with all our relations to his creatures. I am thinking here in part of what Erik Erikson says in *Childhood and Society* about the place of basic trust in a child's life and in the life of the parents.[9]

I would like to enter into this field with the hypothesis or the guess that theology and its understanding and evaluation of the emotions is now at a point somewhat similar to the one at which philosophy had arrived when it deprecated the sensations as yielding nothing but illusion or insignificant knowledge. Might it not turn out that the emotions are as subject to education as seeing and hearing are? May it not be that our religion is the educator, good or bad educator, of our emotions as our speculative intellect is the educator of our senses?

All of that remains wishful thinking, though I hasten to add that when we believe somewhat in the validity of the emotions, wishful thinking is not so derogatory a term as it is commonly held to be in our society. Whatever be the way of future progress, by practical and theoretical theology into the realm of the religious affections and human emotions in general, we have the warrant of the Scriptures as well as our own feeling to testify to us that the love of God and of our neighbor in him is more important than the understanding of all mysteries and all knowledge.

Following these guides we shall not likely go astray, if we think of theology as primarily bound to serve in its own way the increase of that love, always remembering that "true religion, in great part,"—and true life in great part—"consists in the affections."[10]

2

An Ecumenical Vision

The Doctrine of the Trinity and the Unity of the Church

The newer tendencies in theology may be interpreted in various ways. From one point of view they appear to be efforts to recover the Christian theological heritage and to renew modes of thought which the anti-traditional pathos of liberalism depreciated. So regarded they are aptly called by ancient names, being designated as neo-Catholicism, neo-Protestantism, neo-orthodoxy, neo-Calvinism, and neo-Lutheranism. But in many respects they seem more closely related to the present than to the past. If they turn to old ideas they do so for the sake of rethinking man's relations, nature, and destiny as these are put in question by the cultural and personal crises of our day. In all their use of tradition they show that they have been schooled in liberal thought. Hence they may be characterized as post-liberal or as crisis theologies. There is in them, however, usually a third interest. What the new movements attempt to do among other things is to state Christian truth from the point of view of the Church rather than the individual as subject. Far apart as they may seem to be in their scholasticism or their Protestantism they share a common interest in the catholic fellowship and seek to understand life and to formulate faith in the thought-forms of that fellowship. If they turn to tradition, they do so as Church-theologies which carry on in living fashion the tradition of the Church. If they deal with the crises of human existence they do so because the Church and the revelation it employs in all its understanding show the critical character of human existence in all times. So interpreted the newer tendencies are part of the ecumenical and catholic movement and may well be called ecumenical theologies.

One Christian doctrine which had importance in all three respects and which may therefore be moved nearer the center of interest in coming years of theological discussion is the doctrine of the Trinity. Liberalism tended, on the whole, to regard this teaching as primarily of historical and antiquarian interest. "The historic doctrine of three eternal persons who are nevertheless but one divine Being" was, as D. C. Macintosh stated the understanding of liberal theology, "the product of the Greek speculative philosophy of the early centuries of the Christian era—a philosophy which can hardly be said to be the philosophy of the modern mind."[1] Now that Greek thought has come to be regarded with greater appreciation both for its inherent value and for its persistence in the thought-forms of the Western world, such a judgment may be subject to revision. It may be that the doctrine of the Trinity, just because it represented the union of philosophy and faith in the early centuries, will be rethought and restated by a theology which undertakes to reappropriate the Christian tradition and to make explicit what has been implicit in Western thought. The approach to the doctrine of the Trinity from the point of view of man's enduring crisis is of greater importance. The existential problem of God and of man's relation to him leads inevitably to the question about the deity of the Creator of nature, that is, of his goodness, to the question about the deity of Jesus Christ, that is, of his power, and to the question about the deity of the Spirit, that is, whether among all the spirits there is a Holy Spirit. These religious problems are not solved independently of each other by Christian faith. Hence crisis thinking directs attention to the problem and the doctrine of the Trinity. The doctrine, however, also has great importance for an ecumenical theology as a formulation of the whole Church's faith in God in distinction from the partial faiths and partial formulations of parts of the Church and of individuals in the Church. It is with this aspect of Trinitarianism that this article is to be concerned in the way of a preliminary exploration.

The Three Unitarianisms in Christianity

Christianity has often been accused of being a polytheism with three gods and, indeed, the tendency toward such tritheism is probably always present in Christendom. Yet it seems nearer the truth to say that Christianity as a whole is more likely to be an association, loosely held together, of three Unitarian religions. Though we are accustomed to think of Unitarianism as being the doctrine that there is only one God and that this God is the Father, the Creator referred to in the first article of the Creed, a fresh approach to Christian history and to contemporary Christian thinking suggests the hypothesis that there are two other positions comparable to the first. It has often been maintained in effect that the one God on whom men must rely for salvation is Jesus Christ; hence there is a kind of Unitarianism of the Son. And it has often been held in theory and practice that the one God is the Spirit, rather than the Creator known in Nature or the Son known in Scriptures. The common monotheism of Christian faith asserts itself in the first part of each of these statements—there is but one God and God is one. The divergences in Christianity enter with the definition of the nature of the one God and of the place where he is to be found.

The Unitarianism of the Creator seems to be easily identifiable. Its first interest has always been monotheistic. It is a protest against polytheistic and idolatrous tendencies in the Churches. But it has seemed self-evident to this monotheism that the one God whom it is man's duty to worship and on whom he depends for significance and salvation is the reality which accounts for the presence and the pattern and the dynamic of the natural world. He is the Almighty Maker of heaven and earth, the first cause and the great designer. God is the being with whom a philosophy that proceeds from nature to super-nature is concerned and this is the same One of whom Hebrew religion and Jesus Christ spoke. This Unitarianism must always have a large interest in natural theology as presenting the primary approach to the problem of the existence and nature of the super-natural, while historical theology or biblical theology and the theoretical examination of inner experience tend to take secondary places.

Such Unitarianism of the Father or the Creator is not to be identified simply with any particular denomination. It is a strain in all Christian history which comes to overt manifestation in individual thinkers and in special groups which may or may not be called Unitarian. Monarchianism and Arianism in the early Church, Deism and Socinianism and Unitarianism, properly so-called, in the modern period, all seem to share the interests and convictions of this type of Unitarianism of the Father. It numbers among its individual representatives both heroes of faith and philosopher-theologians. Despite the suspicion with which it has been regarded and the persecution it has sometimes suffered, it is a perennial and unconquerable movement in Christianity, for in both its insistence on monotheism and in its particular formulation of that monotheism it represents a fundamental and persistent conviction of faith.

The Unitarianism of Jesus Christ or of the Son is less readily identifiable than the former sort, yet its presence in the practical piety of ancient and modern times has been pointed out by scholars and is readily traceable once attention had been called to it. A. C. McGiffert, Sr., in *The God of the Early Christians*,[2] has summarized the evidence for the existence in the early Church of "a form of primitive Gentile Christianity whose God was Jesus Christ alone, and to which the God of the Jews, the creator and ruler of the world, meant nothing." The interest of these Christians was neither in philosophical explanations nor in questions about man's place in nature but in personal salvation. Christ was the Lord who brought them redemption, hence though they might have in mind the presence of other deities and even of a high God beyond the natural world, their worship was concentrated on Jesus Christ, the Lord. Though this form of piety might more correctly be called a henotheism of the Son rather than a Unitarianism it also had its theological representatives who moved in a Unitarian direction. The greatest of these was doubtless Marcion with his doctrine that the creator of the world and the Jehovah of the Old Testament was not a being worthy of worship as God but that in Jesus Christ "a better God has been discovered," one who is "nothing but good."

The persistence of this kind of practical monotheism of the Son may be traced through the whole of Christian history. The medieval hymns which modern piety uses as its own and which celebrate Jesus Christ independently of his relation to the Creator and the Spirit give evidence of its presence. In them the "Fairest Lord Jesus" is the "Ruler of all Nature"; Jesus is not only the "joy of loving hearts" but "the fount of life," and "life of men." Such expressions are not indeed necessarily exclusive of devotion to the Father and the Spirit, but practically the whole thought about God is concentrated here in the thought about the Son; he is the sole object of worship and all the functions of deity are ascribed to him.

In modern Protestantism the Unitarianism of Jesus Christ appears in many forms. Among them is the Jesus-cult of pietism with its practice of the mystic sense of Jesus' presence, its hymns of adoration, and its prayers addressed to him. For such pietism it is not the Father who "so loved the world that he gave his only begotten Son" or who commends his love to men in Christ, but Jesus is the source and center of love, so that no reference to the Creator is necessary. The love of Jesus for men is the divine reality on which men depend and the Son is ethical rather than mystic in character, though the ethical and mystical forms are often closely related. For the significance of Jesus lies in the fact that he is the Son of Man, the ideal Man, who not only set before men the ideal of a perfect society but undertook by means of his life and death to inaugurate it. This ethical Unitarianism of the Son is often regarded as atheistic since it makes no references to a super-historical or super-natural reality. But in its magnifying of Jesus Christ as the leader and martyr of a new humanity it assumes a definitely religious form. It is at least a sort of hero-cult for which Christ is not only an historical figure but a source of present strength and a real object of adoration.

Archbishop Söderblom, who with President McGiffert pointed out the prevalence of this sort of Jesus-Christ-religion, has called attention to the peculiar fashion in which Emanuel Swedenborg developed the Unitarianism of the Son.[3] The Swedish mystic is first of all a Unitarian, who regards the corruption of the Church and the "insanity of theology" as due to the fact that the "divine trinity has been considered a tripersonal trinity, each person being God and Lord." The first item in the faith of the New Church, therefore, is that "God is one, in whom is a divine trinity, and *He is the Lord God and Savior, Jesus Christ.*"[4] In this thinking the Creator of nature and the Holy Spirit are absorbed into the Son who is the Godhead. As Söderblom also points out, there is in Ritschlianism a comparable tendency toward the sole deification of the Son. While he discerns this tendency particularly in W. Herrmann, for whom communion with God is essentially communion with Jesus Christ, we may trace the tendency back to Ritschl himself. For the latter theologian, as for so many men in the nineteenth century and in our time, the great problem of human existence arose out of man's need to rise above nature. Not in nature and nature's God, the Creator, but in history and in God in history, that is in Jesus Christ, real salvation was to be found. A similar tendency is expressed in the autobiographical statements of the American theologian, George A. Gordon. "The God that Nature gives us," he wrote, "is not the God we need. The Christian religion is God through man, God through the best human beings, God through the ideal man; there is Christianity. The instinct of the child"—he is writing of his own childhood—"revolting from bare, stark, unfeeling, unloving Nature, and returning to humanity aflame with intelligence and love, was in reality life unfolding to the Christian religion."[5]

It is evident that these tendencies toward the Unitarianism of the Son are usually not so much directed against the denial of the deity of the Spirit as of the deity of the Father, just as the Unitarianism of the Father, when it expresses itself in denials, does not negate the Spirit's so much as the Son's deity. From Marcion onward it is doubt of the goodness of the Creator which tends to drive Christians toward the assertion of the sole deity of Christ or of God in Christ. Mated with its motive there is, of course, the inescapable Christocentrism of Christian faith and history. As in the case of the Unitarianism of the Father the Christian character of the affirmations of the Unitarianism of the Son is undeniable. It is their exclusiveness of each other that furnishes the real problem.

The third sort of Unitarianism for which the Spirit is the one and only God, or which absorbs the Creator and the Son into the Spirit, may be the most prevalent of all. Certainly it is so in modern Christianity. All Christian spiritualism tends in this direction. It looks to the reality found in the inner life rather than to the Being beyond nature or to the Redeemer in history for the fundamental principle of reality and value. It does not only say that God is spirit but converts the proposition and usually affirms that spirit is God. The reality with which men come into touch when they turn to reasoning itself, to awareness as subjective, to conscience and self-consciousness—this is the reality on which they are absolutely dependent and from which alone they can expect illumination, purification, perfection. Neither the Creator of nature nor the Jesus Christ of history can redeem men from death, but in the inner life the immortal power which cannot be held by death is manifest. No laws of nature and no counsels of the Sermon on the Mount but only the conscience within can lead to repentance and moral renewal. An objective God, a "Thou" corresponding to an "I," is not to be found amidst the mediations of sensation nor in the historic documents but only in the direct spiritual awareness of religious experience. The way to God, to the one Spirit, cannot be found by means of natural philosophy nor of historic revelation but only through spiritual awareness, through inner knowledge of inner truth and good.

The tendencies of extreme and mild mysticism in all times are toward the development of a Unitarianism of the Spirit. In Joachim de Fiore and the Spiritual Franciscans the doctrines of Unitarian spiritualism were set forth in the terms of a philosophy of history and a program of Church reformation first of all. The Age of the Father, which preceded the coming of Jesus Christ, and the Age of the Son are to be followed by the Age of the Spirit; the institutional, external Church is to be superseded by the *ecclesia spiritualis*. Implicit in these ideas is the exaltation of the Spirit as the final and true nature of deity and of spiritual experience as the true relation of God. One may trace similar tendencies in the Protestant sects, whether or not they had any direct connection with medieval spiritualism and sectarianism. The doctrine of the inner light and the practices of worship in the Society of Friends give evidence of a spiritual Unitarianism. Both Father and Son are assimilated to the Spirit here and spiritual experience takes precedence over both natural theology and Scriptures. The spiritualism of a Roger Williams, which is part of the basis for the separation of Church and state in his theory, is also a case in point.

With the aid of our hypothesis about the three Unitarian tendencies it becomes possible to reassess and reinterpret the tendencies in nineteenth century theology toward idealism and immanentism. By adopting idealism as its metaphysics the Unitarianism of the Spirit was able to identify the Spirit with the Creator while the teaching about the immanence of God was evidently a reassertion in a one-sided manner of the general Christian doctrine of the indwelling Spirit. For this form of Christianity, also, the Spirit and the Son were identified since what gave Jesus Christ his pre-eminence was the presence of the Spirit, of God-consciousness, of religious feeling and moral conscience in him. Though at times this immanentalism seemed to become humanistic, on the whole it preserved its theistic character. But it is not Trinitarian, nor was it interested in natural theology nor in historic revelation in any fundamental fashion. Its theology was empirically based and directed toward the interpretation of the deity found within. Archbishop Söderblom, who called attention in the work quoted above to the religion of the Son, may himself be taken as an example of one who tended toward spiritualist Unitarianism. The religions of the Father, Son, and Holy Spirit, he tended to think, formed concentric circles. The religion of the Father is the most general form of faith; it is universal religion. The religion of the Son is the specifically Christian sphere within the larger circle. But within Christianity there is a special group of people who have special experience of the forgiveness of sins and of eternal life. Here we enter into the holy of holies, into the religion of the Spirit. God, to be sure, must be thought of in relation to nature and to history, but objectivity is to be found in personal religious experience only. Hence the first article of the Christian faith rests on the third and the second, while the second apparently rests on the third, since the meaning of Christ lies in the fact that through him the inner life is developed and clarified.[6] Not only Söderblom but the general tendency of theology since Schleiermacher may be interpreted in this fashion. It was characterized not simply by its use of the psychological and empirical method in theology but by its interest in that divine reality, the Spirit, with which the empirical method could deal. In its development the Joachimite prophecy of the coming of an Age of the Spirit in succession to the Ages of Father and Son seems to have been realized in a measure.

Once more, as in the case of the other Unitarianism, one is forced to recognize the legitimacy within Christianity of the convictions and interests which lead to spiritualist monotheism. It represents a strand in all Christian life and thought; and emphasis upon this strand, on religious experience, on the deity of the spiritual element, has had a salutary effect. The weakness of the movement does not lie in its affirmations but in its denials, not in its inclusions but in its exclusions.

The Inadequacies of the Three Unitarianisms

The three Unitarian tendencies in Christianity have not resulted in the formation of three separate religions with three distinct gods partly because they are logically and historically interdependent. Unitarianism itself, whichever form it takes, has arisen historically in Christianity as a protest against Trinitarianism, but it seems to depend on the existence of what it protests against somewhat as liberalism depends on the presence of traditionalism, and conservatism on the presence of radicalism. In Christianity Unitarianism has been an anti-Trinitarian movement first of all and Trinitarianism has been an anti-Unitarian movement. The polarity of the one and the three which is expressed in the creeds is dynamically exhibited in the movements of faith in history. Unitarianism asserts the monotheism of Christian faith against all polytheism; Trinitarianism protests against the identification of the one God with the author of nature, with Jesus Christ, with the Spirit, but is dependent on the assertion of unity by Unitarianism.

There is another way in which the three Unitarianisms are historically related. Each arises in part as a protest against one of the other forms of monotheistic faith, or against the over-emphasis in Christian piety of the deity of one of the "persons" in the Godhead and one of the ways of approaching God. The Unitarianism of the Creator is always a protest against exclusive reliance on Scripture for knowledge of God and against exclusive worship of the Christ of Scriptures as the object of trust and the bringer of salvation. To some extent, as in English Deism, it may also be a protest against enthusiasm and spiritualism in the Unitarianism of the Spirit. The monotheism or henotheism of the Son often arises in reaction against exclusive concern with the Creator and with rational knowledge as the way to faith. It concentrates on the doctrines of human sinfulness and divine atonement through Christ in conscious antagonism against the teachings about man's good nature as created in the image of God and about his progress toward union with God by virtue of his natural powers of reason and morality. The Unitarianism of the Spirit arises in protest and reaction against exclusive concern with rational and historical knowledge of God as he is known in nature and in history.

The interdependence of the three Unitarianisms is, however, more than historical and psychological. Each of them is logically dependent on the convictions represented in the other forms of Christian faith and this interdependence appears in the way in which one form tends to pass over into another.

The religion of the Creator appears to be a straightforward faith in the goodness as well as power of the author of nature. Looking to science and philosophy as the handmaidens of religion, it bases itself on rational reflections about the implications of nature's being and order. There must be one God, a first cause, a purposer and designer; to him man owes honor and on him man is dependent. But in ancient and modern times, particularly in modern, the question arises whether indeed there is any unambiguous evidence that the power or reality declared in the invisible things of creation is indeed personal, so that it can be addressed, and whether it or he is good. Facing these questions, the Unitarianism of the Creator discovers that it is dependent not simply on reason but also on the faith of Jesus Christ and that the God it worships is after all not simply the God of nature but the Father of Jesus Christ. This Father has attributes not revealed to reason and by nature but declared only in the life of Christ and through Scriptures. The Christian Unitarianism of the Creator is always the religion of the Fatherhood of God, and the nature of the Father is not known save through his relation to a Son. The religious belief in the Fatherhood of God always implies that the Son who is obedient to him to death is not destroyed but remains victorious and powerful. That God reveals his nature and his power in Jesus Christ and not simply in creation, and that he must be known in revelation and not only by reason, is always implicit in the Unitarianism which asserts that the one God is the Father.

The extent to which the Unitarianism of the Creator in Christianity implies the relation of a son to the Father is very manifest in so great a Unitarian as William Ellery Channing. The God he describes as the only true object of Christian worship is the Father of Jesus Christ. So he writes:

> To give our views of God in one word, we believe in his parental character. We ascribe to him not only the name but the dispositions and principles of a father. . . . We cannot bow before a being, however great and powerful, who governs tyrannically. We respect nothing but excellence, whether on earth or in heaven. We venerate not the loftiness of God's throne, but the equity and goodness in which it is established. We believe that God is infinitely good, kind, benevolent, in the proper sense of these words.[7]

Channing and his successors often convey the strong impression that the attributes of the one whom they worship are after all those of Jesus Christ. A favorite text of many of the advocates of the doctrine of the Fatherhood of God as the essence of Christianity is the Johannine text which ascribes to Jesus the statement, "He that hath seen me hath seen the Father." Though the form of the idea of deity is that given in the first article of the Creed, the content comes from the second. Hence also the Patri-passionism which characterizes so many of these Unitarian movements.

For such a monotheism of the Father the recurring problem arises

59

whether after all this God of kindness, benevolence, and Christlike character really exists. Having begun with the rational knowledge of a first principle of nature, but having interpreted that first principle in terms of revelation, or having asserted that the one God is the Creator and then affirmed that the character of the Creator is what is discerned in the Son, this Unitarianism is either required to find in Jesus Christ a reconciler to the Creator or to ask whether the Christlike God has any existence. In its struggles with this problem the Christian Unitarianism of the Father has often turned into a kind of Christian humanism, or into a half-Marcionitic religion of the Son. The inadequacy of its first position is revealed in a tendency to accept the second version of Christian Unitarianism. Jesus Christ, not God, the Father, becomes for it then the central object of Christian interest. He is the leader of a new humanity, the founder of the brotherhood, or the captain of mankind in its conflict with the inscrutable powers of heedless nature. More frequently, however, the Unitarianism of the Creator has made the transition from reasoning about nature to religious experience and from the Creator to the Spirit. The change from the Trinitarianism of the English Presbyterians in the seventeenth century to the Deism in the eighteenth is not greater than the transition of Unitarianism from the rational deism of the eighteenth century to the immanentism and spiritualism of the nineteenth.

The Unitarianism of the Creator has not been able to stand alone. It has had to rely upon and to exchange places with the Unitarianism of the Son and of the Spirit.

The situation is similar in the case of the religion of Jesus Christ. Though it has had no doubt about the goodness of Christ, about his deity in terms of value, it has not been able to avoid the question of his power. But when it has inquired into the power of Christ it has found itself forced back on the question of his relation to the Creator and has found that faith in Christ implies faith in the God who is known through nature, or who rules over nature. In another sense those who begin with the religion about Jesus Christ find that it implies the faith *of* Jesus Christ, just as those who begin with the faith of Jesus Christ cannot evade the question about his religious significance but always take it for granted. Again the relation to Jesus Christ is not maintained as a religious one without recourse to spiritual experience. That there is a spirit in man to which the spirit of Christ makes appeal—a spirit proceeding from the Father—and that the spirit of Christ—a spirit proceeding from the Son—is not confined to the historic Jesus but lives in the community he founded and leads, are ideas which are implicit in the Christocentric faith. In our time the Unitarianism of the Son has tended to pass via a Jesus-mysticism into the religion of the spirit, of immanentism, and religious experience.

The religion of the Spirit, finally, which begins with protest against exclusive reliance on historic revelation and the historic Christ as well as against concentration on rational knowledge and the Creator of nature, always implies convictions about the deity of the author of nature and the historic Jesus Christ. The spiritual life always seems unreal to man unless he can understand nature itself as a manifestation of spirit, and he cannot test what is true and untrue in the realm of the spirit without recourse to standards he has gained from rational knowledge of nature and from history. Kant may be taken as an example, since his position in religion was essentially spiritualist. The object of his veneration and the reality on which he relied for the salvation of man from evil was an inner principle, the moral law and the moral lawgiver in the self. But it was not possible for him to maintain that this spirit was adequate for salvation or that reliance upon it was reasonable unless he could believe that it proceeded from the Father, that is from the Creator of nature. Faith in the spirit must postulate faith in the Creator. In other cases the religion of spiritual experience has sought for assurance that the environment in which the spirit moved, the natural world, was "friendly." Faith in the spirit known in inner experience implies faith in a reality akin to spirit in the natural world. As for the relation to the Son, this has become especially apparent in the need spiritualism has discovered for criteria by means of which to determine what is and what is not divine spirit. What inner experience can be trusted among all the dreams, fantasies and vagaries of the spiritual life? What revelations ought to be believed among all the private revelations men experience in their subjectivity? Here it has been necessary for spiritualism to employ criteria taken from the religion of the Son. It has in practice made its distinction by means of the test Paul used: "If any man hath not the spirit of Christ he is none of his." The Society of Friends has called the *light within* also the *Christ within* and by that identification has secured a test of the validity of spiritual experience. By doing so it has given evidence of its dependence on other than inner experience and on another object of knowledge than the internal God. Experience-theology tends to test the God-consciousness of the individual or the Church by the God-consciousness of Jesus and the individual conscience by its conformity with the historic utterances of Jesus Christ.

In every case it appears true that none of the positions can stand alone but must borrow something from the other positions, that the three Unitarianisms are interdependent. If this is the case, then apart from any other considerations which may lead the Church to the formulation of a Trinitarian doctrine, it must endeavor to do so because it must set forth the faith which is not the realized conviction of any of its parts but rather the common faith. The Trinitarianism of the whole Church must undertake to state what is implicit in the faith and knowledge of all of its parts though it is not explicit in any one of them. It must undertake to correct the over-emphases and partialities of the members of the whole not by means of a new over-emphasis but by means of a synthesized formula in which all the partial insights and convictions are combined. A doctrine of the Trinity, so formulated, will never please any one part of the Church but it will be an ecumenical doctrine providing not for the exclusion of heretics but for their inclusion in the body on which they are actually dependent. Truth, after all, is not the possession of any individual or of any party or school, but is represented, insofar as it can be humanly represented, only by the whole dynamic and complementary work of the company of knowers and believers.

This ecumenical approach to the restatement of Trinitarian doctrine is, of course, only one approach and that not the most significant or promising. But it has its significance and will have its effect on new efforts to understand and state this most formidable and interesting Christian doctrine.

The Church Defines Itself in the World

This paper is an exercise or essay which, it is hoped, will aid the present endeavor of churchmen to define the church. The author's standpoint is that of moral theology and his method is that of reflective criticism. Moral theology (a term I use in parallelism to moral philosophy rather than in its conventional meaning) undertakes to examine critically the mind of the church with particular concern for the practical principles present in it and expressed in its activities. It is not derivative from dogmatic or exegetical theology nor subordinate to either but is a particular inquiry that takes its place alongside such other theological inquiries and remains in dialogue with them.

By reflective criticism I mean that method of self-examination in which one who participates in the faith and work of the church, in its order and life, seeks to bring into his own and his companions' full awareness the principles of individual and communal believing and doing, to analyze the consistency and inconsistency, the origins and consequences of such principles. Such self-examination, I believe, is part of the work of *metanoia* we continually carry on in the church in the hope of purification, clarification, and integration, or holiness. The material with which reflective criticism deals is the practical and theoretical reasoning of the church as expressed in its communication and other action in the presence of the objective reality toward which such reasoning is directed. In this material the scriptural is of first importance. Reflective criticism does not seek to discover the principles of reasoning in the subjective mind of the church in abstraction from the objective reality to which that mind is related or on which it is dependent; it is not concerned with God-consciousness apart from God or with faith apart from the trusted, faithful One. On the other hand, in the method of reflective criticism we do not assume that a relation to the objective counterpart of the church's mind is open to us in isolation from the common consciousness. It seems to me that the subjectivistic error of which Schleiermacher is accused is no greater than the objectivistic error of some dogmatic theology of our time which undertakes to state what the fundamental beliefs are that the church ought to hold on the basis, for instance, of a biblical theology in which it is assumed that the meaning of the Scriptures is available to the interpreter in isolation from a contemporary, interpreting church. For reflective criticism no objects of inquiry are available just in themselves, in abstraction from an interpreting community. This is not to say that the inquirer has no direct relations to the object; if he had none, criticism would be impossible. It is to say that such relations are not separate from relations to a community in which interpretation goes on. Reflective criticism is practical in a situation in which object, subject, and community; or object, subject, and co-subjects; are all present. In such a situation we cannot make an absolute beginning with one of the terms but only with all three.

In undertaking to deal critically with the present activity of the church as it defines itself in the world, we shall try to keep this situation in mind. What is offered is tendered tentatively in a community of critics. We shall proceed in four steps, seeking first to analyze the nature of definition, secondly the character of the present effort of the church to define itself, thirdly offer a critique of that effort, and finally suggest what the principles of adequate self-definition on the part of the church are.

The Nature of Definition

1. A definition always involves the activity of both practical and theoretical reasoning in the subject. (The question of the way it involves activity on part of both subject and object we leave aside.) A definition is descriptive but also normative; it implies decision as well as perception and conception; it is a command as well as a statement. This is probably true of the simplest word-definitions, such as (opening the dictionary at random): "*Machine*—an apparatus consisting of interrelated parts with separate functions, which is used in the performance of some kind of work," or (from Paul Weiss's *Modes of Being*) "An actuality is a being in space."[1] Such statements are highly formal descriptions. They are also commands; in the case of the dictionary a social injunction has been formulated: "When you use the word 'machine' you must mean by it . . ."; in the case of the individual author: "When you read the word 'actuality' remember what I mean. . . ." The definitions also represent decisions.

In the dualities of self and other and of self and community practical principles are expressed in the two forms of decisions and imperatives. In decision the self, subject to imperatives issuing from the Other or the community, chooses to obey or disobey, to value or disvalue; in giving imperatives it counsels or commands others to decide in accordance with the principle. Thus, "The church is the body of Christ" may represent a personal decision so to regard and so to deal with the church; or it may be an imperative, counseling or demanding that others so regard and deal with it.

The involvement of both practical and theoretical reasoning is more significant and more apparent when men define themselves or one of their institutions. Definitions of democracy as government of, by and for the people, or as respect for minority rights are both descriptive and decisive (or imperative). Decision is present in such cases not as resolution to use a word in a certain way but as choice of an essence which is to be conserved or realized. The theoretic statement is formulated as part of a logic in which imperative or decision-sentences will follow description; but decision has also preceded the theoretic formulation. The definition of man as a thinking animal offers another illustration. I do not mean to say that theoretic definition is *controlled* by decision or choice, or the latter by the former, but only that in every case of definition- of ourselves particularly—both elements are involved. When man defines himself theoretically, he also defines himself practically—i.e., he chooses what he wills to be in obedience to imperatives; and he never describes himself in the course of choosing himself. This is equally true of his institutions and societies.

2. Among the decisions that are involved in or precede theoretic definitions are those about purpose, about distinction and about positive relation or context. When I define myself or we define our institutions or societies it is necessary to ask, What was the purpose in undertaking this definition? From what am I concerned to distinguish myself as the object to be defined? To what other realities have I committed myself to relate this object positively? And, are all these decisions or commitments to be maintained or must I begin again on the basis of new or earlier decisions?

As to purpose: Pure science no less than applied science follows on a decision. In pure science the purpose is that of knowledge or truth abstracted from such other values as health, wealth, glory—whether of a self or of another. In theology "pure science" has the "glory of God" for its purpose; applied science here seeks the edification of the church or some other end. But choice of end is always present.

As to distinction: When we define something we distinguish it from what it is not. Except in the case of "being simply considered," we do not distinguish it from non-being but from other being which it is not.[2]

Thus reason is defined in distinction from passion or emotion; or in distinction from sensation. Thought may be defined in distinction from extension or from imagination. Man may be defined in distinction from animal or from God. While the oppositions or distinctions are not *arbitrarily* chosen but correspond to something objective, they are not simply given by the objective reality but involve decision or obedience in a situation. When we define democracy today, we do so as a part of a reasoning in which we have decided (not without imperatives) to distinguish it from totalitarianism and not, as in other times, from aristocracy or plutocracy or mobocracy.

As to context: Together with the decision about what the thing to be defined is not, goes the decision about what it is related to, and to be related to, in a positive way. The selection of such context is again not arbitrary but neither is it simply objectively given. If I begin with the distinction of faith from works (rather than from distrust, for instance) and seek to define the faith that is not works, it is not objectively clear that this reality is positively related to love and hope rather than to vision and hearing. Is Barth's choice of the latter context in which to define faith more objective than Luther's choice of the former? Or, to take a non-theological example: naturalistic definitions of man are not simply the result of a subjectively motivated choice to relate man to other natural entities or processes (and in opposition to supernature); the relations to such entities are objectively present but are not the only ones so present. Further, whether the context in which man is now so defined is that of biological drives, of sex, [of] hunger and fear, or of chemical reactions, depends on the considered choice of the definer. So decision seems to enter into the choice of context as well as into the choice of purpose or distinction.

If it is impossible, as I believe it is, to assign absolute priority to the practical reason in this work of the church, it seems equally impossible to do justice to what we find going on in our thinking and doing by ascribing priority to the theoretic reason. But the tendency to assume the priority of the latter is strong in contemporary theology.

3. Critical self-examination in community never seems able to state exhaustively all the decisions that lie back of a given theory. Hidden presuppositions are always present. We can only try to uncover and re-evaluate as many previous decisions as possible.

4. The decisions that follow on a theoretic definition do not seem to follow directly from such definition only but also from the hidden

66

presuppositions or decisions that lie back of it. Naturalistic ethics is not the simple consequent of a naturalistic definition of man but follows also from the decisions that lie back of that definition and have influenced it. Similarly the definition of democracy in terms of power struggle between interest groups is not the beginning of the power-struggle ethos.

The Contemporary Church's Definition of Itself

1. The effort of the church today to define itself is both a theoretic and a practical effort. Our theological theorizing was preceded, is accompanied, and will be followed by decisions and imperatives. It has been preceded by the decision to seek our unity and looks forward to decisions relevant to the realization in action of such unity. In the theory that follows on the precedent decision certain objective facts about the church have come into view that were not observed in theories consequent on other decisions in other times. But it is not evident that our theorizing is less subject to decisions and wishes than was the theorizing of other periods when other imperatives and other decisions prevailed. The theology of the ecumenical movement is not evidently less pragmatic than the theology of the Social Gospel. Barthian objectivism is not evidently less dependent on decision than Schleiermacher's subjectivism, nor is the latter evidently less obedient to imperatives than the former. The effort of the church to define itself today is both theoretic and practical and we delude ourselves if we deal with it as though we now based decision on an objective theoretic theology whether dogmatic or biblical, while other times were influenced by value-considerations.

2. Among the decisions which lie back of our present effort to define ourselves there is not only the purposive decision to seek our unity in knowledge and action but also the decision to distinguish ourselves *from the world*. We seem to have decided implicitly if not explicitly that we must define ourselves as church in opposition to the world. What we are *not*, is the world. This decision has been made in a historic situation. The German church struggle, the rise of communism, the secularization of political, economic, and educational institutions have all led toward this decision. It is explained in many specific actions, such as the tendency to reject natural theology, concentration on the liturgy of the church, concern for the structure and order of the church in

distinction from the secular society around it, the tendency in the church to accept and even contend that it speaks a private and untranslatable language. The choice of the church to define itself vis-à-vis the world is not an arbitrary choice, since the distinction has objective bases. But it is a choice. There have been times when it defined itself vis-à-vis the state; what the church first of all was *not*, was the state; and this also had objective basis. Or it defined itself vis-à- vis the people of the old covenant; or vis-à-vis demonic power; or vis-à-vis God.

3. In the course of the present effort of the church to define itself, practically and theoretically, certain decisions (often made in relatively unconscious acceptance more than in high awareness of what was being done) about context have also been made. These decisions are related to the choice of purpose and choice of opposition but are not their logical consequences. The tendency of the church to define itself almost exclusively by reference to Jesus Christ and to interpret the Scriptures in Christocentric fashion is doubtless connected with the search for unity. Obedience to the Lordship of Christ, an allegiance to him, is the point on which the various churches can agree. It is accepted also as the distinctive element in Christian belief, separating it from what it is not, namely the world. For some, perhaps many interpreters, Jesus Christ is in such a way the revelation of God that where he is not present there is no knowledge of God; hence church in relation to Christ is opposed to world without relation to Christ, as church with revelation [is opposed] to world without knowledge of God. There are relations then between the various decisions. Yet the definition of the church as related to Jesus Christ has the character of decision and not of necessary consequence of other decisions previously taken. Further, there are certain aspects of the present tendency toward decision that strike one as not necessitated either by anything objective or by previous decision. Among these are the emphasis on revelation in the work of Christ more than on reconciliation, on the deity of Christ more than on the humanity; on the doctrine of Christ more than on the historical actuality of the person; on the incarnation more than on the death and resurrection; on the first more than on the second coming.

4. The tendency in theology today is to regard true doctrine as the basis for right decision. It is the contention of this paper that such priority of the intellect over the will, or better of the speculative or observant over the practical reason, is not self-evident. In making a beginning with true doctrine the church makes a decision, and this

decision is to define itself primarily as a doctrinally believing community or as a community having a certain understanding about the past, present and future, about God and man. It is not questioned that such beliefs belong to a church, but it is contended that to assign priority to doctrine is to make a choice, not to be obedient simply to a givenness in things, whether in Scripture or in human experience. To define faith primarily in terms of belief rather than of trust and fidelity, to define it therefore as intellectual assent more than as practical decision, is possible only on the basis of choice.

Some Theoretical and Practical Consequences
of the Church's Self-Definition

1. It is not my contention that theories can have only pragmatic truth or that they are primarily pragmatic statements. The argument is rather that what is known and knowable of objective realities is limited by the intent and decision that precede and accompany theory. Interest in unity opens our eyes to unitive elements in the church's life; it limits our vision at the same time; other embodied values, particularly those connected with diversity and with conflict, do not come into view. A definition of the church that is preceded by the decision to seek its unity is not more or less objective than one preceded by the decision to seek its self-preservation, its power, or its holiness. In every case what is attended to in the object has been limited by the purpose.

Similarly practical decisions consequent on earlier decisions are still made in freedom, but the freedom has been limited. It is with consequences in this sense that we are now concerned.

2. A consequence of the decision in our time (whether made with a high sense of responsibility or with relatively low awareness in assent to the current of the times and to social imperatives) to define the church in opposition to the world has been the tendency to ignore or deprecate the "worldly" character of the church and "churchly" character of the world. We seek to find the essential marks of the church in elements that are peculiar to it when distinguished from world; we regard those elements in its phenomenal appearance that relate it positively to the world as unessential or as foreign and deleterious. Its Agape must be wholly different from Eros; its theology from philosophy; its revelation from knowledge. Combining this tendency with the one consequent on the decision for unity, we tend to think of the

69

factors that lead to division in the church as not only "non-theological" but as non-Christian while we close our eyes to the operation of such "non-theological" factors in the movement toward unity. Since by definition such factors belong to the world, we cannot take them seriously as agencies through which the grace of God as well as the power of sin may manifest itself. But a church defined without reference to such factors tends to become an ideal church, an eschatological church invisible to our time. Practically we tend, in consequence of the definition of church in opposition to world, to cultivate a church life in separation from the world.

3. The corollary definition of the world as non-church leads us to ignore the churchly character of the societies of the world. We do not attend to their election into being, the summons issued to them to be covenant communities and to fulfill missions in the realm of God. We tend also to ignore the responses of individuals and communities to such elections, being made more aware of demonic forces and faith in the demonic in this realm than in our own.

4. Our decision or our concern to define the church positively by relation to Jesus Christ only has led us into situations in which we tend to define Jesus Christ by his relation to the church only. Our understanding of the church as related to God as Creator and to God as Holy Spirit is being limited by interpreting Creator and Spirit only through Christ and not Christ also through Creator and Spirit. We tend to overlook the fact that the church we know is a religious community expressing movements of the human soul toward God (in the cry for aid to supernatural power, in the need for ecstasy, in the sense of the holy) which are part of man's created nature and which are expressed also in other religions. We try (and in doing so ignore many facts about ourselves) to derive everything in our churchly existence from Jesus Christ.

We do not in this limited perspective take much note of the work of Jesus Christ outside the church or of the obedience rendered to him on the part of those who do not explicitly call him Lord, nor do we rejoice very often in the confidence in God, the fidelity to him and the hope of glory introduced into human rather than church history by Jesus Christ.

5. At all these points I believe our present movement finds itself in conflict with certain fundamental imperatives and decisions heard and made at critical junctures in the life of the church, recorded in the

Scriptures or in [the] church. I believe that something like the decision Israel had to make about the meaning of its election is being re-enacted in our time. It is the decision whether the election is for witness and service or for special salvation. It seems also to be a decision not unlike the one made by Paul and the other apostles regarding the future of the church, whether it was to maintain itself as it had been begun, or, becoming [a] missionary movement among the Gentiles, risk the danger of losing itself. And Jesus' observations about his losing and finding of life, about seeking first the Kingdom, and about those who say "Lord, Lord" ring in one's ears at such a moment.

Second Thoughts about Church and World

1. We cannot easily translate our personal or group decisions before divine imperatives into imperatives for others, as we cannot easily and uncritically accept the imperatives that human institutions or companions give us as divine imperatives. If I cannot accept as divine imperative to me in the present moment the social imperative to seek the church's unity first of all, neither have I the right to say that it is God's will for all churchmen not to be anxious about their unity. But as a moral theologian who undertakes to help men interpret their own situation before God, I have the duty to ask whether they do not hear what I hear and see what I see in our situation. Hence everything now to be said must be said confessionally and in the first person.

2. I believe that the decision to seek our unity in the church must be put into a different perspective than the one which frequently prevails. (a) Church unity ought to be dealt with as a gift to be appropriated rather than as achievement to be won. It ought so to be regarded because the fundamental decision of the church is not to be church but to let God be its God. The obligation follows from a commandment and a decision prior to the commandment and decision for church unity. Unity is a gift which has been given, is being given and will be given to the church as it has, is and will be given to whatever is made in the image of God. A gift, of course, must be appropriated; no gift is received without activity. We must rue the fact that we have neglected the gift and now try to understand what has been given, and try to use it in service. But church unity, like personal integrity, like faith, is not something we can seek or decide to achieve. We can only thankfully accept, understand and cultivate in service the gift of grace while we

71

pray, "Increase our unity." (b) Church unity is not to be treasured more highly than any other reconciliation of parents and children, of husbands and wives to each other, in reconciliation of God; the reconciliation of nations to one another in reconciliation to him; in short, the coherence of everything and all things in God is the gift for which thanks are offered and for which we pray; the gift also we seek to appropriate. (c) The basic orientation of the church, in law and Gospel, is toward the oneness of God not the oneness of any creature. No unity achieved or given in integration around any principle save the one God can really unify or endure. Insofar as we seek a unity in Christ otherwise than in his oneness with the Father and the Holy Spirit, or confess him Lord otherwise than to the glory of God the Father, we are in peril of worshipping the principle of our Christian unity, not the principle of the unity of being.

3. The tendency of our thinking and acting today in distinguishing the church from the world ought also to be put into a different perspective. It is true that we are not the world. But the imperative to separate ourselves from the world and the decision to do so are subject to a prior imperative and a prior decision. That prior imperative is present in the confrontation of the church—or of mankind in the church—with the sovereign God and that prior decision lies in the rejection of the temptation to try to be like God, especially in the knowledge of good and evil. Though it sounds paradoxical it seems nevertheless to be true that the important difference between the church and the world is that the church knows itself to be "world" before God while the world does not know this but thinks that it can be like God. Perhaps it would be better to say that the church consists of that portion of humanity which, knowing God, knows that man is not God and has made the decision before God that it will not play God but let God be Lord. We may use various scriptural phrases, such as image of God or body of Christ, and say that the church has defined itself and defined man in opposition to God as only image, or in distinction from Christ as only body not the head, not the spirit. In any case all definitions of the church in relation to the world as not world are secondary to definitions of the church as not God.

4. In the light of fundamental distinctions we see the context in which we define ourselves as the context of created world and especially of humanity. We stand with the rest of the world before God as that part of the world which, sharing in the world's unbelief, hopelessness

and self-love, has begun to believe, to hope, and to love God. We are not that part of the world to which Jesus Christ has come in human form but we are that part of it which recognizes him as sent from God to redeem the world. Insofar as Jesus Christ is seen by us as seated at the right hand of the Father, as very God of very God, the distinction of ourselves from Jesus Christ is primary; we are not Christ. But we identify ourselves with the Christ who has identified himself with man and mankind. We are related to the Christ who is related to the world; and who is not related to the world through us but by his own action.

5. With respect to the definitions of ourselves as one, as not God and as part of the world, everything, it seems to me, points to the need for remembering and renewing our early decision in the church to begin our thinking and acting in the presence of the One God who is Father, Son, and Holy Spirit, and not to begin with a reduced confession that Jesus Christ is God. It may be said that the former confession is implied in the latter, but if it is not made explicit, it is easily forgotten and becomes ineffective. Insofar as it is forgotten we tend to separate ourselves as church from the created and inspired world; we seek to understand ourselves as creations of Jesus Christ in a certain isolation from the Creator of all things and the inspiration of all things; we depreciate what is not recognizably related to Jesus Christ directly; we misjudge the world that is without knowledge of Christ as without any awareness of God.

II

HISTORY

3

The Meaning of History

A Theologian's Approach to History

In our age of specialization and of the separation of [a] onetime unified knowledge into many divisions the work of relating the fragments is of great concern and interest to modern scholars. We reflect on each other's specialties and in doing so occasionally make contributions to the companions from whom we are divided. But quite as frequently the efforts are profitless because we cannot construct a unity of what has been atomistically conceived and developed (like a *Cambridge Modern History*) or because specialization has left us in great ignorance of fields of learning beyond our own gardens. A physicist's comments on politics may afford the political scientist new perspectives or insights but they may also make clear that the physicist, just because he is a specialist, knows less about political realities than does a shopkeeping alderman. His reflections on politics may be less those of a physicist than of a man who has been kept ignorant of politics by his concentration on physics. So when a man who by profession is a theologian approaches history, he may, if he is fortunate, offer the historian some aid to self-knowledge, but he may also because he is a specialist theologian be so ignorant not only of the story of the city of earth but of the methods and problems of those who seek to understand it that instead of offering theological observations on history he may present his recollections of the history he knew as a high school student before he was a theologian. The subject assigned for this paper was therefore judiciously phrased when the committee passed by the obvious statement: "A Theological Approach to History" and carefully entitled it "A Theologian's Approach to History." The formulation doubtless reveals the wariness of historians rather than the modesty of theologians, as in the case of the accompanying paper the formulation may indicate theologians' recollections of past offenses against them more than historians' expectations of being able to bring light into the darkness of theology. With this warning in mind I shall modestly use the first-person singular and say what I think about history, leaving it to you to decide whether these reflections are theological or simply the reflections of a man who as theologian has become vastly ignorant in the course of devoting himself to a special inquiry. What then is history as I see it from my specialized point of view? How do I the theologian get along with my often helpful and sometimes irritating partner in the university, the historian? How do I relate his search for wisdom to my own? What contributions has historical science made to me in my theological work?

The phrasing of those questions has already made somewhat clear what I think of when I think of history. I do not envisage so much the course of human events in their larger or smaller connections as I do historical work—the resurrection, the re-enactment, the understanding of these events in their small and large "*Gestalten*" by the historian, be he academic or literary. Hence I do not ask directly about the role of the past or of my personal or social recollection of things past in my work as theologian. I am concerned rather with the present activity that makes the human past its object, with history as present re-creation and re-enactment.

Before trying to state what I think this history does for me in my work, I must sketch in outline my general understanding of the situation in which we human beings know anything at all and of the manner in which our various types of knowledge are related to each other. That understanding or theory of the human knowing has grown out of my conversation with history to no small extent.

I begin with the inescapability of the subject-object situation and its dialectical character; hence with the untenability of either complete objectivism or complete subjectivism as an explanation of any knowledge. The knower and the known are bound together till death parts them. I can analyze no event as an occurrence in the object only nor any that can be reduced to a wholly subjective process. We are engaged everywhere and always in a dialogue between subject and object, whether we inquire into the American Revolution, the occurrence of a hallucination, or the creation of the world; whether we ask about nature, society, or God. Yet knowledge does not happen in the subject-object dialogue unless the subject is also related to another knower, to a companion or companions engaged as he is in dialogue with objects and also engaged in dialogue with him. All knowledge contains an element of interpretation, and it is all social. The forms and categories with which we come to our objects are *a priori* so far as individuals are concerned, but their source seems to be not in a "pure reason" so much as in the social mind; and they are mediated to us by our companions from childhood onward. These ideas or forms are not so fixed and established that they cannot be modified in consequence of our individual and present experience of objects, yet the social categories are indispensable to any experience. Furthermore, we depend on our companion knowers for verification. Purely private knowledge, not subject to social verification, remains so dubious as to be almost hallucination.

Now in this situation in which as knowers we are engaged in a double dialogue—with their objects, on the one hand, with our fellow knowers on the other—we may direct primary attention to the one or the other dialogue. Hence arises a great division in the human sciences between those which are directed primarily to the common objects which have engaged in conversation with a sensible and intelligible present objectiveness and those which are concerned *primarily* with the fellow knowers, fellow artists and artisans. I may regard a human being primarily as an object or primarily as a fellow subject. In the former case I am a physiologist or psychologist, in the latter case a humanist. I may try to know a political society from the outside, as subject engaged in a dialogue with this object; but I may also try to think with it or its members, participate in its common life, practice empathy [and] engage in dialogue with its members as [a] fellow subject. In the former case I am a political scientist, in the latter probably a historian.

It will be clear from that last statement how I think of history. It is, as I see it, a humanistic study in which the effort is made to think the thoughts and do the deeds of fellowmen after them. It is the re-enactment of their subjective encounters with the objects. It is possible only because as an intensive dialogue with companions it is accompanied by my own dialogue with the same objects or similar ones that they encountered. But the emphasis lies on my understanding of their encounters and responses, not on the objects of those encounters. The earthquake of Lisbon, so far as it has left traces of itself in the conformation of the earth's crust, is an object of geology; but the concern of the historian is with the human experiences of and responses to that earthquake which have left their traces in the writings and legends of men. He can understand these human reactions only because he has some experience, direct or vicarious, sensible or imagined, of earthquakes. Yet he is trying to understand not the movements of the earth, but the movements of men. I do not wish to say that history is the only inquiry of this sort in which the effort is made to understand our social companions, but this seems to me to be the most helpful of all inquiries of this sort. Hence the emphasis in history for me does not lie so much on the pastness of the events into which it inquires as on the subjective element in those events, on the humanity in them. I find the greatest illumination, it will be evident, in Collingwood's definition of history as the re-enactment of past experience.[1] But instead of thinking of its purpose, as he does, as the attainment of self-knowledge, I see it as participation in social knowledge and so as contributing, among other things, to knowledge of our present objects as the latter knowledge, in turn, is contributory to history.

Having offered these rather schematic reflections on the two dialogues in which man is engaged and the two sorts of emphases or specializations in our knowing, I turn more directly to the question of theology and history. What is theology, first of all, and then, how is it related to history? I believe that the object of that whole series of inquiries we call theology is always man before God and God before man. It is the counterpart of natural science which in its many varieties and specializations has as its object nature before man and man before nature, and of the social sciences which have as their object man before men, responding to men in their institutions, communities, and individual behavior—or the institutions, communities, and persons to which men react. I will not undertake to defend the actuality of the object of theology—man before God and God before men. The definition of what is meant by "God" in that phrase is at least as complex and difficult as the definition of *nature* in the case of the natural sciences, of *society* in the case of the social sciences. That men's ideas of what they confront in the determination of their destiny, in the why and wherefore of their existence, vary widely is well known; that what the believer calls God is called Fate or Chance by the unbeliever; or sometimes Life or Nature, we all know. Ideas of nature also vary widely, yet we assume that men live in and before the same nature, no matter how widely their interpretations of it and hence their responses to it differ. As theologian this is my object—God before men and men before God. Objectively stated, it is God as he is in himself; subjectively stated, it is human experience of God; but I cannot separate object from subject, and hence I say my object is God before men, including myself in my subjectivity before this object, and men before God, including God in the objectivity before these subjects.

How I come to this object of my inquiry with categories, ideas, patterns of relationships, with certain *a prioris* of experience—these I have derived from my society. In part they are categories of faith. The determination of destiny, the ultimate reality in which I am absolutely dependent for existence, is one and it is faithful. It is the creative principle, in the artistic sense of creativity. This man before God is made in his image, made to reflect him. I come with the more specific postulates and hypotheses of Christian faith. But I also come with the contrary expectations of unbelief which I have no less derived from my society. As social unbeliever I expect that God before men will let me down; he will be far off; he will demonstrate his unconcern; he is impersonal.

In this situation, becoming aware of the *a prioris*, the antecedent and conflicting ideas with which I face and interpret my object—God before men and men before God—I may try to take the Cartesian way, i.e., dismiss the "towering and magnificent palaces" of the social faith, the social patterns, as "having no better foundations than sand and mind," and determine henceforth "no longer to seek any other science than the knowledge of myself or of the great book of the world."[2] I am tempted to dismiss as did Hume not only the work of the historians, but more significantly the whole apparatus of patterns, ideas, and interpretations with which I came to my object and to start fresh. But that is impossible, as Descartes's example, particularly in the field of theology, illustrates. My other choice is to become critical, to try to understand *a priori* categories and patterns and principles with which I came to the interpretation of my objects, to understand their origin, their development, their degradations in my past, my social past, and to do this by constant reference to my present experience of objects to which my human companions of the past responded in their own way and with their own interpretations, which finally yielded the *a priori* patterns with which I have come to my experience.

So as theologian I turn to history as the necessary accompaniment of my theological inquiry. I turn to the history of the recent past, not only of the particular religious community from which I derived my patterns of interpretation, of existence before mystery, but of the human community from which I have derived patterns of unbelief. I turn further back to discover how these ideas have fared, whether earlier forms comport more readily with my experience of my object than do their successors. I turn to the period when the leading patterns seemed to have their origin. By means of the re-enactment of the experiences and ideas of the past, I free myself from some of that past which has led me to interpretations of the present object which were rationally unsatisfactory and I recover other patterns of interpretation from communities and associates no longer living, which give some order and coherence to my present encounter with my object.

History has so become for me the great critical inquiry which enlarges my community of discourse with my companion knowers of my present object, which enables me to compare my patterns of interpretation with those of men with other perspectives, which helps to give me in the situation of men before God some understanding of the value or disvalue of the patterns with which I approach the interpretation of, and with which I guide my responses to, present realities that exercise force on my life.[3]

I note also that history seems to play a similar role in the other main inquiries of contemporary men. It is so closely related to the social sciences that it is often itself regarded as a social science, though its connection with the theological and natural sciences seems not less intimate. Political scientists use history not only because their objects, the organized societies and the communities, have a past, but also because they, the scientists, have a past, a set of conventions, patterns of interpretation of what is before them, and need to come to awareness of these patterns, to learn to modify them and to unify, replenish, refresh, and enlarge them by conversation with and re-enactment of past encounters with society. To an increasing extent, it seems, natural science as it becomes conscious of its methodology, of its structures of interpretation, turns to history for an understanding of itself and recognizes the historicity of contemporary as well as past ideas of nature.

The younger sciences, psychology and sociology, often seem less self-critical and hence for the time being also less historical. But their growing maturity appears in the increase of reflection on their past.

Each human inquiry into compresent objects turns naturally to history, to the re-enactment of its own past, for the sake of understanding itself in its relation to its objects and so also for the understanding of its objects. But the belief in the unity of knowledge, in the unity of the knowing mind and of the known object, of the presence of a One in the manyness of subjectivities and objectivities, is also with us. Into the origins or nature of that conviction we do not now inquire. We acknowledge its presence and its great importance even when we set up such programs as this—when theologians speak of history and historians of theology. The immanent drive in human reason toward unity and relation seems close to the central spark of our human existence. If it does not give life and interest to what we are doing in all our searching and researching, it is at least a sign of the central dynamic principle, which seems to be so much more than our animal curiosity.

That thirst for unity, for the understanding of relations, drives us back also to history, to the re-enactment of the thoughts and deeds of men whose specialized labors had not yet led to the erection of dividing walls between the workshops. We find in the recovery of our history, or in our conversation with social and individual wisdom of the past the evidences of the unity from which we came and toward which we aspire in all our aspirations after wisdom. History in this aspect, not as the history of ideas or of the specialized thinking [of the] men and societies who are our companions, but as *human* history, fulfills its critical role for us as it leads us into living conversation with historians who were theologians, and with theologians who were historians, and who being both were sometimes also natural scientists and social philosophers. They do not represent for us an ideal after which we can or would aspire, but in thinking their thoughts after them we are led to criticism of our partialities and are enabled to combine our self-knowledge with a sense of the wholeness of all knowledge, however vain our efforts at synthetic understanding of ourselves and the universe.

Reflections on the Christian Theory of History

Theory of History and Ethics

A theory of history is always at the same time an expression of faith and an aid to the guidance of life. The relation between religious faith, theory of history, and ethics is *triadic*. The New Testament view of history may be taken as an example. It represents, on the one hand, in its affirmations and denials, an expression of faith in God and in his rule. God is king, despite appearances to the contrary, and his rule is to become manifest in history. The ethics of Jesus is based upon the same faith in God; it is not dependent upon the eschatology [of his day],' but it is an ethics of faith which can express itself in the terms of wisdom-thought as well as of eschatology. Yet the theory of history does give guidance to life; how this faith will issue in conduct here and now seems to be partly determined by the eschatology. Similarly, the modern theory of progress is an expression of faith in the divinity of the human spirit as the source of life's meaning and as the conquering and organizing force in existence. Modern ethics, whether in utilitarian or idealist forms, is based upon that same faith. It is not founded upon the theory of progress, but it is supported and modified by it. Marxian ethics and Marxian philosophy of history are similarly related to each other and to Marxian faith. The class ethics is not dependent upon the economic theory of history, nor vice versa. They are both dependent upon faith in economic value as the source and foundation of all values. But the theory of history gives guidance to the ethics.

The meaning of this observation lies in the fact that it seems to offer some help in avoiding two errors in developing a theory of history and ethics. The first error is that of making [history] the foundation of [ethics]. In that case theory is developed independent of action, that is, speculatively. It tends then to become an expression of faith in such a way that all events are regarded as equally the product of divine determination (whether the god be the Christian god or one of the ancient or modern pagan deities). The resultant ethics is likely to be one of quiescent expectation, whether of the Kingdom of God, or of progress, or of the revolution. The opposite error is that of making the theory of history dependent on ethics, while the latter itself is based upon itself or upon desire. The result is Utopianism and the wishful interpretation of history. History is made dependent on human teleology, and the latter has no guidance save that which it derives from its wishes. The ethics of modernism and of Marxism have led to perversions similar to those found in some Christian interpretations of the Kingdom of God at this point.

The theory of history seems to be able to fulfill its proper function only when it is developed strategically. That is to say, when it is developed neither for the sake of justifying the ways of the god to man, nor speculatively, but for the sake of understanding the situation of man in history, in order that he may know how to conduct himself. It is not the function of the Christian theology of history to explain to man the whole strategy of the divine campaign in order that man may rest content, assured of the victorious outcome, but rather to set forth so much of the divine strategy as is discernible and as is necessary in order that the ethics of faith in God may have some guidance in understanding what is required of man in the immediate situation.

Human History as an Individual Event

The event with which the Christian theory of history is concerned is the event "mankind." It is not creation in general, temporal existence as a whole. Men may have some intimation of the meaning of that total history, of a "creation that groaneth and travailleth in pain until now," of a "fall of the angels." But apart from the faith that all things have their source and goal in God, this total history lies beyond human comprehension, and the understanding of it is not necessary to man. Thought about it seems to lead to mythological or philosophical speculation without relevance to human duty. On the other hand, the history with which Christianity is concerned is not the history of a culture or of an individual person. These events doubtless enter into consideration and the problem of their "direct relation to God" is a genuine problem for theology. Yet the Christian theory of history regards mankind itself as having a history with a beginning, a middle, and an end. It is not a succession of individual histories, whether of persons or of cultures. It has unity and meaning as a single event, unique and unrepetitive.

From the point of view of individualism or of cultural pluralism the history of mankind is a sort of eternal background for these histories. Mankind itself has no true history. The destiny of persons or of cultures is the all-important thing. Insofar as Christianity has become person-

or culture-centered it has tended to lose sight of the meaning of human history as one event. In consequence it has had difficulty in doing justice to its early apprehension of creation, salvation, and judgment as unique and non-repeatable occurrences. History conceived as a series or congeries of many personal events, or of cultural and national histories, needed to deal with many creations, salvations, and judgments. From this point of view the meaning of Jesus Christ lies in the general law which his life and destiny illustrate. Considering the life of mankind as a single limited event, [however,] Jesus Christ's significance does not lie in the general law but in the fact of his appearance in that life at one unique moment.

Christian ethics oriented by such a view of history is concerned with the effect of individual life and action not only upon persons or civilizations but upon mankind. Sin affects the race; salvation deals with mankind. Evil and good are resident in the whole of humanity.

The Meaning of History

The essence of the pagan religions, ancient and modern, is their location of the source of life's meaning within that life itself. In the modern paganisms or secularisms the individual derives the meaning of his existence from his participation in the life of the nation, of civilization, of a race, a class, or of mankind as a whole. But these gods are regarded as absolute; they derive their meaning from nothing beyond themselves. The attempt may be made to find meaning in history, in the life of the race, by relating it to values, defined as eternal essences. Such values, however, represent abstractions from the life in relation to which they are values. In every case the assumption is that the life of the race, or nation, or class is eternal. Mazzini's utterance, "Nations, like individuals, live and die, but civilization cannot die," and Feuerbach's reference to the eternity of the race are characteristic assertions of the dogma.[2]

The Christian theory of history is first of all negative in its rejection of this assumption of the eternity of anything temporal. One abiding meaning of New Testament eschatology lies in its recognition of the fact of death as a fact not only in individual life but in national and especially in human life as a whole. The belief that this eschatology has been disproved by the failure of the end to put in its appearance in the generation of the disciples is as respectable as the belief that a

86

child's vision of death is disproved by the fact that it continues to live through many crises. The acceptance of death as the end of humanity as well as of persons and cultures means that intrinsic value is denied to these events. No reason for living can be found within life itself. In this sense the cross is the revelation of the end and of the futility of history.

The obverse of the Christian denial of the intrinsic meaning of history is the affirmation of its derivative meaning. Life is not worth living for its own sake, and this is true of the life of the race as of the life of any individual. Yet it is worth living as a life which has its source and goal in God. Creation and resurrection are the affirmation of the meaningfulness of history, as an event which not only refers beyond itself but represents the outgoing love of God. In the central event of history, in Jesus Christ, this meaning comes to light; it is revealed. But it is not revealed in the so-called historical Jesus whose end is death; it is revealed only to faith in the Jesus Christ who is resurrected from the dead. "If in this life only we have hope of Christ, we are of all men most miserable" [1 Cor. 15:19]. But the resurrection is not an event in history, in the sense that it means the return of Christ to the history of mankind. Such an event would not represent a victory over the cross.

The Christian theory of history, moving between this denial and affirmation of the meaningfulness of human history, is in constant danger of developing into an other-worldliness in which the rejection of this world predominates over acceptance, or into a this-worldliness in which affirmation is unaccompanied by eschatological denial. A two-world theory also, in which dualism replaces the dialectic, is a perversion of the Christian view.

The Determining Force in History

The Christian interpretation of history must be distinguished from both the naturalistic or materialistic and the teleological or spiritualistic interpretations. According to the former, "compulsory" factors determine history; according to the latter, the "persuasive" factors are primary. Naturalism sees history as a causal process, of which mind and will are a part. But even Spengler and Marx must make some room for teleology. Spiritualism finds the directing and determining factor in the human mind which moves toward an end, distant or in view. It recognizes the reality of the causal process and its necessity, yet regards it as fitted to mind or open to teleological guidance.

In recent years the spiritualistic interpretation of history has often been confused with the Christian view. But there are many points at which naturalism is more closely related to Christianity than such spiritualism is. Yet the Christian interpretation is distinct from both in that it finds the determining force in history neither in nature nor in culture but in a third type of determination, in the rule of God. The priority of this determination does not involve the denial of the reality of either the causal or of the teleological sequences but it does deny their claim to primacy. The relation of this divine determinism to nature and to culture may be conceived somewhat in analogy to the relation of culture to nature. As human teleology absorbs and transforms the causal sequences without abrogating them, so the Kingdom of God may be said to absorb and transform both.[3] In this sense the Kingdom of God [as] divine determinism transcends history; it is not in history, though the whole of history is in it, and it reaches into the causal and teleological sequences so as to modify them. This way of describing the situation, however, rests upon abstractions. The process of history has causal and teleological aspects rather than that it is made up out of the addition of teleology to causality and of the Kingdom of God to teleology.

Where does divine determinism appear? There are intimations of this divine determinism in events which seem to outrun their causes or the purposes which preceded them. Emergences in the historic life, the pure givenness of historic individuality, the fatefulness of the "I, Here and Now"—these suggest a determining factor beyond nature and culture. Yet this factor is not thereby proved divine nor is it desirable to maintain that causal and teleological determination may not be found in these events. The demonstration of the reality of divine determination is found by faith in miracle. But miracle cannot be interpreted either as interference with the causal sequence or as the abrogation of the teleological process. It is rather the transformation of both by their inclusion in another pattern. The miracle is miracle of faith as well as miracle of demonstration and intuition. Where men think to do evil but God thinks to do good; where nature leads to death but God brings to life—there is miracle. The great miracle of human history is the salvation wrought in Jesus Christ. This event Jesus Christ may be interpreted naturalistically or teleologically by reference to the ideal which Jesus taught and lived. But a super-naturalistic and super-teleological interpretation, recognizing the former aspects, sees the miracle here in the operation of the divine determinism which absorbs and transforms a life ending in death into a higher pattern, into a life-giving process. Here again the evil and good intentions of men are transformed and death is swallowed up in victory.[4] This appearance of the rule of God in Jesus Christ remains the criterion by which Christianity judges history. Apart from such a salvation the emergence of life, mind, conscience, individuality, then history, would not be interpretable as revelations of God's rule, since all of these creative emergences end in death and nothingness and meaninglessness.

How is the divine determinism apprehended? The rule of God remains hidden to a view which deals with the causal sequences, just as the teleological factor is not discoverable so long as we remain bound to nature. We apprehend freedom only as we are free; we can see design only because we are designers. To any point of view wholly within history the Kingdom of God is hidden; and we are all in human history. The Kingdom can be apprehended only insofar as we surrender to the divine determination, only by faith, not as belief that it exists, but as trust in it. This is not to say that faith creates the Kingdom; the "miracles" of God are objective, but they are hidden save to faith. The Christian interpretation of history requires participation in that history as a divinely ruled life of mankind. Apart from such participation the interpretation remains a more or less interesting speculation. But this is true of all interpretations of history.

How is human teleology related to the Kingdom of God? In the spiritualistic interpretation of history God's determination of life is channeled through human teleology. God exercises his rule through men who share his purpose. We have rejected this interpretation as inadequate if not contrary to the Christian point of view. How then does man, or rather the citizen of the Kingdom, co-operate with God? Not directly but tangentially, as it were. Man could scarcely make God's purposes his own, even if he knew what they were. But he can act in his own sphere in the light of what God has done and with the hope of what He will do.

The Kingdom on Earth

Though the telos of the life of mankind lies beyond history, as the telos of every individual life lies beyond that life, there is an irreducible truth in the millenarian strain in Christianity. As individualistic Christianity in its mystic and pietist-evangelical forms insisted upon a present vision of God, a present conversion, a present anticipation of the eternal fulfillment, so millenarianism—though often in mistaken ways—has insisted upon the anticipation in the here and now of the eternal fulfillment, of human history. The dangers of this insistence lie in the tendencies to make this relative fulfillment the true goal, to regard some partial conversion or vision or organization of society as perfect, to seek it without reference to the divine determinism. On the other hand the dangers of the traditional view, which refers only to the eternal fulfillment, are those of compromise with the world of sin, of relative satisfaction with the relative institutions of a sinful world. Millenarianism in the social scene, like monasticism and pietism in the individual, has rightly emphasized that Christian faith must make a profound difference here and now in the total organization of life.

The Christian faith calls not only for a life lived between the two revolutions of the salvation wrought in Christ and the end with judgment and resurrection but for the penetration of the life of humanity here and now with the ethics of faith in God, and all that flows from this. But such penetration of human life is possible only at times of crisis when the destruction of faith in half-gods occurs or, to use Tillich's phrase, when the spirit of self-sufficient finitude is broken. Such crises are to faith judgments of God. They offer the opportunity for pressing into the kingdom. They present men with forced options, with either/ors.

In this sense every moment of great crisis is a millenarian moment. The opportunity is created by God; but whether his rule will be the judgment or the salvation of men depends, from the point of view of human freedom, upon their acceptance or rejection of the opportunity. It seems to me, however, very important to remember that the conversion of mankind is not something which can happen so as to give men security. The doctrine of the Christian revolution is a doctrine of permanent, continuous revolution.

Reinhold Niebuhr's Interpretation of History

I approach the task of reviewing Reinhold Niebuhr's interpretation of history with much hesitation. The theology of history offers many difficult problems, and I remain confused even about the questions that can significantly be asked in this realm. Since I grope my own way uncertainly amidst its mazes, how can I adequately describe another man's course through the labyrinth? My hesitation is increased by the knowledge that my relation to the interpreter has a history of its own and that I shall not be able to describe his interpretation as a thing-in-itself but only in the context of my complex responses to one who since the time of an historic but only partly remembered childhood has been hero, friend and co-worker, fraternal rival and theological foil, someone to be depended upon in all crises and one from whom independence needed to be gained. Such complexities may characterize any interpretations of history. Certainly they are present in this case.

But the hesitant venture must be begun. I shall begin by asking Reinie certain questions that seem to me to be significant and by extracting the answers as best I can from his books on the interpretation of history. I shall confine myself to those two volumes on the subject which represent his ripest thought, *Human Destiny*, the second volume of the Gifford Lectures, and the Beecher Lectures on *Faith and History*.[1]

The first question is: What is he interpreting? History is a notoriously ambiguous term, as Reinhold himself points out; it means both a course of events and the recording, remembering and re-enacting of events. But the ambiguity cannot disguise the fact that some interpreters of history direct primary attention to a course of events, seeking to find patterns, relations and definable directions in it, while others concentrate on the activity of the recorder, rememberer and interpreter of events. The former seek for meaning in the course of noting how one event points to another or to something common in them. The latter ask, What does it mean that men remember, re-enact and interpret events? What value does this activity have? To what does it point? To be sure, the study of the object and the study of the subject cannot be divorced, but they can be distinguished, and it seems to me to be important to discover whether an interpreter of history is concerned first of all with historical activity or with its object, whether he is a philosophical historian, like Hegel or Toynbee, or a critical philosopher of the historical reason, like Croce or Collingwood.

When I go to Reinie's books with this question I get no clear answer at first. He is not interpreting the work of the rememberer and reorganizer and re-enactor of the past; it is very rarely that one is able to substitute for the word "history," as he uses it, the phrase "remembrance or re-enactment of things past." Memory interests him primarily as an aspect of man's freedom; it "represents man's capacity to rise above, even while he is within, the temporal flux."[2] Such specific memories as Israel's recollection of the covenant and the Christian memory of Jesus Christ are primarily significant in connection with freedom. They enable man to act in a universe, to be free and yet realize the limitation of freedom. Reinie, then, is not interpreting, primarily, human or Christian activity in recalling and reorganizing the past, though he has a secondary interest in this. It is easier to substitute the term "the course of human events" for the word "history" as it is used in most places in his writings, but not always. The phrases "social process" and "social actions" fit better. History and society seem to go together so that individual life can be contrasted with history as in the statement, "If history cannot find its meaning except in the disclosure of a divine sovereignty, which both governs and transcends it, it is implicitly . . . assumed that history, however meaningful, cannot give life its full meaning. Each individual transcends and is involved in the historical process. In so far as he is involved in history, the disclosure of life's meaning must come to him in history. In so far as he transcends history, the source of life's meaning must transcend history."[3]

My effort to find an answer to my original question comes to this result: What Reinie is interpreting is not the "course of human events" nor yet the activity of the rememberer but the conception of social process as this is present in the mind of an ethical agent. Hence his questions about an interpretation of history are always questions about its ethical results insofar as it modifies conduct and somewhat, too, about its ethical origins, insofar as it has its sources in human faith or pride. The idea of a correspondence between the theory of the social process and its actuality is not lacking but seems to be secondary to the ethical idea. The interpretation of history which we have here is, then, neither of the order represented by Toynbee nor yet of the sort represented by Collingwood, but rather like Marx's or Comte's. Hence also the problems in the Christian interpretation of history in which he is interested are not the sort of problems that arise for an Augustine or even a Joachim. The question, What ought I do in the social process? always seems to have priority over the questions, What can I know? What may I hope? What do I trust in? Every interpretation of history doubtless moves between the polarities of contemplative and practical reason, but there are significant differences here between those who regard the course of events with worshipping wonder and those who look at it with the concern of doers of deeds. It is the difference between the 105th Psalm and the Book of Daniel, perhaps the difference between Augustine and Joachim. It is characteristic that the former theological interpretations turn more to the past, though with reference to the future, and that the latter turn to the future, though with some reference to the past. In the polarity between past and future, Reinie is drawn always to the future, I believe, rather than toward the past.

The second question one may raise about an interpreter of history is, Whose history is he interpreting? or What are the limits of the process in which pattern and interrelation are sought? As it is characteristic of the so-called modern interpretation of history that it maintains that the intelligible field of interaction beyond which it is unnecessary to go comprises natural events and human actions, [and] as it is characteristic of the pluralistic interpretations to assert that such interactions within a civilization are intelligible, so it is characteristic of Christian interpretations that they assert not only the necessity of taking the whole human process into account in all the interactions of men with all of nature, hence universal history, but the interactions of all finite wills with God, who is not a third force alongside of man and nature but always the Other who is encountered in all human and natural challenges. That Reinie's interpretation of history, as ethical, is Christian in this sense of being universal is indicated on every page of his writings. His polemic against modern and classic interpretations is carried on partly in attacks on their pluralism and their effort to discern intelligible patterns and guiding principles of conduct in social affairs by attending only to such abstractions as the natural process, or the national process, or the human process.

Our question may be reformulated in another way: Is this one-world history or two-world history? Do all the actions that realize value and disvalue take place in the sphere of the visible, tangible world and of human freedom? Or do they take place in a sphere beyond our knowledge and freedom? Or do they take place in interaction between the human and super-human? Reinie's ethical interpretation of history with its polemic against both this-worldly and other-worldly beliefs about its character is evidently two-worldly. History is the realm of both human freedom and human limitation by something distinct from nature and from the fatalities pointed to by astrology and its modern counterparts. The meaning of our actions in the social process cannot be understood if they are not related to actions that limit our freedom and also limit the power of nature. Meaning in history is discoverable only at the intersection of mystery and intelligibility.

That leads us to our third question: What active powers are distinguished as participating in the process called history and what is the role which each plays? The answer to this question which I find in Reinie's writings is exceedingly complex. Against all naturalism he asserts the power of human freedom. Man "is a creature, subject to nature's necessities and limitations; but he is also a free spirit who knows of the brevity of his years and by this knowledge transcends the temporal by some capacity within himself."[4] Man's freedom, however, is not only the freedom of the knower, it is also the freedom of the doer, though I am not quite sure how the transition is made from the freedom man has as one who knows to the freedom which he has as one who can change the course of natural events. But he has the "freedom . . . to be creative in history," "to transmute every physical impulse," to choose himself at his end, to identify himself with particular causes.[5] His freedom, then, is not only the freedom of contemplation but also a liberty of choice and that ability to create and destroy which Dostoevsky and Berdyaev have underscored. Reinie seems to rest his case for freedom on the ability of man to transcend himself as knower of his deeds but it is evident that this is not the fundamental freedom of man for him, as his attacks on the separation of soul and body clearly point out. The inadequacy of progress philosophy is not due to the fact that it discerns the power of human freedom but to its over-estimate of that power. Secondly, the power of non-intelligent forces in the historical process is recognized, for what is wrong with naturalistic interpretations is not that natural forces do not exist but that they are over-estimated both as to their power and as to their ability to bestow value.[6] To be sure, Reinie does not pay much attention to the powers that are in things, to the energies pointed out by those interpreters of history who see in weather and geography great formative influences, but I do not think that he is disposed to deny the reality of such powers in history. He is more concerned with the potencies and powers which are in man as a part of nature and which are strangely blended with his reason. He notes what Marx and Freud and Hobbes have noted— the presence of non-individual, non-personal forces in man, the "vitalities" as he calls them, the power-drives which limit the rational will even while it limits them.

Beyond these natural potencies there are active in history, according to Reinie's conception, great social combinations of reason and power, structures of justice which are at the same time structures of injustice. It is false to conceive the institutions of society, laws, property, the specialized functions of priesthood, economic groups, the military, as rational organizations under individual control. They are not wholly rational but "more or less stable or precarious harmonies of human vital capacities . . . governed by power."[7] They mold individuals though they are subject to some modification by individual action. They are not simply structures but dynamic movements and the irrational dynamism in community life comes to expression in such movements as Nazism and Communism.

But history is not a chaotic conflict of these various relative agents, individuals and institutions, reason and vitality. Unity and continuity are given to the social process by a negative and by a positive principle. Negatively all this conflict of forces is characterized by the prevalence in it of "the force of human sin, the persistent tendency to regard ourselves as more important than anyone else and to view a common problem from the standpoint of our own interest."[8] This "evil is a force within history itself and not the intrusion of the necessities of nature into the historical." It is the universal inclination of men "to make their own life into the center of history's meaning."[9] Positively, history is unified by God, though the fact that this God exists is known only in faith. Negatively, the truth that not-God does not exist is apparently knowable, apart from faith, by the impossibility of framing either an intelligible or a meaningful view of history without postulating Him, in however hidden a manner.

How does God act in history? It is erroneous to say that he acts as though he were an agent alongside other agents. He acts upon the whole social process prescribing to it its limits. He sets an outer limit to the human defiance of his will by so ordering the whole that forms of life which make themselves their own end, in isolation or dominion, destroy themselves.[10] This ordering, however, is such that God judges and destroys the rebels by raising up against them social powers and forces, which, themselves ambiguous and sinful, become executors of his will. Men do not know this action of God's in judgment, because they do not apprehend the final word spoken in all the words of men, they do not "interpret the defeats to which they are subject from an ultimate standpoint." It is faith which descries the action of God in history. The divine action so discerned is an activity of creation, government and redemption, but the emphasis in Reinie's interpretation seems to fall on government, for the significant element in the creative action of God in history is that limits are imposed on the created. "The idea of the divine creation of the world . . . when taken profoundly, describes the limits of the world's rationality and the inadequacy of any 'natural' cause as a sufficient explanation for the irrational givenness of things."[11] Creation means "that nothing in the world should be considered absolute."[12] The positive idea that God's action in history as apprehended by faith consists in the introduction into existence of ever new and always *good* forms of being is implied, sometimes made explicit, but is not at all emphasized. It does not seem of much importance to Reinie, or it is important only as stated negatively, that nothing is good in itself.

God's redemptive action in history is mediated by Jesus Christ, though perhaps not only by Jesus. Hence the question arises, What is the role of Jesus Christ as an agent in history? Fundamentally it is that of the revealer. The cross of Christ is the revelation of the wisdom of God. Jesus Christ reveals the falsity of the hope that man can redeem himself in history by his obedience to the law, or that the righteous man can give meaning to history. He reveals the sinfulness of man and the fact that only by the suffering love of God Himself the contradictions of history can be overcome.[13] Secondly, Jesus Christ makes possible, through his revelation of the limits of human virtue, wisdom and power, genuine renewals of individual and social life in history, though these are always only provisional renewals.[14] Thirdly, Jesus Christ redeems men in history from meaninglessness by pointing to the judgment and redemption which lie beyond history.

The final question which I shall put to Reinie, before I undertake to interpret him to myself, is, What periods of history do you distinguish? Here I believe the answer is evident. The periods which need to be distinguished are not those of history itself but the mythologically stated periods of the Pre-Historical, the Historical, and the Post-Historical. This scheme underlies his discussion of the perfection of Christ[15] and the discussion of the original righteousness of man,[16] as well as his interpretations of the end.[17] The historical, middle period, is the time of the fall. Sin is permanent in it. It is the fact which we always need to take into account; its prevalence is symbolized by the myth of the Anti-Christ who appears at the very end of history. Though Jesus Christ's entrance into history makes a certain division of the historical process into Before- and After-Christ periods not unimportant, Reinie seems more aware of the dangers which follow from such a schematization than of the good which may come from it.

I am aware that this sketch of Reinie's interpretation of history compares with the richly wrought-out fullness of his thought as the rough drawing of a skeleton compares with an actual living body. It may, however, serve to call to mind certain of the features of a compact body of thought which the members of this group know directly, and so be of some use.

II

When I ask myself what I think of this interpretation of history as a whole, I find myself perplexed. There is so much here that is important for any Christian interpretation, and so much I want to hear said that seems to be lacking. Yet what is lacking seems somehow to be present by implication. Reinie's thought appears to me to be like a great iceberg of which three-fourths or more is beneath the surface and in which what is explicitly said depends on something that is not made explicit.

If I look only at the explicit statements, then I am inclined to say that this interpretation is very much like a pre-Christian eschatological view of history, expressed in the three great affirmations that God rules, that His rule is hidden by the reign of the powers which are interposed between Him and us, and that His rule will be made manifest. The eschatologism of this interpretation does not consist so much in its constant reference to the end, though that is important, but in its awareness of the presence of the powers, partly demonic (sin, the structures of justice, communities), partly simply independent (nature), to which adjustment must now be made, though it is evident that they are not final and must not be taken as final. What distinguishes this interpretation of history from such pre-Christian eschatologies is, first, the elimination of every trace of particularism and, secondly, the absence of any contention with God about his justice or his wisdom in allowing the powers to continue to rule in the interval before the final revelation of his Kingdom. It is pre-Christian eschatology in the sense that the emphasis falls on the two ideas that sin and the "demonic" powers now reign and that only in the "end" will there be fulfillment. It is Christian eschatology in the sense that the first coming of Christ has judged man and the powers so that in faith it is now known that they do not have any final dominion and that God will make his justice, love, and mercy manifest in the end. It is Christian eschatology in the sense that the time of the interval is the time of repentance and faith made possible by the coming of Jesus Christ into the flesh.

Something is implicit here that is not made explicit and which if it were made more explicit would, I think, somewhat change the emphasis. What seems to be said is that the cross as judgment stands in the very midst of our history, though as forgiveness it stands at the end of history so that man in history can live in repentance and in the hope of forgiveness. But the resurrection does not explicitly stand in history, though the faith which is now in history according to Reinie presupposes the resurrection. It seems to me important that all the references to Jesus Christ as having come are references to the crucified Christ, to "suffering love" which must "remain suffering love in history" and that there are so few references to "triumphant faith"—not necessarily the triumphant faith of the Christian but of Jesus Christ.

This is near the center of the difficulty I find in appropriating Reinie's interpretation of history as my own. Jesus, he says, reinterprets the "eschata." Jesus attributed the qualities of the suffering servant to his first coming and the qualities of the triumphant Son of Man to a second coming. Hence Reinie makes history between the first and second comings an interim in which love continues to suffer but in which men partly know the true meaning of history and so live in faith and repentance. But it seems to me that the Christian reinterpretation of the "eschata" must be distinguished from Jesus' reinterpretation, that the resurrection means that Christ has come again and come with power, that the interval between the first and second comings was very short and that the interval in which men now live is not between crucifixion and resurrection but between the resurrection of the first fruits and the final resurrection.

I want to try to say this in another way. It is evident to me that for

Reinie himself Christ's resurrection is a fact in his own history. He believes that God is good, that Jesus was not destroyed; he does not quarrel at all with the justice of God as he would need to do if he did not believe that Jesus Christ is risen from the dead. For him faith is not only that man-to-God movement by means of which he apprehends God beyond the limits of human experience but the God-to-man gift that has been put into his life and the life of his community by the resurrection of Jesus Christ from the dead. Yet he speaks to men who do not know that they live between the resurrection of Jesus Christ and their own resurrection; they think that they live after the crucifixion only. And in speaking to them he takes their ground and does not make explicit the whole content of his interpretation of history. History is in fact for him not only the history of sin, suffering, love, and repentance, but the history of faith as a gift of God and faith is not only wisdom of God but power of God. Of course, the recognition of this fact can easily be perverted into the fido-centric heresy which substitutes faith in faith for faith in God, but this does not cancel out the fact that through Jesus Christ triumphant faith in God has been introduced into the world.

Closely connected with this problem of the place of the resurrection in the Christian interpretation of history are two or three other problems which arise for me in trying to understand our history with Reinie. The first of these is the problem of myth. So far as I understand his use of this term it means that an effort must be made to state in story form what is in fact not a once-and-for-all event but a pattern in repeated events or an aspect of human existence. Creation means the ever-present limitation of the finite; fall means the ever-repeated and inevitable succumbing of the spirit to the temptation of pride; the end of history means the beyond-history reference which is necessary in every moment as reference both to the judgment and the meaning which came from beyond the finite.[18] By the same token it would seem that Jesus Christ as revelation of God might be a mythological figure standing for suffering love in history. Sometimes Reinie seems to come near this position. But he stops short of it, warning only against the tendency to ascribe to the humanity of Jesus what is characteristic of the second person of the Trinity. This suggests to me, first, that actually for him the coming of Jesus Christ into the flesh is a profoundly significant, once-and-for-all historical event which makes the distinction between A.D. and B.C. exceedingly important and does not quite permit

99

the treatment of all human history as equally subject to the reign of sin and equally characterized by the defeat of suffering love. Secondly, it suggests that if he himself wants to avoid that cyclical interpretation of history which he elsewhere attacks, he needs to ascribe to creation, fall, and end more than mythical meaning. These terms refer, first, to once-and-for-all events and, secondly, serve as categories by means of which to interpret repeated events. This seems to me implicit in his view but is not made sufficiently explicit to my understanding.

Again there is implicit a theology which is negatively stated and which I should like to see made explicit. In his chapters on the biblical understanding of history he faithfully describes history as dramatic encounter between God and man in which the initiative always lies with God. But when he turns to the interpretation of contemporary social action he seems to use the eschatological more than the prophetic pattern and God is dealt with as hidden and veiled, *Deus Absconditus.* "Moral judgments are executed in history; but never with precision." "The virtuous and the innocent may, and frequently do, suffer more rather than less in the competitions of life and history, precisely because of their virtue." "There are . . . tangents of moral meaning in history; but there are no clear and exact patterns."[19] Etc. All these things can and must be said insofar as God is *Deus Absconditus.* They cannot be said insofar as he is *Deus Revelatus.* For as *Deus Revelatus* it is clear that his righteousness is not that of rewards and punishments but of forgiveness, and in the light of revelation, history is illuminated not simply as the scene of sin and of the ambiguous powers which rule over men but as the action in which we are being created, chastised, and forgiven. It is illuminated as the place where God now rules and does so with precision. I would like to see this positive theology which underlies all the negative statements in this theology of history made explicit.

Finally, I must raise a question about the significance of the church for Reinie. I find myself in hearty agreement with all his criticisms of the churches' tendencies to find the fulfillment of history in themselves and of a spiritualism which seeks to escape temporal conditions. Yet I think that this whole interpretation implies the reality of an invisible community of faith which is in history, living by relation to the risen Christ. The reality of faith in history is not the reality of individual faith only, but of communal faith. If the significance of faith as mediator of divine power in history needs to be made explicit, the significance of the community of faith must also be made clearer.

Perhaps the statement of these problems I encounter in interpreting the interpreter only indicate that each of us has his particular task to do and that when Reinie undertakes to speak to the secular mind of today about the Christian interpretation of history he must leave unsaid what others of us who are trying to understand what we believe find it important to say; or that when one seeks to set forth an interpretation of history that is relevant to Christian action in civilization one must deal with other questions that arise when one tries to state what is relevant to Christian faith within the church.

4

Historical Interpretation

Theology in a Time of Disillusionment

I

The subject chosen for this lecture requires more than a formal apology. We are all more than a little weary of keeping our religion up-to-date, of adjusting and adapting our theology to changing intellectual fashions. We have had gospels for an age of doubt, theologies for periods of social reconstruction, religions for the era of science, faiths for democratic civilizations and philosophies for modern life, until we have begun to wonder whether there is such a thing as a faith for life and a theology for man, a gospel for the common human situation. We have admonished ourselves so often that we must be "up and onward" in our religious thinking if "we would keep abreast with truth" that we have cause to confuse truth with mobility, and we have grown weary of mere mobility which keeps us in exerted quest without defining where we are going. We have, in Professor Ralph Barton Perry's phrase, invested much religious capital in scientific novelties—and have been caught in a bear market—so that like most investors in these days we have grown cautious in the use of our remaining funds, if indeed we have any funds left to our account. All of this is part of the disillusionment which theology cannot escape, of which, whether we want it so or not, it is bound to take account; and all of this may be part of a situation in which theology can turn from the relative and the changing to the absolute and the abiding. To speak of theology in a time of disillusionment may mean, therefore, that we can speak of a theology which does not ask us to adjust ourselves to the latest change in intellectual climate but of a theology which is forced by a change in the cultural outlook to turn away from the changing, transient flux of things to the permanent and the abiding. Such a theology may conceivably contain no more of the absolute in the last analysis than the theology which a period of optimism and progress produces, but it cannot help but contain elements overlooked in times of enjoyment. Like religion in the hour of need, so theology in a time of disillusionment contains an urgency and a reality which appear to be lacking in softer hours with their easier faith and their less urgent demand for reality.

The disillusionment that has come creeping upon modern Western civilization during the past decades may not be its most characteristic feature when this period is viewed from the vantage point of centuries, but when our days are regarded from the shorter perspective of a hundred years gone by, that is their most striking attribute. It is not a disillusionment which can be identified with awareness of the maladjustments and toils of a post-war period, though these have added the necessary high relief which revealed the significance of discontent and disappointment ignored in a previous period. It is rather an attitude which has been long in preparation and which now, like a conversion, arrives at its apparently sudden revelation.

We may note that fact when we think of the primary disappointment in our culture—its disappointment in man. The liberalism and romanticism which laid the foundations of nineteenth century culture had for their fundamental dogma the optimistic faith in human goodness and rationality. On this foundation they built a political theory which promised Utopia to those who would trust in the innate wisdom of the common mortal, an economic practice which held forth the hope of universal wealth if only the native urges and rational self-interest of natural men were allowed to have full sway, and a philosophy which exalted the human mind as the point in which alone eternal reality could realize itself. If the faith was not produced by the success of man's industrial and scientific enterprise and by the victory of those middle classes which were advancing and expanding from the middle of the eighteenth century onward, it was at all events supported by these experiences. And theology no less than philosophy was persuaded to accept the new dogma which replaced trust in God and love of man with trust in man and the love of God.

In that trust our civilization has been disappointed more or less effectively. For more than half a century it has been voicing that disappointment, but today the measure of its disillusionment has been filled up. As has been the case in many another period of history, the men of literature, novelists, dramatists, poets and essayists, were more responsive to the new temper than the professional philosophers and historians of civilization. Scarcely had the voice of Whitman left off praising the grandeur of man than the novelists began to pry behind the scenes and to display with ill-disguised glee the tinsel and the paste disguise of human majesty. In place of romantic descriptions of souls harmonious with harmonious nature they offered us sketch-books showing man as the discordant product of a nature which was not only "red in tooth and claw," but also rather grossly sullied with the mire from which it had emerged. These heretics were suffered for a time while the new orthodoxy of the divinity of man continued to hold sway in the mass of Western civilization and especially among those middle classes which ruled the cultural process. But the volume of voices increased. If Henry Brooks Adams's disillusionment was a rare occurrence in the later nineteenth century, it was received in the twentieth as the significant experience which mirrored the experiences of thousands. If naturalism and realism seemed a disease of European letters to Americans of the nineties, in the twenties we received *An American Tragedy* and the realistic description of our own *Main Street* with a grim appreciation.[1]

What the novelists began the psychologists continued. Perhaps they have contributed even more than their more literary brothers to the destruction of liberal orthodoxy, to the abandonment of romantic faith in man's innate sublimity of mind and conscience, and of the liberal's trust in his power to help himself out of every situation. One needs only to recall the pertinent terms of the new psychology as contrasted with the old to note the change. Instincts for faculties, reaction patterns for free will, rationalization for reason, the unconscious for the conscious, libido for the will, suggestion for conviction, these with their countless corollaries mark the passing of the creed by which idealism lived and the growth of the great disappointment. And in all of this, psychology may be reflecting less the results of experiments carried on in academic laboratories and more the outcome of the great social experiment of the nineteenth century, which built on faith in man and found the structure it had erected broken and tottering, a house of many discontents.

After novelists and psychologists, biographers followed in the train. One by one they have taken the idols to which men pointed with pride as the sufficient miraculous proofs of the truth of their doctrine, of the certainty of man's divinity and goodness, and have demonstrated that even these paragons of humanity were created considerably lower than the angels. Our school-day heroes, who once established our faith by their demonstration of what glory and honor crown humanity—Washington, Lincoln, Grant, Queen Victoria, Florence Nightingale, John Wesley, John Calvin, Martin Luther—have been subjected to cynical examination and have been found wanting. Nor have Jesus and Paul been spared. From Strachey's *Eminent Victorians* to Masters' *Lincoln* the line of criticism runs steadily downward to reveal the error of our misplaced faith.[2] If the psychologists have generalized the findings of the novelists to show statistically that the Main Street–mind is the mind of the race and not an exception, then the biographers have undertaken to show that there are no exceptions to the new generalization, as it is written, "There is none righteous, no, not one; there is none that understandeth; there is none that doeth good, no, not so much as one" [Psalm 14:3].

And the significant thing is not that novelists, psychologists and biographers say these things; the significant fact is that we receive their statements with approval. They reflect what the modern man thinks about himself—or about his neighbor. And so one of the arch-foundations of liberal theology has been torn away. Once we could believe and could count on the presence of the like belief in almost all our world that in modern man we have a creature, as Fiske said, "different in kind from his predecessors and fit for an eternal life of progress, for a closer and closer communion with God in a beatitude that shall endure";[3] or we could speak with George A. Gordon of the "dear, eternal humanity of God" and proclaim as our faith that "the humanity of God is given in the humanity of man," "that we ascend to God through man and his sovereign leader."[4] If humanity is what today we believe it to be, what kind of a God is that to whom we can ascend or descend through man? We have learned and are learning in our school-rooms, from our newspapers and our literature that man in essence is not the Godlike being in whom liberals and romanticists trusted, but as the late Professor Bennett once had a fabulous student summarize his academic knowledge "man is a ratlike savage, suffering from demoniacal possession."[5] Or we may choose an astronomical view or say with Professor Vernon Louis Parrington that he is a parasite infesting the epidermis of a midge among the planets.

Our disillusionment with man is paralleled by our disappointment in his civilization. It was not long ago that churchmen were identifying the Kingdom of God with culture and praising every new success in man's conquest of the physical environment as a meaningful advance toward the coming of the rule of love and peace and joy. We sketched the rise of civilization from savagery to modern life and, with our faith in man, combined the dogma of an eternal progress ever upward and onward. The faith in progress ignored many salient facts, but it was based on some very striking experiences and supported by an alliance with a scientific theory. Preceding the theory of biological evolution, the social basis of faith in progress was the expansion and growing power of the middle classes who had in their hands not only the industrial but also the academic and religious life of the later eighteenth and of the nineteenth centuries. In the growth of wealth, the successful combat against many diseases, the provision of ever new mechanical miracles which enabled the mind and the body to expand their life and their sovereignty, the suggestion was powerfully presented that the movement toward control of the universe was automatic and inevitable. In religion a this-worldliness, which sometimes took on the character of humanitarianism but which more frequently remained satisfied with a humanism that trusted the inevitable laws of progress to wipe away all tears, replaced the earlier orthodoxy and proclaimed that the immanent God was realizing himself in the processes of culture. Warning voices began to be heard as the nineteenth century grew older. Marx saw the road to progress leading through revolution though he remained committed to his own proletarian version of the middle class dogma. Henry George associated poverty with progress. Dante Gabriel Rossetti warned against the folly of presuming "to be glad in his gladness who comes after thee"; Emil Du Bois-Reymond inquired into the meaning of progress for the last man roasting his last potato in the last fire on an arctic planet. With Bertrand Russell's "Free Man's Worship" the skeptical and disappointed note arose more clearly and poignantly but was valued as a sad melody is appreciated, as a thing of beauty rather than as a statement of truth. Men could continue to console themselves with the reflection that though the cosmic process did not hasten their advance or have any concern for their ideals, yet their own nobility and love of truth made up for any lack of cosmic support, that they could carry their ideals to victory in time if not in eternity, and that, at all events, the "vast death of the solar system" which would involve in ruin "all the labor of the ages," "all the noonday brightness of human genius," was some millions or hundreds of millions of years distant.[6] Moreover, so long as faith in man's nobility and genius persisted the cosmic drama was felt to contain at very least the significance of noble tragedy.

We have not been allowed to lay this flattering unction to our souls for long. Loss of faith in man has robbed the idea of progress of its dynamic and has made the end of the mundane process appear less a noble tragedy than a strange and futile interlude. It has made the question of the meaning of life incredibly difficult and at the same time greatly increased its urgency. Yet the disillusionment of Western mankind with its new orthodoxy had other sources besides this one. The same science which furnished the belief in progress with a convenient mythology and an appropriate dogma raised its voice in criticism of the faith which far outran the underlying facts which science had revealed. When men filled with enthusiasm for the new doctrine began to study history and anthropology for the sake of finding data to support their hypothesis they came across facts which could not be too readily incorporated into their system. They discovered that there was little evidence for the theory of a continuous biological improvement of the human race during the period covered by history. And they found, furthermore, that all surveys sketching the line of progress were infected with the vice of relativity. Drawn from the point of view of a present which could not help but regard itself as nearer to perfection than the past, such surveys were all biased in their selection of historical data. The relativity of all schemes of progress became even more evident, however, as a result of increasing contact with other civilizations than that Western culture which had arrogated to itself the full significance of history. Contact with the civilizations of Greece and Rome as a result of the nineteenth century's painstaking research and with the cultures of India and China as a result of its imperial and industrial expansion, brought home the relativity of the doctrine of progress, while dispassionate historical study revealed the declines in Western and Eastern history which had been no less significant than the advances.

Yet all this was less effective in bringing about the great disillusionment than the actual failures of civilization, the experience of great negative instances. It is almost as characteristic of human nature to generalize its sorrows as its joys; if in times of expansion we are prone to believe that progress without end is our lot, we are nearly as likely to assume in times of gloom and sorrow that all of life is mournful and all this world a vale of tears. The sorrows and disappointments of our generation have apparently outweighed its joys; certainly it has been deeply disappointed and so it has lost faith in civilization and in its advance to perfection.

What the death of twenty-six million combatants and noncombatants, the loss of millions of private fortunes and the substitution of the sense of insecurity for certainty—all as the result of the war—have meant for the changing of our mental climate, it is difficult to estimate. But no matter how much influence in the creation of the modern mood we assign to these factors, we are not likely to *overesti-mate* their weight. Combined with these sorrows is the great disappointment in democracy to which the fascist movements of the Old World bear witness, but which is scarcely less pronounced in the cynicism with which the New World has come to regard corruption in national and municipal government. And these social experiences are supported as Parrington and others have pointed out by a realistic psychology which "with its discovery of morons and its study of mob tendencies," with its intelligence tests, turns "the whole romantic theory of democracy to quicksand under our feet" so that it is "no wonder we are bedeviled by doubts and uncertainties." "Our jauntiness is gone."[7] Utopias no longer seem so close at hand as they did; plans and specifications for the ideal commonwealth no longer seem simple matters to be drawn by any competent social carpenter.

Our disappointment with the machines which clatter round about us is perhaps even greater. It is difficult now to recapture the sense of deliverance and the enthusiasm with which men hailed the advance of the machine some twenty, thirty, fifty years ago. Sometimes one happens across a voice out of that past in a Sunday newspaper supplement or in a sermon that clings doggedly to the old faith and calls up once more the miracles of steam and electricity, of aeroplane and radio with the same stubbornness with which the miracles of loaves and fishes or of water turned to wine are recalled by those with a somewhat longer memory. It is in the Russia of today that one recaptures with the poignant regret of old age, in the presence of happy, but soon to be disillusioned youth, this memory out of our past. For it is only a memory. We are grievously disappointed in the machines that promised to make us happy but have brought us much sorrow, as well as distraction, which promised wealth and have brought a new kind of urban poverty to millions, which promised freedom and have enslaved so many in a new bondage, which were to give us that most craved-for gift for our short life—time—but seem to have taken time away from us. We blame the machine for much for which it alone cannot be held accountable. No matter, we must have our Satan. We are disappointed in our creature. Whether it be Satan, whether it be a fallen creation, it has helped to banish us from Paradise, and we condemn it. Even when we are not afraid of our Frankenstein or disappointed in our mechanical savior, we have grown callous to its miracles. We are not encouraged; the zest of faith in a progress that was to come *on wheels* is gone.

There is little need to sketch the whole story of our disillusionment— of our disappointment with the processes of a business enterprise which once we regarded as the source of all wisdom and which now stands revealed as ignorant as well as greedy, as mendacious as well as shortsighted; of our disappointment in reforms which promised much and have brought many evils, many perplexities; of our disappointment in the church which seems to offer so little guidance and to be so much a part of the whole past which has lost authority over us. Even that lode-star of modern civilization which appeared to promise us guidance out of all perplexities—science—has somehow become obscured. Men can no longer look to it for the revelation of almost tangible certainties, but feel that it increases their perplexities. There is some similarity between the trend of science in our days and the development of medieval philosophy. The subtleties of modern physics leave the old believer as bewildered as did the subtleties of later scholasticism. Even here a glory has passed away from the earth.

The completeness of the disillusionment which has crept and is creeping upon us may be no more justified than the completeness of the optimism which preceded it. But it is a sociological and a psychological fact and it rests upon experiences which are certain, though less inclusive than the pessimistic dogma which they support. Theology cannot escape the influence of the great disappointment any more than philosophy, sociology, history or ethics can evade it. And in fact the evidence of its effects on our religious thinking are to be seen on every hand.

II

The most evident effect is the passing of liberal theology. Not that liberalism in theology is dead. Theological movements are cursed with the fate of the wandering Jew; they can never die. Every theological movement from Gnosticism to eighteenth century rationalism seems to continue a more or less shadowy existence in some remote or populous corner of our modern world. But the spirit of the liberal theology which gloried in the "dear humanity of God," which looked forward to the ethical perfection of mankind in its mundane generations, which built its edifice upon faith in the divine spark in man is not at home in the world which is now coming into existence. The fruits of liberal scholarship, its critical analysis of history, its painstaking study of religious psychology, its discovery of the ethical values resident in religion, its orientation of faith in the world of science, have become part of the theological capital of the future and cannot be sacrificed. But in one aspect liberal theology is part of the whole liberal movement of the nineteenth century, an expression of the faith in man, and in progress which found correlate expression in economics and in liberal political theory. And with these it built upon a faith that has not been validated, which on the contrary is now being rejected. Furthermore, it has its own great failures to record: its failure, despite all emphasis upon the Social Gospel, to divorce itself from the social ethics of economic liberalism and the dominance of middle class morality. Under the rule of liberal theology in the church the progressive alienation of the growing working population of the West from religion has gone steadily forward; the immersion of the church into civilization and its use as a means for the support of the existing social system with its nationalism and its castes, its war, its poverty has become well-nigh complete—in many of the areas of civilization at all events. The ethical failure of liberal theology has been partly paralleled by its religious insufficiency. To a period which has lost faith in man and in progress it reveals little to cling to, little of meaning for life. To countries and to sections of the population which must make their account with death its message of abundant life in mundane terms has little to offer. Hence the turning away from liberal religious thought in the country of its birth, in Germany.

The rise of religious humanism in America, which represents an extreme form of liberalism, seems to run directly counter to the European movement and [to] invalidate the observation that liberal theology is passing. From the point of view of our analysis humanism is the last stand of liberalism and a vain effort to command retreat to the waves of one of those great popular movements of thought which seem to rise so mysteriously in history, but which nevertheless have their sources in the storms that blow upon our planet. As an ethical movement humanism seems subject to the same impotence which has afflicted the liberal theology throughout its course, the same inability to capture the religious imagination of the people and the same failure to unite with the strong forces of human need and yearning which alone make a theology capable of directing as well as expressing the religion of the human heart.

With the decline of liberal theology and liberal religion and the disillusionment with the dogma of progress and faith in civilization, a rather curious return to the primitive has set in, in some of our religious thinking. The return to the primitive in literature, music and the plastic arts may have passed the period of its greatest flowering but it is symptomatic of our situation, and this is true also of the return to the primitive in religion. The vogue of Rudolf Otto's *Idea of the Holy*, primarily in Germany but also in England and America, may be at least partly explained from this point of view, and a significant statement in one of Brunner's books to the effect that Christianity is more closely related to primitive religion than to Buddhism and other religions of civilization is indicative of the same fact.[8] As in other developments of the theology of disillusionment, it is the most completely disillusioned country of our time, Germany, which represents this tendency most evidently. In [Paul] Tillich, most promising of the new generation of German theologians, the return to the primitive is presented on the one hand in an effort to recapture the meaning of the demonic and to translate all religious thought into terms of mythology, upon the other hand in the attempt to recapture a primitive realism in the apprehension of divine qualities in the world of natural and aesthetic objects. The ideas of mana, of awe and mystery, of the sacred and the demonic are once more made to live outside the pages of textbooks on the history of religion in the religious experience of modern men.

The return to the primitive in theology is far less evident in English and American religious thought, just as the revolt against civilization is far less pronounced in these more fortunate environments. But revolt against civilization is not absent here and the return to the primitive in religion may come in time to have meaning for us also. This much must be said for it—that when we cease to think of mankind as a progressive series of generations rising one above the other, and begin to think of it as made up of individuals and societies who needed and need to face at all times some of the same great problems and who are always under the urgent command to find the meaning and the reality of their life, then we must look not for the marks of religious progress so much as for the marks of the religion of the common human situation. And in this religion, as in art and ethics, we may discover that primitive man is also among our teachers. The theology of a day of disillusionment with progress is likely to become a theology of the common human situation, not the theology of the successful final generation. It needs to raise the question of the meaning of life not from the point of view of a distant future, but in its immediate relation to eternal reality. It needs to live far more completely in the present and hence it is likely to value every present moment, including a primitive present, not as a stepping-stone to another era but as a last stepping-stone on the brink of an ultimate abyss. And, furthermore, the theology of a time that confronts mysteries, because it has lost dogmas, and which sees the world once more in a strange and unfamiliar guise as the realm of irrational as well as rational manifestation of reality feels a new kinship for the awe and the tremor of primitive man facing wonder at the boundaries of his intelligence.

This renewed appreciation for the transcendence of the object of religion is probably the most characteristic and valuable feature of the theology of a day of disillusionment. If the watchword of the philosophy of religion and of theology in the nineteenth century was immanence the characteristic term of the new tendencies in the new religious thought of today is transcendence. The theology of crisis which has left a deep impression on most contemporary German thought about God and which is not entirely ineffective in America built upon this foundation. It has been called forth and has been able to exercise so great an influence as it has only because transcendence in its negative aspect—as the absence of immanence—is so much a part of the experience of this period of history. For transcendence is primarily a negative concept, the statement of a void in life rather than of a fulfillment. It is the virtue of this Barthian theology that it has rediscovered the religious significance of the void. If we have been inclined to combat the novelist and the biographer whose hatred of human nature seemed to make them the enemies of religion by destroying our faith in the immanence of God in man, this theology reminds us, as Whitehead also does, that religion is transition from God the void to God the enemy and from God the enemy to God the companion, but that access to the companion may be too cheaply purchased to be real when it is not gained by way of the void and the enemy. The history of our faith, at all events, reminds us that men have found their way to God, as often if not more frequently, by way of disillusionment with man and in the divine immanence as by way of the creation to the creator. The theology of transcendence is, however, first of all a negative theology which, accepting disillusionment, points to the grave of our humanity to tell us, "He is not here."

But the theological tendencies of a time of disillusionment may also put a positive meaning into transcendence. The failure of the relative points us to the absolute and if it makes the discovery of the absolute more difficult it also makes it much more urgent. The revelation of the transiency of the transient points us to the permanent and requires us to find the anchorage of life in a rock of ages that is not in the age. It is significant that the theology of our time engages with the deadly earnestness of Jacob at the ford of Jabbok in the wrestle with the ultimate, that it turns from God the epitome of our values, God the divine ideal, to the permanent ground in things, to the unconditioned source of being and of meaning, to that which "stands beyond, behind and within the passing flux of immediate things." Not that this sense of God as ultimate Fate has ever been absent from theology, but that disappointment in the immediate makes the ultimate more urgent and that disillusionment with the immanent makes the transcendent more effective in our thinking. Now more than ever the problem of theology is the problem of God and the problem of God is the problem of our ultimate fate, of the constitution of the universe.

Yet a theology of transcendence begins to function positively not when it traces the relationship of our life to its last, unconditioned source and meaning, and so becomes a theology of faith. Its function in history and in our time also is the interpretation of another sort of religious experience, of the experience of condemnation. It is the *theo-*

ria of God the enemy. There are several ways in which we can deal with our disappointments; we may interpret them as mere disappointments, as failures of the world to meet our expectations, or we may regard them as our failure to meet expectations which the world has rightly had of us. We may regard them as deceits or we may experience them as judgments. The typical mood of much of our generation is the former; it is the mood of the war-play which is more significant of our present temper than of the temper of fifteen years ago. We curse and carry on. We curse the whole sorry scheme of things in which we are caught up; we indulge ourselves—as much recent literature does—in a passionate hatred of this environment which has let us down. And we carry on as best we can observing the rules of fair play and decency in a game that has been lost but in which there are fellow players to be considered; or we retire to the sidelines to develop a stoic wisdom in our contemplation of the spectacle; or we elaborate a little scheme of conduct on the basis of a noble pity for those who with us are condemned to play the game which has lost meaning. There are less disciplined ways of dealing with the disillusionment but of these we need not speak. But all these ways are an evasion—an evasion of the judgment involved in our disappointment, a failure to face the necessary transition from the void of God to God the enemy. When we have faced the fact that meaninglessness is intolerable only because there is a prior meaning, and that relativity is insufficient only because there is an absolute, that our whole disappointment has been possible only because faith is more fundamental than disappointment—or when, at all events, we have cause to regard our disappointment in the light of a possible eternal meaning, an ultimate, last fact, we cannot deal with failure any longer as an inconsequential thing in an inconsequential universe. Our pettiness, our meanness, our futility, face the enemy, the judgment. Our social system, its war, its poverty, all its brutal carelessness of life and finer values, no longer appears as a betrayal of our hopes but as our betrayal of God. It is not we then who have been betrayed but we who have betrayed.

The theology of disillusionment, therefore, recaptures a meaning which has scarcely ever been absent from Christian thinking but which has been toned down and allowed to sink into semi-obscurity during the time we believed in our virtue and in our power to achieve whatever it was desirable to attain. In this theology the social note becomes not less but more urgent than in a theology of immanence. There are tran-

scendentalists today, to be sure, who flee from the judgment by translating the whole action once more into the personal and mystic sphere,
who confine the experience of God the enemy to men in their solitar-
iness, and there are others like the Barthians who succumb to the temptation of pessimism to the extent that they deliver this whole world with
its institutions and social arrangements into the hands of the devil,
requiring of the individual who seeks his justification, that he bear the
burden of injustice, as its agent or its patient, and look for relief only
to the eternal miracle of the Word which can never really become flesh
in an evil world. But the experience of judgment taken by itself requires
a more radical and a more urgent dealing with our social injustice, not
a more passive one, than characterized the past. More radical because
the distinction between the righteousness and the justice which is demanded and the actual evils and injustices of our world are set over
against each other in antithesis rather than accommodated to each
other, in a scheme of development, because the Kingdom of God is
allowed to appear again as an absolute demand while the kingdom of
this world shows its distance from the Kingdom of God far more clearly
than when it was regarded from the point of view of its promises rather
than from that of its failures; the task is more urgent because the significance of the present generation is no longer found primarily in the
future, nor are we given the infinite centuries of upward progress in
which to fulfill our work. So far as our particular task is concerned we
understand once more what Jesus meant when he said, "This generation shall not pass away until all things be accomplished" [Mark
13:39]. This generation, this life is for us the decisive and the only
decisive moment; we can neither presume that we or that others shall
be glad in the gladness of those who come after us nor that our labors
will be completed by others. The theology of disillusionment becomes
a theology of the present moment, individually and socially. As a theology of the present moment it has its own particular historical task to
perform both as theory and as pointing to practice. In its theory its
urgent and inescapable task lies in its attempt to realize the eternal
significance of the present stage, to point out the places where the
eternal breaks into our time. In the practice to which it points, its duty
lies in discovering and defining the sort of life, individual and social,
in which the present may realize its relation to the eternal—in some
form of faith and religious experience and in some form of justice.
Recognizing the relativity of every formulation of the ideal of the King-

dom of God, it will nevertheless know that the absolute can be heard within the relative and that the eternal must become concrete in each present moment.

In other words the chief task which faces theology in an age of disillusionment does not lie primarily in the religious interpretation of disillusionment, though this has its important place; it lies rather in building upon the foundation of disillusionment—not by its denial— the theory of an immanence which is present and which yet must be attained, in making the transition from God the enemy to God the companion, or to God the savior. That transition has not been effected in contemporary theologies of disillusionment save as the dogmatism of Barthian theology may be said to have effected it. We may anticipate the development or, rather, sketch the task which confronts us, by saying that the transition may most promisingly be sought in three spheres, all interdependent—in continued wrestling with the problem of Jesus and the historical meaning of the revelation of God in history, in continued realistic analysis of religious experience and the search for divine reality in actual religious life, and in ever more urgent effort to realize the eternal will of God, as we must see it from the relative point of view of the present moment, in some form of social and personal justice which will carry within it, as immanent, a revelation of the God who yet remains transcendent, which will be adequate to our own situation but which will contain the absolute demand. And so by confronting our disillusionment in theology and preaching in the spirit of a critical realism which will be no less critical than realistic and no less realistic than critical—both with respect to man and in regard to God— it may be that we can attain to a more adequate definition for our time of the eternal revelation in time and of our urgent task as those who face not only eternity but also their own time.

The Kingdom of God and Eschatology in the Social Gospel and in Barthianism

The problem assigned in the title given above has baffled me. What is it that the committee wants me to discuss? Here are four unknown quantities, meaning many different things in different contexts. I suspect that the question is a very simple one, like "Who chased whom around the walls of what?" to which I could return an unambiguous answer if I only knew the story to which the question referred. But my education has failed to provide me with the key. I can remember the walls of Jericho but no chase connected with them; I recall a story about the pursuit of Absalom but there are not any walls in that account; so there's something in my mind about Kingdom of God and eschatology in the Social Gospel, but Barthianism does not fit into that, etc., etc. Hence I must set myself a problem which is intelligible to me and, since I cannot speak of what I'm asked to talk about, tell another story to disguise my ignorance. I shall discuss the problem of divine and human action as illustrated in the doctrines of Kingdom of God and eschatology in Social Gospel and Barthian theology.

Divine and Human Action in the Social Gospel's Conceptions of Kingdom of God and Eschatology

Theologically the character of the Social Gospel was determined by its concentration on the doctrine of the Kingdom of God. "If theology is to offer an adequate doctrinal basis for the Social Gospel," Walter Rauschenbusch wrote, "it must not only make room for the doctrine of the Kingdom of God, but give it a central place and revise all other doctrines so that they will articulate organically with it."[1] Not only he but his associates, predecessors and successors reinterpreted Christology, soteriology, anthropology and theology proper accordingly.

But despite its use of the symbol "Kingdom of God" the Social Gospel was not theocentric. Two things were denoted by the term ["Kingdom of God"]: teleology and a specific standard of values. As against the causal theology of earlier Protestantism (e.g., predestination, providence), the social gospel was teleological, emphasizing the direction of life by means of a goal; as against the individualistic teleology of late pietism it made the goal of society primary; as opposed to other-worldly teleology it was this-worldly. "The Kingdom of God," said Rauschenbusch, "contains the teleology of the Christian religion"; and this was [Albrecht] Ritschl's thought too. But the *telos* was not God, it was "humanity organized according to the will of God" in a kingdom of ends, that is, an association in love of intrinsically valuable persons.[2]

This goal (which was often conceived in Aristotelian fashion as a kind of *activity* rather than a *structure* and as *present* therefore as well as *future*) was to be realized by human and divine activity. The Social Gospel found its enemy above all in *laissez faire* philosophy in the Christian church, according to which the kingdom of love would be the indirect by-product of action directed toward selfish spiritual ends. [However,] "since the Kingdom of God is the supreme end" [of God] "all problems of personal salvation must be reconsidered from the point of view of the kingdom."[3] [Only] the kingdom would provide satisfaction to the individual, it was believed, but [satisfaction] was [to be] the by-product [the Kingdom the end]. The Kingdom would not come without intense activity and this activity needed to be consciously directed toward the Kingdom as end. The emphasis on teleological striving was, we may say, something the Social Gospel shared with the whole of industrial culture and with activistic Protestantism, Calvinistic or liberal; the definition of the goal as social was its specific characteristic. As teleological religion of this special sort, it reinterpreted, then, the whole of Christian thought as a teleological metaphysics and ethics. The meaning of Jesus was found in his human striving after the realization of the Kingdom of ends; his death was martyrdom in that cause; his prayer and the Christian's prayer "Thy will be done" meant, "Let us do thy will," i.e., seek our social ideal.

When then did divine action come in? It is fallacious, I believe, to call the Social Gospel humanistic; it carried with it too great a heritage of faith in God; it reinterpreted the democratic, humanistic ideas of modernism too much in the light of the New Testament, to allow for such a reduction. But divine action was recognized really only in two forms and primarily in the form of religiously motivated human action. God was conceived as the author of nature, the teleological factor in the universe, the divine and superhuman cooperator, without whom the human enterprise lacked all guarantees of success. But primarily he was the one who acted in history through those who "did his will" which meant those who had the good purpose. God was always the religious object; the Social Gospel was as dependent on the religio-empirical theology as on teleological ethics. Its social interest was the distinctive thing about it in this respect also, but it was, after all, a movement within the general movement of religionism. In any case God's action and man's action are conceived by it as either immanent, the one in the other, or as parallel. Right action is one-way action directed toward an "end."

The Social Gospel approached the traditional eschatological teachings of the church from this point of view and reinterpreted them not only in the light of the conviction that the goal of life was social, but also in the light of the other convictions that the goal was the object of striving in religious man. In other words it was not only as *social,* but also as *teleological,* and as *religio-empirical* that it reinterpreted traditional eschatology. As social it conceived a new appreciation of the Apocalypse and other biblical documents which described the future in terms of human destiny rather than of individual immortality; as social it also apprehended the pertinence of eschatological ideas of judgments in history. But as teleological and religio-empirical the Social Gospel was deeply suspicious of the catastrophic, pessimistic, and other-worldly elements in eschatology. Whatever the explanation may be, it dealt with Christian eschatology in highly eclectic fashion and did not succeed in really reinterpreting it.

It was in connection with eschatology that the Social Gospel revealed how impossible it was to comprehend the whole of Christian theology and to interpret or guide actual experience by means of its grand hypotheses that life was fundamentally a teleological striving for the attainment of a Kingdom of ends. In eschatology, though not only there, the idea of a divine initiative, of a divine action not channeled through religiously motivated human action was expressed, and this idea the Social Gospel needed to hold fast without being able to make it a part of its real scheme. In actual life the experience of endings which were not goals, of wars and death, and of the importance of actions which were not religiously motivated, resisted inclusion in the grand plan. The labor movement, with which, as social, the Social Gospel had so much sympathy, suggested to it on the one hand that there was a justice in historical events which ran counter to human teleology, and on the other hand that the way to what it had called Kingdom of God, to equality in fraternity, did not lead through love and moral striving but through coercion and self-interest. On the one hand [Leonhard] Ragaz and [Paul] Tillich needed eschatological rather than teleological categories for the interpretation of socialism in history; on the other hand

Harry Ward and Reinhold Niebuhr needed to wrestle with the problem of motivation and to abandon in one way or another the identification of divine action with loving human action.

Kingdom of God and Eschatology in Barth

The distinctive difference between Barth and the Social Gospel is not that eschatology takes precedence over Kingdom of God in his thought but that divine action, which eschatology symbolizes, takes precedence over human action. It is not the social character of the end that he questions, it is its teleological character. Or in other words, Barthian theology is not a reaction against Social Gospel; it is a criticism of teleological theology of which the Social Gospel was one variety and for the decline of which it prepared the way by its recognition of the importance of social destiny, and of non-religious action.

Barthian theology is always dialectical and its own history, particularly in the case of Barth himself, indicates that truth cannot be expressed in a single proposition. Most interpretations of Barth that one hears are fallacious because they fail to take this fact into account. Negatively Barthianism asserts that there is no road from man to God and the early Barth emphasized this point; positively it asserts that there is a road from God to man and that man can begin on this road; throughout the nineteen-thirties Barth has been emphasizing this and criticizing the one-sidedness, not the untruth, of his earlier statements. In connection with the doctrines of the Kingdom and of eschatology Barthianism does mean, in contrast, to the teleology of the Social Gospel, that human action both as finite, temporal, and as sinful cannot lead to the realization of the reign of love among intrinsically valuable persons; that the very conception of the future state as the act of finite sinful man is a finite, sinful act in which human pride and self-evaluation try to determine the end for God; that God sets a limit to all human action and that this limit does not coincide with the ethically conceived telos. Kingdom of God means that man is not king; eschatology, the doctrine of the end as "finis" not "telos," is the radical "NO" which God utters in response to man's petition "Let my kingdom of liberty, fraternity, and equality come." So also the idea of eternity is the negation of the absoluteness of man's time which the doctrine of progress in the Social Gospel seemed to accept. The meaning of "Kingdom of God" and "eschatology" in Barthianism is to be understood, then, from the point of view of the central doctrine that God acts, and first of all in this way, that God's action is negative—the denial of human action with its purposes. So approached all the concepts of Christian theology have a purely negative content. Eternity is Not-Time; Kingdom of God is Not-Kingdom-of-man; Salvation is not-conservation, etc. All this is best symbolized by the doctrine of the "end," so that early Barthianism may be understood as the reinterpretation of the Kingdom of God idea in a theology which makes the end, as "finis" rather than "telos," central.

But there is another side to the Barthian position; the positive affirmation is that there is a road from God to man and that God has taken, is taking, and will take this road. God stopping man's teleology is God pursuing his own teleology. And the divine teleology can become man's hope though it cannot be his telos. The Kingdom of God in this Barthianism is not to be described as either social or individual, as either this-worldly or other-worldly. Insofar as these terms may be applied both parts of each pair must always be used; the Barthian point is that it is the Kingdom which *God* establishes, has established, and will establish. The question raised is not whether we shall think in teleological or eschatological terms but whether we shall begin with *our* purposes and goals or with *God's* as these are revealed, known, and believed through God's act of self-communication in Jesus Christ.

The real question which Barthianism raises for us then is not about Kingdom of God and eschatology but about the relation of human action to divine action in human history. According to a popular interpretation of Barthianism, emphasis on divine action not only excludes the human initiative in determining the goal of existence for both God and man, but also all significance of human action. Barth's statements on politics are then regarded as unconnected with his theology. But Barth's own statements, particularly in the second volume of his *Dogmatik*, indicate that this interpretation rests on a misinterpretation or on the use of a different understanding of the nature of human action than he employs. Christian action is to be understood not as parallel to divine action in the common striving after a common telos, nor as counter-action to God's action, but as response to the divine activity which precedes, accompanies, and awaits human action in history. Kingdom of God means that God is pre-temporal, super-temporal, and post-temporal; it means that time is bounded by eternity on every side, but it also means that eternity enters into and conditions time and calls for the response of the temporal at every moment. In accordance with the faithfulness of that response the conditions in time must vary and in that sense temporal man may enjoy more or less of the benefits of the "Kingdom of God." The temporal is not eternal but eternity is forever ingressing into time. That it is ingressing and what it is in character is known through revelation by the Christian, whose life must consist of response to the eternal rather than of a seeking after it, or of an ascetic denial of the temporal.

Such a life of response to divine action is life under the Kingdom of God, it is life in hope of the Kingdom and life in reliance upon it. God's eternity, says Barth, cannot be expressed as mere transcendence of time, though when that eternity is identified with human values of one sort or another, transcendence must be emphasized. But neither can it be expressed in simple terms of pre-temporality as the Reformers tended to do, or super- or co-temporality as the eighteenth and nineteenth centuries did, or of post-temporality as the Social Gospel tended to do. Eternity in time must be spoken of in all three ways. God is the one from whom and to whom and in whom all things are an act.

I believe that Barth has become the legitimate heir of the Social Gospel by placing its social understanding of life in a context in which it can live. He has saved it from perishing with utopianism and offers a more consistent alternative to that redefinition of the Social Gospel which splits its intraworldly ends from its supernatural faith and continues to think in terms of human action directed toward temporal, though now unsatisfactory, goals.

The Anachronism of Jonathan Edwards

We have met today to honor in memory Jonathan Edwards, pastor of this church from 1727 to 1750, missionary to the Indians at Stockbridge, Massachusetts, from 1751 to 1757, president of New Jersey College, now Princeton University, for some two months in 1758. He died at Princeton on March 22nd, 1758, at the age of 55. The bicentennial of his death will be two weeks from yesterday.

The harvest of his life of study, preaching, and pastoral work was gathered at Stockbridge where he wrote the treatises that established him as our greatest American theologian. But the ground was tilled, the seed sown, the rising plants that issued in that harvest were cultivated here at Northampton during twenty-four years of a ministry that was marked by two great events—the revival of 1740 and the tragic dismission of the pastor in 1750.

The memories he has left behind him these two hundred years are varied. A highly popular, widespread impression is the one recently reproduced in *Harpers Magazine* in verses by Phyllis McGinley.

> Whenever Mr. Edwards spake
> In church about Damnation,
> The very benches used to quake
> For awful agitation.[1]

A somewhat less impressionistic portrait, though drawn also from folk memory more than [from] life, was offered a generation ago by Vernon Louis Parrington in his *Main Currents in American Thought*. In that history of the liberal mind Jonathan Edwards is described as the great "anachronism." He was an anachronism to Parrington because in him the conflict of ancient dogma with the new liberalism was re-enacted and resolved in favor of the old. The brilliant idealist metaphysician warred in him with the traditional theologian; and the theologian won. The Emersonian mystic "consciousness of the divine life flowing through and around him, making him one with the Godhead" fought in him with the Calvinistic theocrat;[2] and Calvin won; the new churchman, opening the doors of the sanctuary to all seekers after peace, contradicted in him the loyalist to ancient discipline, for whom the company of the faithful was the selected band, the trained shock-troop of the Kingdom of God in a rebellious planetary province.

Parrington concludes his account in these words:

123

As one follows the laborious career of this great thinker, a sense of the tragic failure of his life deepens. The burdens that he assumed were beyond the strength of any man. Beginning as a mystic, brooding on the all-pervasive spirit of sweetness and light diffused through the universe, with its promise of spiritual emancipation; then turning to an archaic theology, and giving over his middle years to the work of minifying the excellence of man in order to exalt the sovereignty of God; and finally settling back upon the mystical doctrine of conversion—such a life leaves one with a feeling of futility, a sense of great powers baffled and wasted, a spiritual tragedy enacted within the narrow walls of a minister's study. There was both pathos and irony in the fate of Jonathan Edwards, removed from the familiar places where for twenty years he had labored, the tie with his congregation broken, and sent to the frontier mission at Stockbridge to preach to a band of Indians and to speculate on the unfreedom of the human will. . . . Cut off from fruitful intercourse with other thinkers, drawn away from the stimulating field of philosophy into the arid realm of theology, it was his fate to devote his noble gifts to the thankless task of re-imprisoning the mind of New England within a system from which his nature and his powers summoned him to unshackle it. He was called to be a transcendental emancipator, but he remained a Calvinist.[3]

Later writers, notably Professor Perry Miller, have corrected this account in certain respects. College students, introduced to Edwards via other routes than the sermon on "Sinners in the hands of an angry God" can set Phyllis McGinley right.[4] But in the main the judgment stands in America, in American Protestantism, in literary and academic, even in most theological circles: Jonathan Edwards was a great man but he was wrong on almost every issue for which he contended—the gloriousness of inscrutable, almighty, universal, majestic, wrathful God; the depravity and corruptness of the human heart; the need for the reconstitution of the church not as catholic and all-inclusive but as the selected group of the convinced; the determinism, the unfreedom of human existence; the glory of God as the chief and only end of being, which in reconciliation man serves willingly as a "cosmic patriot," but will serve in his unwillingness by his destruction, as Hitler's patriots in their catastrophic ending may be said to glorify the rule of justice.

Since the judgment stands, and is no doubt explicitly represented in the thoughts of many of us here as it is implicitly represented in the value standards of the great dominant majority of Americans, and American Christians, and of American intellectuals, we must ask by what right, with what rightness can we honor Jonathan Edwards today on this bicentennial of his death?

By what right do we join the funeral procession, stand beside the grave, intrude ourselves into the company of those who mourn him? When we think of his exile from Northampton and his more inclusive exile from the company of all right-thinking modern men, we must apply to ourselves on this occasion the indictment that Jesus made of "hypocrites" who "build the tombs of the prophets and adorn the monuments of the righteous, saying, 'If we had lived in the days of our fathers, we would not have taken part with them in shedding the blood of the prophets' " [Matthew 23:29-30]. We are quite sure we would have been less gentle with him than our neighbors or forebears. When we read the story of his dismissal from this church and then think of the temper in other New England towns two centuries ago, we cannot honestly say that he would have fared better elsewhere. The Cambridge and New Haven that offered him no alternative to life at Stockbridge would probably not have suffered him as long as Northampton did, had he been pastor there. If small-pox had not removed him quickly from Princeton, how long would he have remained an honored head of the College in New Jersey? When we move from the eighteenth century down to our present time we cannot really convince ourselves that if Edwards now lived among us he would be more respected in the 1950s than he was in the 1750s.

The issues on which he was then tried and found wanting seem to have been so universally decided against him by the court of American and Christian opinion that they scarcely remain issues today. What hearing could he gain if he stood in this pulpit today, or in any pulpit in America and spoke to us now about our depravity and corruption, about our unfreedom and the determination of our lives, about the ineffable floriousness of God, and about the awfulness of his wrath? About the necessity of reconstituting ourselves a holy community?

By what right do we, who seem to disagree with him more strongly than his contemporaries did, now honor him? Can this commemoration of his death—not in Northampton only and in his old church— but in New England and in American Protestantism, be an honest gesture of respect or does it merely express the desire to be in the company of the great, for the sake of sharing in a superficial and reflected glory? This question a speaker at such an occasion as this must ask himself even more than his fellow celebrants.

Let us raise in another way the question of our right to honor Edwards. If we met in his spirit today, if we wanted to honor him in a way that would be acceptable not to his human vanity, for which he would need to do bitter penance, but to his central purpose and will, how would we go about it? His own conduct at the time of David Brainerd's death—his son-in-law, missionary to the Indians—gives us a clue. We cannot honor him at all except we do so in the context of honoring what he stood for, of honoring the cause to which he wanted above all else to be loyal. Have we any right to honor him otherwise? To exalt him as a great thinker, as though he could take delight in being praised for having honed his mental tools very sharp, no matter what they cut; to speak admiringly of him as an excellent orator, as though adeptness in the use of images were an enviable thing, no matter what they imaged; to do him reverence as a great student who learned from Newton and Locke and the Platonists, from nature itself, no matter what he learned—to honor him thus is to do him *no* honor that he could accept—or which, accepting, he would not thereafter bitterly rue. So to honor him would be as though we commemorated Nietzsche as a great Christian, or praised George the Third as a great American. It would not only be irrelevant, it would be contradictory to the intention, the understanding, the spirit of the man. To Edwards the desire of man to be great in himself, and to be honored for his eminence, to stand out in comparison with his fellows, to be more loved than his companions—even by God—this is man's pettiness, his perversity, his pustulant sickness, as he might have said.

There is no really honest and consistent way of honoring Edwards at all this day except in the context of honoring, of acknowledging and renewing our dedication to his cause. That cause was nothing less than the glory of God. I do not know whether this is the audience which can hear the summons to think in the terms of that theme, to lift up mind and heart into regions of thought and imagination so majestic, to dedicate itself to a cause so tremendous. I only know that your preacher is not adequate to preach upon the text that Edwards himself would have chosen for this occasion:

Now unto the King eternal, immortal, invisible,
to the only wise God—
be honor and glory, forever and ever. Amen.
(I Timothy 1:17)

Since it lies beyond the scope of my mind and spirit to direct your meditations so to honor Edwards in the only context in which he can honestly be honored, we may venture to try to do him less adequate justice by letting him, or rather our imagined reincarnation of his spirit, speak today to his detractors.

The first charge against me, he might say, is this, that I have demeaned man in order to glorify God. "You charge me with having said that our experience teaches us the truth of the scriptural saying, 'There is none righteous, no not one' (Romans 3:10). 'They are filled with all manner of wickedness, evil, covetousness, malice. Full of envy, murder, strife, deceit, malignity; they are gossips, slanderers, haters of God, insolent, haughty, boastful, inventors of evil, disobedient to parents, foolish, faithless, heartless, ruthless.' You charge me also with saying, again pleading the support of the Scriptures, that though we humans have many kindly affections, love of children, love between men and women, love of country, all these too are corrupted and defiled; and that though we have very agile minds, able to penetrate into the mysteries of nature, we put this gift and attainment to ignoble uses."

Some, Edwards could say, have dismissed my indictments as wholly false. Particularly from the men of the generation that succeeded his, he could have heard much praise of men. Using Shakespeare instead of [the] Scriptures as the sources for their text, but without reading the passage to the end,[5] they said with Hamlet—

What a piece of work is a man! how noble in reason! how infinite in faculties! in form, and in moving, how express and admirable! in action how like an angel! in apprehension how like a god! the beauty of the world! the paragon of animals!

But a strange thing has happened. A later generation has revised the judgment of the romantics. Its experience of the extent to which human brutality can go, of the fury that can be unleashed when the human animal is attacked, its acceptance in wry cynicism of the venality of great and small; its acceptance, too, of a psychological analysis that tends to show how slight the power of reason, how great the strength of obscure passions; how corrupting of children the possible love of mothers and the wrath of fathers; its portrayal of men and mankind in bitterly disillusioned novels and in shuddering chronicles of man's inhumanity to man;—in all this the twentieth century has perhaps gone beyond anything that Edwards said in dispraise of men, individually and in the collective. But though on the surface this generation seems to accept something that is like the Edwardsean estimate, it still rejects Edwards no less than the Emersonians did, though for other reasons.

How would Edwards speak to this situation? He might answer something like this—: " 'With what measure you mete you shall be measured.' You resented my measuring man by the standard of his position before God; you resented that I said: as a loathsome insect is to man, so man is to the Holy One that inhabits eternity. You applied the standard of man's position before other men; or before himself, and having begun by saying: man to himself is like a god, you are now tending to say, he is like a devil to himself; he will destroy himself."

Now who demeans humanity? The one whose standard for man is small or the one whose standard is very great? The one who judges him as a domestic lover or as a citizen of a universal commonwealth? The one who looks on him as faithful or unfaithful administrator of lawns and stores, of stocks and bonds, or the one who sees in him the steward of eternal riches? What is greater, a neatly painted, well constructed five or eight room house or the ruins of the Forum or the Parthenon? What Edwards knew, what he believed in his heart and with his mind, was that man was made to stand in the presence of eternal, unending absolute glory, to participate in the celebration of cosmic deliverance from everything putrid, destructive, defiling, to rejoice in the service of the stupendous artist who flung universes of stars on his canvas, sculptured the forms of angelic powers, etched with loving care miniature worlds within worlds. In the light of that destiny, in view of that origin, because of the greatness of that calling, it depressed him, angered him that men should throw away their heritage and be content with the mediocrity of an existence without greater hope than the hope for comfort and for recognition by transient fellowmen. Man who had been made to be great in the service of greatness, had made himself small by refusing the loving service of the only Great One; and in his smallness he had become very wicked, covetous of the pleasures that would soon be taken from him. *But in the end, man could not make himself small, Edwards knew, for the way of man is not in himself.*

That leads us to the second charge against him, namely that his understanding of the sovereignty of God left no room for human freedom. This charge, like the previous one, is frequently so understood by unbelievers who cannot follow the logic of belief that they equate theocracy with priestliness. They think that Edwards, believing in government by God, must have derived from that premise the conclusion that therefore preachers were his lieutenants on earth and should be recognized as gods. This is about as illogical a deduction as one can imagine. The consequence of the premise that God rules is, for the believer, "therefore I must obey," not "therefore I must rule." Because His will is to be done, therefore my will is to be denied. I believe that any reading of Edward's life, including the story of the sad controversy in Northampton, will make quite clear that he was no self-willed man taking the name of God in vain to fortify his wishes. But this is the minor print of the charge. The major complaint was that in Edwards's world of determinism no room was left for human freedom.

How would he reply today to this charge? I think it is quite possible that, zealous student of philosophy as he was, he might admit that the way he argued his position was somewhat overly indebted to the mechanical thinking of his time and of the Reformers. But his main point would stand; and as in the case of the charge about demeaning man, time has reversed the opinion of his antagonists though it has not reversed men's opinions about Edwards.

You were concerned, Edwards might say, about the freedom of the will, to choose its goods, to choose good or evil, God or the devil. You were concerned to say that man was somehow the master of his fate, so that without his will God himself was unable to save him from disaster.

Look now, he might go on to point out, how you have conceded my point that man is determined by his strongest motive and that his strongest motive is so much the love of self, self-interest, that there is no way of moving him to anything at all save by touching this spring of his action.[6] Regard your society, the free enterprise system, the operation of the hidden persuaders and of the open ones. Who is free? Man is free to follow his self-interest. But is he ever free from his self-interest? Is he free to follow any road but that of self-interest? Or consider your international politics. Do you not recognize that national self-interest is a law the nations obey with such invariableness that you must base all your calculations on how to maintain your own nation on the assumption of that law? Or consider your freedom of religion; is it not the freedom to be religious or irreligious, to worship or not to worship, in accordance with your self-interest, whether you think it is good for you or not? Your free religion of self-interested men has made God into an idol. How are you free to love God, since you are bound to love yourselves, even in religion?

The will is as its strongest motive is and its strongest motive is self-interest and so man is determined and cannot by any new freedom at his disposal change his determination by self-interest.

After two hundred years there are very, very many who agree with Edwards on the proposition about our freedom and our bondage. Many who accept this determinism still think, however, that self-interest will continue to ensure for us the enjoyment of our civil liberties. We have seen other nations, to be sure, in which self-interest has made itself felt as an invincible motive for the giving up of what we call such freedoms. And when we think of this we begin to wonder whether civil and religious liberty can indeed be based on the position of Edwards's opponents or only on the kind of foundations he provided not in but in connection with his determinism.

Edwards on human unfreedom is not so anachronistic as he was. Yet for some reason we do not dare to follow his logic even when we accept some of his premises, such as this one of our determination by our strongest motive.

A third count of the constant indictment against him has also lost something of the persuasiveness it once had. The threat of destruction, of hell, which Edwards used to stir his people toward, that revolution of thought and conscience which could be the occasion for the entrance of new freedom has always called forth strong reaction. Preaching about hell is always resented by men of so-called liberal mind. How could the infliction of torment be rhymed with the rule of a merciful God? What human wickedness deserved such a consequence?

Yet on this point also in some ways Edwards seems less anachronistic than he did. If you will read again his Enfield sermon you will note that the emphasis does not lie on hell but on the terrible uncertainty of life. "Thou hast set their foot in slippery places"—that was the text.[7] There is no guarantee anywhere, he points out, that this comfortable life of ours will go on and on and on. What awaits us is death, and it may come at any moment—and death is not nothing. It is the beginning of another state of being.

Now we find it difficult to accept the mythology of Edwards, though we may need to accept again something like it, when we come to the full acceptance of the realization, that as we did not and cannot elect ourselves into existence, so neither can we elect ourselves out of it, if the inscrutable power that cast us into being wills to keep us in being after our biological death.—But aside from that, we have a mythology of our own. We see before us in social, if not in personal terms, the real possibility of a future hell. Of a state of existence in which surviving souls, condemned to live, crawl about scrofulously among the radiations of insidious poison, among emanations of noxious gases, on a planet unfit for habitation which they must nevertheless inhabit. Or we envisage the possibility of that anarchy in which every man's hand is raised against his neighbor; where there is no truth but only deception and lies. Or the hell we envision is that of Huxley's *Brave New World* or Orwell's *1984*, or the culmination of the life of Organization Man.

The mythology has changed. The possibility that Edwards saw before man is now our possibility, though in a different setting. Those critics of his who saw no other alternative before man than progress toward perfection and heaven on earth have become rather quiet. They are not even greatly stirred by the prospect that we shall export our wars with our machines to other planets and re-enact on a larger scale the kind of history with which we have become too familiar.

We tend to agree more with him also on the tenuousness of the hold we have on ordered life. Our feet, we know, are set in slippery places. A single trigger-happy or nervous bomber, flying now with a load of destruction in the vitals of his plane, can inaugurate at any moment the beginning of our end. A missile gone astray by the failure of a tiny and fragile device may shoot us into the inferno. Or a statesman's unthinking remark may begin the debate that will end not in death for us but in an unforeseeably long process of destruction.

Edwards is not so anachronistic on this point as he was; not so anachronistic as his nineteenth century critics now seem.

But at the central point he remains alien to us as to them, more alien than he was in the eighteenth century with its Benjamin Franklins. And because he is alien at that point the sorts of agreement we may be able to achieve with him on other ideas seem superficial and unreal.

The anachronism of a commemoration of Edwards's death in 1958 is the anachronism of Jonathan Edwards in 1958.

We will concede perhaps that man is as wicked as Edwards said. What we do not know—or do not yet know—is that God is as holy as Edwards knew him to be. We have in our wisdom substituted for the holy God a kind Heavenly Father. A holy God will not suffer his plans for a vast, stupendously intricate, marvelous creation and the men designed to be his sons to be flouted and destroyed by self-willed and proud little delinquents, aged 60 as often as 16, called nations or civilizations as often as persons. Or we have substituted for the holy God, the sovereign source and determiner of being, Being simply considered, the Constitution of the universe, a wildly running chance. Our feet are standing in slippery places, to be sure, but we are not being held this side of destruction by holy power and determined will; it is chance that keeps us from slipping. There is no wrath in heaven directed against us, because there is no holiness, no will for wholeness, for integrity, and for glory. And since there is no holiness there is no hope for us except the hope that we'll get by a little longer with our compromises and our superior animal cunning.

Edwards used to say that the trouble with men was not that they had no ideas of God, but that they had little ideas of God. We might add that they are ideas about little Gods. The anachronism of our Edwards celebration is not so much that we try to honor him in a time of atheism, when men do not believe in God; but that we seek to know and respect a servant of the Almighty, of the Lord, the Source of Being itself, of Power beyond all powers, in a time when our God is someone we try to keep alive by religious devotions, to use for solving our personal problems, for assuring us that we are beloved. He is without wrath, because we have made this image wrathless; his love is not holy love because we have painted the icon without holiness.

If Edwards's God is not with us, what meaning is there in our agreement with his propositions about human wickedness, human determinism, about the threat of destruction? Our sense of wickedness is without repentance, our sorrow over it is not a godly sorrow leading to life, but cynical and accepting, leading to death. Our knowledge of our determinism is without struggle, because we know of no power that can set us free to be free indeed; our visions of possible life amidst destruction are unaccompanied by visions of possible life in the presence of glory and everlasting joy.

But now a possibility presents itself to us as we remember Edwards and remember man's remembrance of him. We have changed our minds about the truth of many things he said. No rather, our minds have been changed by what has happened to us in our history. We have seen evil somewhat as he saw it, not because we desired to see it, but because it thrust itself upon us.

If that has happened, why shall we not hope—and fear—that what has not yet happened will also occur.—That once more, by no sudden event it may be, but by the same kind of accumulative experience that has made us aware of the evil emptiness that surrounds us, we shall be lifted to see and know—in our time—the Holy One that inhabits eternity and yet is near to the humble and contrite in heart. Then we shall be able to meet in the presence of Edwards, saying

> Now unto the King eternal, immortal, invisible,
> to the only wise God—
> be honor and glory, forever and ever. Amen.

Address on Martin Buber's Eightieth Birthday

You have conferred honor on me by asking me to express on behalf of Protestant Christians their thanks and mine to Dr. Buber on his eightieth birthday. I am pleased by this honor. I rejoice more over his presence in our world and in this occasion when so many honor him. I am grateful to him for his person and his work. Grateful to God who has chosen him into existence and equipped him. And this gratitude I believe is representative of many, very many of my companions in the Protestant churches.

But, as always, joy is tinged with sadness and gratitude accompanied by desire for what has not been given. The sadness in this joy is made up of many elements but an important ingredient in it is the knowledge that even on such an occasion and in our celebration of the work of such a man, we cannot give ourselves in utter wholeness to each other. This "I" rejoicing in that "Thou" presents himself and is presented not as "I" but as Christian and Protestant man, and he must confront "Thee" not in unique selfhood but as Jewish or as Catholic man. Why must the hopes that separate us and partly make us strangers to each other appear in the very moment of our meeting as "Thou" and "I"?

Moreover our thanksgiving is a little less than complete because it is permeated by a sense of hunger for what has not been given. We give thanks here for integrity and truth in the inward parts; and for the call to integrity and truth that has come to us through Martin Buber. Yet as we do so we are aware that there is a rift in us and that we cannot give the thanks of the single-minded, the pure-hearted, because we desire honor on this occasion not simply for Martin Buber but for ourselves—for our Protestantism, or perhaps our Judaism, our Christianity. There are always purposes besides the recognition of the other; not selfish purposes necessarily but self-regarding or in-group- and out-group-regarding purposes. So in the moment of thanksgiving to Dr. Buber, we are aware of our hunger for a single-heartedness and a truth in our selfhood that has not been given.

These things one must confess at the outset lest our thanks to Dr. Martin Buber be corrupted by pretensions to a simplicity and single-heartedness that have not yet been given or achieved by the "I" and by the "We," even through his mediation. Yet, granting that the rift is present even in the meeting of companions who largely trust each other and that double-mindedness must appear even in the praise of single-heartedness, these sad reflections cannot be allowed to take precedence over the joyful ones, these regrets about the self permitted to overbear our joy in the other.

More than any other person in the modern world—more even than Søren Kierkegaard—Professor Buber has been for me and for many of my companions, the prophet of the soul and the witness to that truth which is required of the soul, not as solitary but as companionable being. What he has done in other realms of understanding and in the field of scholarship others than I must celebrate. For me and those for whom I can speak he has been a Socrates who has helped to bring to us, helped us to recognize and acknowledge a knowledge present in us but often unpossessed—the knowledge of ourselves and of one another as selves.

In a sense he has been a voice crying in a wilderness, for these selves are strangers and aliens in the modern world. "I" and "Thou" are doubtless always foreigners in the world of things. But it seems to us that they are ignored, passed by, treated as unwelcome intruders more in our twentieth century than has been the case in most other times in human history.

They are the banished ones, the excluded beings, the ignored in our inquiries into the nature of reality and of what composes the universe. Our knowledge of the forces moving in the world of nature, of their modes of behavior, of the patterns in their conjunctions, of the action and of infinitely small and infinitely large fields of forces, grows with increasing speed. But in all this knowledge there is no place for "I" 's and "Thou" 's. These terms and these realities must not intrude into our explanations and descriptions of the world in which we live and of the forces we seek to use for our benefit. And we acknowledge that it is right that this be so, that our science of things confine itself to things and introduce into its impersonal descriptions no confusing hypotheses about "you" and "me" and "him." But the excluded self—if there in these activities we call science, present as the "I" of the man who is the scientist and who must live in decision of devotion to truth, of truth-telling to his companions, of confusing devotions also to nation or civilization—the self is present but excluded from consideration. It cannot be banished; but cannot be recognized. It is an alien and a stranger, not unreal, but not a member of the accepted community of things that really count.

We turn to man, and our understanding of him seems also to be vast and intricate and to increase with rapidity. But in the science of man also there is no place for "Thou" and "I." The psycho-somatic being, this intricate process in which many movements of physical and ideational and emotional forces interact, is better known to physicians and psychologists and through them by ourselves—than was ever the case before. But where in all this complex of forces am "I"? There are available explanations of the content of my thought and yours, of your habits, conduct and mine, of the normalities and abnormalities of our physical processes, for the emotions that stir within us. But where in all this is the self? This "I" in this here and this now, this "I" a Christian or a Jew, an American or an Israeli, twentieth century "I" [brought] into existence now and not then, here and not there—this ["I"] remains the stranger and the alien.

Or it may be that I seek to understand myself as member of society. And then I am made aware of all the roles I play—the role of the churchman, the role of the teacher, the role of a representative of Protestantism, or the role of the American. I identify myself with all the parts I play upon life's stage. And I am led to understand the roles, to understand by whom or what the lines were written, by what the costumes prescribed. But the "I" that plays the role remains outside the knowledge. I–Thou's [existing] more as unknown, unacknowledged strangers through all their parts and roles. As bit players or stars upon the stage they are known and recognized—but the selves behind the masks remain lonely wanderers, unacknowledged, unwondered about, unsaluted by superficial and insensitive knowers.

The self that is an alien in the community of knowers is a foreigner also, an unnaturalized citizen, in the commonwealth of man. His skills are employed, his achievements rewarded, but he remains at the fringe of awareness. He can be passed by. We move about or are moved about as instruments of purposes not under our control. We acknowledge the man as banker, artist, technician, salesman, teacher. And we are aware that behind the work there is the stronger self. But the awareness is flawed, attention is distracted. He does not figure in our efforts as we try to achieve the ends of common or personal enterprise.

Perhaps the sadness of modern man is largely due to this estrangement. It is not that he is a stranger to himself, though this may also be true. It is not that he moves among men who are strangers to each other and to him, though this is true. But rather the estrangement, the alienation is that of all souls, all selves in the world of action and of understanding. The "I" is a stranger to the thinking mind; the "Thou" a stranger to the will. I do not try to think [as] an impersonal, common, disinterested mind thinks about you and us but about common patterns. I will, but do not will thee to be and to be thyself, nor will myself to be truly myself. I will—but I will what is external to you and to me.

The "I," the "Thou" are always present; and always alien. If they were simply absent, we should not be sad. Our sadness as selves is that of beings who are present but who do not belong.

It is in such a world, whether the modern or the perennial world, that Dr. Buber has come to us as prophet of the soul. Others have warned us of our penchant for passing by and failing to salute the values that are all around us. But he has gently, insistently called to us to regard these aliens among us, the selves who are more than values. And the words in which he spoke have been reduplicated in his actions. When I have read what he has written it was something like a letter addressed to me. It was not some missive directed "to whom it may concern"—but to me. It was not an epistle to the Christians. It was to me that his words came, who am a Christian but first of all a self. And I became aware that what my Christianity had meant for me and means for me is that it calls on me to be myself and reconciles me to my companions. And the letter was signed not "a Jew" but "Martin Buber" and I know that the Judaism he served had served him in calling him to selfhood and to manhood. And beyond my Christianity and his Judaism I was made aware of the "Thou," the transcendent "Thou" by whom he and I and you are called to be living souls.

We speak of the mystery of selfhood, the mystery of the soul. We might therefore speak of Professor Buber as one who has made us aware again of the mystery. But it seems better to speak of the revealedness, of the openness, the clear presence of selfhood, of you and me, of I and Thou. Is it not so that we have made a mystery of what is not hidden at all but very clearly present in every moment? And is not Professor Buber's work that of pointing to present revelation, not to mystery? Has he introduced strangers to each other? Or has he helped to reconcile old friends, divided by suspicion, alienated by the slight they have inflicted on each other as they passed but without acknowledgment? He has been no purveyor of mysteries, but a prophet pointing to what is revealed; no introducer of strangers, but revealer of friends.

I have called him a witness to the truth and am reminded of the umbrage Kierkegaard took when a Danish bishop was called by that title. Kierkegaard's sense of truth was outraged by the description of one who was perhaps a great bishop, a great speaker, perhaps a man who knew much and communicated his knowledge truly, but who was not a witness to the truth. Among all of us Professor Buber's sense of truth is like Kierkegaard's, and I hope he will not be offended by my use of the term in connection with him. But his sense of truth is more like the Hebraic Psalmist's than like Kierkegaard's. "Thou desirest truth in the inward parts; and in the hidden part thou shalt make me know wisdom" [Psalm 51:6].

In our world of objective truth, that inward truth is almost as alien as the self. It is not absent, but it is unacknowledged. It is not banished, but is not invited and cherished. We know other members of the truth well. We cultivate truth as true relationships between theory and fact, between propositions and the states of affairs to which they refer. We welcome and rejoice in truth as coherence, logical order within our statements, among our various theories. We seek it out as such in our efforts to bring together in unity our various sciences, our philosophies and theologies. When truth as coherence among our thoughts is lacking we bemoan its absence and ask what we can do to bring it home again. Pragmatic truth is far from being a stranger to us. It is an intimate and loved friend. We honor the truth that works and brings us benefits—benefits for body and mind.

But there is a form of truth among us that along with selfhood remains an alien. It is necessary to us. As the other strangers in our gates, our existence depends upon its presence. But we do not seek it out; we do not welcome it. We will vote no crash programs, make no billion-dollar appropriations to realize it. Perhaps we do not so much ignore it as fear it—this truth in our inward parts, this correspondence of ourselves with ourselves, this coherence which will make necessary the recognition of all our self-deceptions, self-contradictions, our deceptions of one another. Such truth is not only the correspondence of our utterances and self-manifestations with our inward intentions, though it is that. It is the coherence also of our inward intentions with each other. It is not the coherence of our ideas about things, but the unity of our willings, it is the purity of heart that wills anything. It is the truth on which the lives of selves depend. It is the truth that works to maintain selves in being.

It is truth also as the fidelity of self to self. That every man should speak truth to his companion, act truth toward him, be true to him, is the demand that is written into our nature, our society. But it is an unwanted truth, not dearly loved; it is barely accepted, grudgingly acknowledged and slighted. Alongside our boasted love of objective truth there stands in our human world the love of the love. Alongside the increasing enlightenment of the areas of ignorance the shadows of deception fall further and darker on the landscape. We cannot welcome personal truth, the subjective truth, truth between "I" and "Thou" as we welcome scientific, impersonal, objective truth.

How can we defend our lives in a world of enemies and deceivers, defend our nations against internal dissension and external aggression? How maintain our great and small business enterprises? How promote our religions, how keep order in our growing generation, if we do not deceive with little and large evasions of the truth about ourselves and the truth among ourselves and truth in ourselves?

This indispensable but always alien truth presents no particularly modern problem; it is the human problem. The magnitude of the tragedies it brings to modern life may be unusually great. And there is a peculiar discrepancy between the modern passion of our search for truth in thought and in our relations to things, on the one hand, and the lack of passion for truth in will and in interpersonal action, on the other.

This is the situation in which Professor Buber has worked among us as witness to the truth, namely to truth in the inward parts, between companion selves, trueness of man before the trueness of God. The witnesses to this truth cannot be honored. Their work is harder, their rewards are smaller. Yet this is as it must be. And Professor Buber would be the last to regret the fact.

I will not venture to speak of what has been present beyond all this in the meeting of men of our generation with Martin Buber, as a meeting with and before the Eternal "Thou,"—alien and stranger to us more than self and truth; present always, always ignored, always passed by: the Affirmer who is denied, and affirmed in denial.

To Him we give our thanks for Martin Buber and for one another.

III

CULTURE

5

Religion and the Democratic Tradition

The Relation of Christianity and Democracy

To speak again of the relations of Christianity and democracy is to
venture on ground well-trodden by angels and fools. If we would avoid
the folly of the latter as well as the greater folly of pretending to an
angelic wisdom beyond our reach, we shall do well to define our terms
and to limit our discussion. For both words—Christianity and democracy—are basket-words, containing all sorts of meanings and lending
themselves to vagueness in thinking. *Webster's Collegiate Dictionary*, for
instance, defines the word "Christian" as meaning: "1. One who believes, or professes or is assumed to believe, in Jesus Christ. 2. A human
being as distinguished from a brute. . . . 3. A decent or respectable
person."[1] Any daily newspaper offers enlightenment on the variety of
meanings associated with the words "democrat," "democratic," and
"democracy." They may refer to a political party, or to an attitude of
respect for all human beings, or to certain principles, variously conceived as rule by the majority, liberty of speech, press and conscience,
absence of interference by government in business enterprises, or a
host of other such claims.

The confusion in this field is doubtless largely due to the emotional
and valuational character of both terms. We rarely speak of Christianity
and democracy when we refer to simple facts. The facts have value for

us and we are more concerned in general with the values than with the facts. We tend to become so devoted to Christianity that we do not inquire too diligently into its character; we love democracy so dearly that we do not ask it too many questions about its heredity, its religion, its virtues and vices. We find beauty in both because we love them, as well as love them because they are beautiful. Defensiveness increases confusion in this realm. We recommend Christianity to ourselves and others, we defend our churches, by trying to show how valuable they are for democracy; on the other hand we endeavor to prove that democracy is good by proving that it is Christian. In such defensive use the words become ever more general and vague.

Some of these dangers may be avoided if we will inquire not into the relationship of Christianity and democracy but into the connections between the faith that God, the Father of the Lord Jesus Christ rules, and the political device of rulership by the people. We shall not undertake to say that faith in the Father of Jesus Christ[2] is *the* essence of Christianity, or that reference to the people as the final source of political authority is *the* essence of democracy. But for the purposes of this discussion we shall so define Christianity and democracy and shall undertake to set forth the relations of this faith to this political device. If the terms be otherwise defined—if Christianity, for instance, be regarded as the teaching of Jesus and democracy as the teaching of Rousseau or Jefferson—then other relations will obtain; but these are not now our concern.

I

When we ask about the relations of such a religious faith to such a political system the first answer is obviously that there is little direct connection between them. This faith has existed for more centuries in monarchic and aristocratic societies than it has in democratic commonwealths. It has apparently been found compatible also with the non-political existence of men who, like the monks, abjured all interest in the maintenance of civil authority and sought to live in a sort of philosophical anarchy. Faith in the Father of Jesus Christ has not, in this apparent indifference to government, simply yielded to the pressures of history—the pressure by the powerful, for instance, to banish religion from political life—but it has also followed the example of Jesus. His most famous utterance on the subject of politics—"Render unto Caesar the things that are Caesar's, and unto God the things that are God's" [Matthew 22:21]—indicates an indifference to political questions which his conduct confirms. It contains, as his behavior at the trial implies, a dispassionate acceptance of Roman monarchy and foreign rule; it contains his definite refusal to associate himself with those rebellious forces in Jewish society which believed that political self-determination, whether under hierarchic or Davidic leadership, would somehow bring the rule of God nearer than it was under Caesar. If the statement definitely separates God's rule from Caesar's empire it no less definitely rejects the identification of a Jewish kingdom or republic with the rule of the Father.

This apparent indifference of Jesus to the form of the political state is faithfully mirrored in the writings of the early church. These counsel obedience to magistrates and nowhere condemn or commend a form of government directly, though of course the Apocalypse expresses early Christian animosity to the persecuting Roman state in emphatic manner. When Paul writes, "Let every soul be subject unto the higher powers" [Romans 13:1] and when the first epistle of Peter counsels Christians to "fear God" and "honor the king" [1 Peter 2:17], they exhibit the same fundamental attitude that the Jesus of the Synoptic Gospels does. Even the Apocalypse is far from being a revolutionary document, since it calls for endurance rather than democratic or any other kind or revolt.

This apparent indifference to forms of government, including self-government, is rooted in the faith and cannot be satisfactorily explained away as relative to first and second century conditions. It has been said that Jesus simply evaded the political question when he counseled payment of taxes to Caesar; he wished to avoid complicating his simple gospel and to keep first things first. But when one takes the political situation into account—the issue which had been made of paying taxes to Caesar, the demand of the Zealots for self-determination, their identification of rule of God with Jewish hierarchical rule—then it is evident that Jesus was not evading at all but declaring very directly that obedience to the rule of the Father did not require the establishment of a new government in place of Roman monarchy. Again it is maintained that the apparent indifference of Jesus and early Christianity to the form of the political state was due to their eschatological expectations. They did not think that it was worthwhile to concern themselves with temporal systems which were soon to pass away. But neither Jesus nor Paul gives an eschatological explanation of his political statements. Just as Jesus' words about anxiety for food and clothing are non-eschatological in character, being based on the conviction of the natural presence rather than on the apocalyptic imminence of God's rule, so his attitude toward the state is founded not on the expectation that God will rule soon but on the certainty that he is ruling now. The explanation of Jesus' and Paul's statements about the state is to be sought in prophecy rather than in eschatology. Like the prophets they believe that God is ruling *now*, though he acts through wicked men and nations; they insist on present obedience to the divine king and present loyalty to his kingdom, within a political life that despite all appearances is under his control.

The Fourth Gospel reports that Jesus said to Pilate, "Thou wouldest have no power against me, except it were given thee above" [John 19:11]. Whether or not he used these words, they express the prophetic attitude which characterizes his whole behavior. So Isaiah had understood that the Assyrian, whatever his intentions, was a rod in the hand of God and that under all circumstances the important thing was to be obedient to the divine rule which did not exist alongside of Assyrian or any other power but overruled them and ruled through them [Isaiah 10:5]. The attitude is similar to the philosophic position represented by a Socrates who is obedient to the unjust state not because it is unjust but because behind the injustice of its representative there stands the justice of the laws; it is to the latter that he renders his suffering obedience, not to the former. Jesus is obedient not to an abstract law, but to the living Father who gives power to unjust Pilate. The instance illustrated the universal, prophetic principle. Faith in God and obedience to him are not dependent on the existence of any quality or type of human government but are to be exercised under every form of government. God always rules, no matter how hidden his Kingdom; to his intentions and activity, transcending yet immanent in all human intentions and activities, exclusive attention is to be given. The universal will expresses itself only in particular occasions, but faith responds to the universal in the particular, to God who is active through Assyrians and Pilate, and it ignores the particular intentions of Pilate or the Assyrians.

As we note this fact it becomes clear that "indifference" is the wrong word to apply to Jesus' attitude toward the state. The state does not lie outside God's sphere of action. He is not the God of religious life but of all reality. Faith in this Father is faith in one who rules in the social world, in history and nature. What is important is that he be trusted and obeyed in the here and now, whatever the form of political rule, whatever the natural conditions. Trust and obedience cannot be deferred until some other human rule or some other nature has been established. A Christianity which centers in such faith must always be a religion and a politics of the present moment. It will not look to the past or to the future for the Kingdom of God but will act in the confidence that God rules now. Hence it will use the demands of every present government as occasions for obedience to the Father and for demonstrations of loyalty to the universal kingdom. It will obey God rather than man not only when it refuses to yield active obedience to human law but also when it conforms to the latter's requirements. For it will observe the laws not as though they emanated from interested and wicked men—as they always do—but as though they came from God. It will pay income taxes and obey labor laws not grudgingly nor of necessity buy cheerfully and with the heart because it will attend less to the self-interestedness of the politically powerful, expressed in such laws as in all others, than to the universal demand for the repayment of obligations, for the exercise of self-limitation, for the practice of love and charity. It will go two miles with the law instead of one because God and not the soldier makes the demand. And when it is impossible to obey political power positively in obedience to God, then such faith will be passively obedient, accepting the suffering inflicted, knowing that what is done *to* us is as important in the universal Kingdom as what we do, or that God's rule not only requires men to do something to others but also to have something done to themselves. It will transcend bitterness by accepting suffering as coming from the hand of the ruling God rather than from the hands of the short-sighted and sinful agents through whom he acts and who, like ourselves, do not know what they are doing.

It should be evident, but it needs to be made very explicit, that this principle of Christian suffering and obedience is wholly perverted when it is applied to others rather than [to] the self, as when white men recommend it to negroes, when rich men preach it to the poor, or coercionists proclaim it to conscientious objectors. Such a use of the principle is defensive and perverts it utterly. Under God's rule there are some things men can only say to themselves and this is one of them. The defensive use of the principle of obedience to God in all situations has been the scandal of Christianity at all times and has made it a tool of the powerful. But the fact that the principle can be so abused does not detract from its significance and necessity.

The first point, then, is this: confidence that the ruling power in the world is our Father, of that the Father of Jesus Christ actually rules, and response to his action in all our actions is possible and required under all forms of government. While Christians live, they live in the Kingdom of God; and this depends for its existence no more on democracy than on monarchy or aristocracy. If democracy fails, God does not cease to rule but even that fall is evidence of his justice and goodness, for this kind of government is also of sin as well as of grace. The relation between this faith and this form of government is no closer than were the relations between the faith and Davidic rule or between it and the Holy Roman Empire. We cannot avoid this conclusion once we have abandoned a way of thinking which always begins with human initiative and have begun to think first of the divine initiative and of the problem of response to it.

II

A second point is equally important. The apparent indifference of faith in the Father of Jesus Christ to democracy or any other form of government turns into antagonism when a finite political power is made absolute, as when the voice of the people is declared to be the voice of God. Faith in the Father of Jesus Christ is no more compatible with religious reliance on the good will and power of all the people than with such reliance on a monarchic individual or an aristocratic class. When democracy, instead of being a limited and pragmatic device of government, becomes a religion, when the people begin to worship themselves as though they were their own beginning and their own end, when they are not obedient to a law higher than themselves but regard their wishes or ideals as the source of the moral law, when the people become the measure of all things—then faith must challenge democracy. It is evident to democrats that faith in God is incompatible with absolute monarchy and absolute aristocracy; genuine Protestants recognize that it is antagonistic to the claims of an absolute church; but what is often forgotten is the fact that such faith denies the absoluteness of any creature, even of mankind as a whole. There is only one who is absolute incarnate was one who emptied himself of all claims to either goodness or power. The attempt of any individuals, or institutions, or whole peoples to think of themselves as powerful enough to rule without being overruled and as good enough to declare the moral law otherwise than as subjects of that law, is a great illusion which results in disaster for themselves as well as in the crucifixion of the innocent. When the divine absolute is acknowledged, all human absolutes appear as dangerous usurpers of the Kingdom of God. This internal, logical antagonism of faith in the Father of Jesus Christ to the absolutizing of the relative, the sanctifying of the sinful, is one source of historic Christian suspicion of democracy as it is expressed in the writings of many Christian thinkers. It is not the only source, of course, since Christians are sinners like all other men and tend to set one finite absolute against another. Sometimes they have resisted democratic absolutism only because it imperiled ecclesiastical absolutism, and sometimes because they preferred absolute monarchy. Nevertheless there is a true issue between absolute democracy and the absolute God as well as between this God and absolute monarchies. If Lincoln's phrase, "of the people, by the people, and for the people," be taken simply and literally—as Lincoln himself did not take it—then Christian faith must question it as an adequate definition of government.[3] No people can live in the world of God who live for themselves, who consult only their own desires in making laws, who are their own last court of appeal, their own beginning and their own end. If the last will in the world is the will of the Father of Jesus Christ, then the general will of the people is relative and not truly general; it must subordinate itself to, criticize itself by, and integrate itself with the truly universal will.

III

When all this has been said, it remains true that there is an intimate and close relation between those measures of government by the people which have appeared in history during the Christian era and the faith in the Father of Jesus Christ. If that faith is indifferent to forms of government insofar as it always refers to the transcendent ruler present at all times, and if it is as antagonistic to democratic absolutism as to any other sort, yet it is a parent of government by the people so that one may say that faith in the Father of Jesus Christ leads to democracy, in a limited and pragmatic sense. Government by the people is not a stage on the way to the Kingdom of God, but realization of the actuality of divine rule does lead to government by the people. Democracy is a gift which is added to men who seek first the Kingdom and its righteousness.

The first point in this connection is not wholly decisive so far as democracy is concerned. It is simply this: when government is regarded dispassionately, when men abandon the religious interest they have in defending certain political traditions and forms as though their salvation depended on these, when they understand that no government can either imperil or hasten the Kingdom of God, then they have freedom to work out rationally those political devices which are best suited to serve the limited ends of the human state. In politics as in every other sphere faith in the Father of Jesus Christ frees men from that jealous regard for their particular social idols which they must have so long as they see these as the centers of meaning and worth. Released from the necessity of defending institutions because they are ours and because we think we can justify ourselves by them, our minds are set free to consider the forms of government critically and to work for the establishment of the best form possible under the circumstances. A Christian citizen, statesman, or political scientist is like Paul, free to give up the traditional law and to devise in liberty those measures which, according to reason and experience, best serve the limited, temporal ends of a limited political society. Roger Williams offers a good illustration of the way in which such freedom operates in the political sphere. He was an extraordinarily able organizer of political life partly because he did not stake too much on the outcome of his political experiments. His hope for the salvation of mankind was not tied to the realization of Old or New Testament or any other patterns in political life. He proceeded to organize Rhode Island on a pragmatic basis, knowing that government could neither save people from ultimate destruction nor satisfy their deepest needs, knowing at the same time that it could do some very necessary and important things. If it could not convert the minds and souls, it could protect the bodies of men; if it could not lead to the peace of God, it could preserve a relative human peace; if it could not make a law out of the Gospel, it could provide a law that maintained some order in society and put no barriers in the path of evangelization. Faith in God did not prescribe the form of government; reason and experience operating against a background of faith indicated what was to be done. Hence the common law of England rather than the Scriptures was Williams's guide in political construction. But one must add that this objectivity and freedom from personal involvement was accompanied by a great earnestness. If Williams avoided the fanaticism of Puritans and Quakers, he also avoided the quietism of a Lutheranism which so separated religious faith from political reason that it abjured the exercise of the latter. Prophetic faith gives freedom to the political as to scientific and economic reason, but is also requires the intense use of that reason so that men may discharge their responsibility to God faithfully.[4]

It will not do to say that the free use of reason and experience in politics leads to democracy. We cannot so bind reason or anticipate experience. It is well known, moreover, that many of the best political thinkers in history have not arrived at a democratic conclusion. Free reason lives in time and practices an unselfish expediency. But it can be said that in modern history, under the conditions of modern life, the development of democracy, like that of natural science, had been due in considerable measure to the work of a reason which had been set free through the Protestant revival of faith in God from timid dependence on an absolute church and from the defensive attitudes of traditionalism. One thinks in this connection not only of churchmen such as Richard Hooker and Roger Williams, but also of political philosophers and statesmen such as Locke, Althusius, Grotius, and James Madison.[5]

The positive relation between Christian faith and democracy is, however, more a moral than intellectual one. Whenever confidence in the rule of God is vital in a society it leads to the limitation of all human power, to increased participation by the people in government, to the willingness to grant liberty to men, and to the political recognition of human equality. Whether or not these are the marks of true democracy, they are features of the political organization of nations which have been influenced by Jewish and Christian faith. If they constitute democracy, then faith in the Father of Jesus Christ leads to democracy.

It is evident that a faith which refers in every event of life to a rule above the power of kings, traditions, institutions, and all human authorities must result in the limitation of political power. It does so in theory, for it affirms that there is a higher obligation on the part of men than their obligation to the state, and furthermore, that the latter is itself obligated and not autonomous. With its long-range view this faith points out the incontrovertible fact that all power is actually limited and that when it does not recognize these limitations it must come to early grief. All eternal empires are limited in time; the injustice of arbitrary power leads to revolt; they that take the sword will perish by the sword. But it is further true that where the faith is actual in men an immediate human limitation of the state also ensues. The latter discovers that it cannot indeed exercise power over men who are subject to a higher obligation. These men, by martyrdom, by protest, resist the political power when it transgresses its limits and interferes with their supreme loyalty. It finds that it has not dominion over them. They limit it also insofar as they constitute a church which tenaciously preserves or recaptures its independence; they limit the state by putting themselves on the same level with their governors when they demand that the latter also obey the higher law. Faith constantly appeals to an ultimate court of justice, to an ultimate law, and an overruling executive.

The effect of prophetic faith in history has always been the limitation of government. Through a long series of events and in many different ways the Christian movement and community, like the Jewish nation before and with it, has acted as barrier to the development of human absolutism and in some times has positively forced back into narrower confines the claims of the politically powerful. Early Christian martyrs who refused to worship Caesar, the monks who maintained their independence by abandoning all things over which despotism could exercise power, the Roman church with its self-sufficiency and its principle of natural law, Protestantism with its loyalty to the Scriptures, the sectarians with their resolute obedience to conscience—all these have barred the path to absolutism. The existence in human societies of a community which maintains, in however broken a fashion, a loyalty beyond political loyalty always prescribes a limit to state power. Furthermore the convictions and practices associated with faith in the rule of God have led, when there was opportunity for new construction and when theocentric faith was strong in society, to the legal recognition of the principle of limitation. Thus constitutionalism, the limitation of political power by written law considered as prior to the power, has been reinforced by a faith which seeks to obey a God whose will is known by revelation and by reason. Catholic interest in natural law and Protestant biblicism have made available to all citizens knowledge of the law to which governments are subject and have helped to create a constitutionalist frame of mind, which compares the edict of power with the principles of right. Again, the prohibition of state interference with religious worship, which we call religious liberty, represents a limitation of the state that arises in part out of the loyalty of faith in God. James Madison recognized more fully than any other American founder the difference between religious toleration which does not limit the state and religious liberty which does limit it. He insisted on the latter. "It is the duty of every man," he wrote, "to render to the Creator such homage, and such only, as he believes acceptable to him. This duty is precedent both in order and time and degree of obligation, to the claims of Civil Society. Before any man can be considered a member of Civil Society, he must be considered a subject of the Governor of the Universe: And if a member of Civil Society, who enters into any subordinate Association, must always do it with a reservation of his duty to the general authority; much more must every man who becomes a member of any particular Civil Society, do it with a saving of his allegiance to the Universal Sovereign."[6] Such religious liberty is not a right granted to citizens but the acknowledgment on the part of a government that it is not supreme and that it must not transgress certain limits. When religious liberty is regarded otherwise, as a privilege bestowed on citizens by democracy as though democracy had the right to grant or withhold it, when it is based not on prior duty but on the arbitrary freedom of the individual, then its connection with faith in God is tenuous at best.

It may well be that the principle of *limited* government—of government limited to secular end, limited by law based on reason and revelation, limited by the division of powers and by the independence of church, press, conscience—is a more essential feature in modern political systems which are called democratic than is the reference of authority to the people. Apart, however, from that consideration, it is true that Christian faith requires the limitation of political power and, if this be democracy, tends to establish democracy.

Faith in the Father of Jesus Christ leads to participation in political functions. The prophet who felt himself responsible to God became a statesman not out of ambition nor by the free choice of a career but out of necessity. A critic of kings and judges, an instructor of the nation in justice, a tribune of the oppressed, he was the original democrat in the sense that he accepted responsibility for what was going on in the common life. He did not wait for the establishment of government guaranteeing freedom of speech and conscience before he undertook to speak to the people or to denounce the inequities of power. He exercised political function not because he had a political right to do so but out of duty to God. The right was pre-political since it was founded on a pre-political duty. So it has been with the successors of the prophets throughout the centuries. Now when a nation, a whole people, has really conceived faith in God so that it knows itself to be subject to a higher authority than that of the political rulers, then its members cannot help but prophesy in the measure of their loyalty and confidence. They participate in government by being the outspoken critics of the mighty and the instructors of their fellowmen. They are not revolters who seek to establish themselves in power, but the loyalists of a higher government which is actually in power. When participation in government does not arise out of such a duty to a higher source of obligation but represents merely the claims of independent individuals to a share of temporal goods, faith in God can have little interest in it. Such general participation in government may indeed be preferable to tyranny or oligarchy; it may be the best of many bad forms of government and an expedient device for preventing things from becoming as bad as they might be, but it has little relation to faith in God. But democracy based on the higher duties of all citizens is a wholly different thing from democracy based on private claims.

Participation in government is a consequence not only of obligation but also of gratitude, of love and charity. The faith which recognizes the ruler of all things to be a father, which induces some measure of self-forgetfulness while it enhances the value of every neighbor, must undertake with Jesus the task of seeking and saving the lost, of doing good to all men. Living in the Kingdom of God it does not wait for the invitation of political power before it enters into the service of the community. It begins to perform functions in the common life which do not so much run counter to political action as they anticipate [it]. Christianity has more frequently participated in government in this fashion than through the state. Its direct service to the community in education, social welfare, and evangelism has been more important in creating a common mind and developing a sense of mutual responsibility than its indirect approaches to the common life through political agencies. Whether or not such service has eventually led to political measures in the narrow sense, it has represented participation in the actual government of the community. Christian people, insofar as they have faith, cannot be kept out of such participation in government, whatever the official state may do or fail to do. In this way, also, faith leads to democracy. One may state the idea conversely, saying that when people do not take such active interest in the affairs of a community, it is evident that they have little actual relation to the God whom Jesus loved and obeyed. They may be Christian in some other sense—lovers of perfection, spiritually minded—but the rule of the Father is not actual for them.

Again it appears that faith leads to the practice of equality in the common life and to the demand that the state deal equally with men. The democratic doctrine of equality by nature is difficult to understand or explain; but the idea of equality which stems from faith in the creator and judge of all men is truly self-evident, granted the faith be present. Perhaps it is not a doctrine of equality at all, since it does not measure men by men or by some common human standard; it affirms rather that all men have immediate worth to God, the last measure of value, whatever be their worth or lack of worth to each other and to society. It demands of the believers not that they treat all men alike but that they deal with each person as uniquely sacred and ignore all claims to special sanctity. Seeing all men before the final judge, faith discounts all temporal privileges and claims and in this sense treats all men as equal. There are tendencies in all human law toward the principle of equality. Christian faith with its sense of the sacredness of every being intensifies these but clarifies them as well by relating men to a reality which transcends nature as well as temporal society. It leads to the recognition and practice of equality also by convicting men of their sin, humbling the proud and privileged while exalting the lowly.

Since the time of Paul "liberty" has been a watchword in a part of the Christian movement. But this Christian or spiritual liberty is often regarded as unrelated to political liberty. They are certainly not identical yet their close relation seems indicated by history. Whenever the Pauline strain in Christian faith has been the active one, as in the time of the Reformation and of the Protestant revivals in the eighteenth and nineteenth centuries, political freedom seems to have increased among men. On the one hand, the conviction of direct obligation to a living God rather than to a static law has required the breaking of certain confining laws; it has led to the actual practice of liberty under obligation. On the other hand, the knowledge of one's own sinfulness and of God's gracious activity in the world has induced willingness to grant liberty to others to develop, think, and speak in accordance with their own gifts and obligations. Faith has created an atmosphere in which political as well as religious liberty could flourish. So the Great Awakening in America had little to say about political liberty and yet seems to have contributed considerably toward the liberal movement in politics. Whenever the church, whether Protestant or Roman, has had little faith in the activity of God it has endeavored to increase its control of life and to extend the scope as well as the rigor of law. When its faith has increased and it has trusted its ruler, knowing that he employs other agencies than the church and the law, it had been impelled to grant larger liberty to other human powers and organizations. And what is true of the church is true of Christians as individual citizens. Once more it appears that Christian faith, which leads to liberty and the democratic doctrine of free men or of free societies, are two different things, but also that Christian faith leads to a freedom which in a broad sense may be called democratic.

These are some of the ways in which faith in the Father of Jesus Christ seems to work toward constitutional, limited, equalitarian, liberal government in which all citizens participate. Such democracy, if this be democracy, is a gift more than an achievement, a consequence of the performance of higher duty rather than an assertion of rights which precede duty to the state. But we cannot say that modern states, called democratic, are simple consequences of Christianity. They contain many features which are not traceable to faith at all and some which are, indeed, indirectly contradictory to its demands. In these states we meet measureless claims to freedom by individuals and groups which recognize no higher obligation; we encounter a pure individualism that supplants the idolatry of the state by the idolatry of the self; we find a pure commercialism which resents restraint and a pure sectarianism that guards religious liberty only to prevent some other ecclesiastical group from gaining public advantage in the competition for power. We shall do well then to avoid not only the identification of Christian faith with the doctrine of the absolute goodness and power of the people but also with the character of modern democracies.

IV

The true inquiry of Christians in democracies cannot be whether Christian faith and democracy are compatible or whether democracy represents the rule of the Father in political life. It can only be an earnest search after what the Kingdom of the Father requires of us now, since we live in democracies. Faith requires of us neither the defense of itself by reference to its worth for democratic institutions, nor yet the defense of the latter by reference to their worth for faith. Insofar as faith is loyalty to a living God rather than a belief that some being corresponding to our ideas exists, it cannot be defended. It is like love, a wholly active thing which either exists as an outgoing energy or does not exist at all. Faith that is act cannot be possessed but only acted. All that we can possess are the ideas in which faith clothes itself and hides itself and which it must cast off again to assume other garments. So also with the character we call democratic with the habits of participating in government, of limiting the self and all human absolutes, of practicing regard for every man before the law and outside the law, of giving liberty rather than seeking to impose our patterns on other individuals and nations. Such virtues also exist, under the rule of God, in act or not at all. We can as little defend the democratic virtue of respect for minorities as we can defend the Christian virtue of love of neighbor. The only way to retain the latter is to love the neighbor; the only way to defend the former is to defend minorities. It is more democratic to defend Jews, Poles, Czechs, conscientious objectors, etc. than to defend democracy, by which we usually mean ourselves with all our vices as well as our virtues. It is more Christian to care for the neighbor than to be anxious about the principle of love and to defend the "ethics of love."

Insofar as the question about Christianity and democracy is a problem of mutual defense it is a wrong and dangerous question. It is always an illusion to believe that we can retain our inheritance from the fathers in any other way than by active use. It is always a self-deception to think that we can hold fast within limited confines to a principle which is infinite in its demand. Trotsky is right rather than Stalin: revolution must be permanent or it betrays its principle. Whether or not this be true of the communist revolution, it is true of the Christian revolution and of any democratic revolution based on Christian faith. A conversion that is not continuous throughout life cannot be a turning of the whole soul to the infinite and eternal God. If we do not rise we fall, there is no standing still in faith or in the social life that is based on faith. The demand of the Father to whom faith is directed is infinite, continuous, new in every moment. It is never satisfied by any attainment.

In the past faith has felt required by divine goodness and power to limit ecclesiastical and political absolutes. But since Christians act not only in faith but also in sin they help to enthrone new finite absolutes when they assist in the casting down of old tyrannies. So Protestantism assisted in the development of absolute individualism and of autonomous economic power. Now faith is required to limit by criticism and by law the infinite ambitions of the economic man, to seek in this new realm the recognition of the sacred worth of all beings, to win liberty for those bound in a new slavery. Tomorrow another usurper may take the place of the absolute priest, the absolute monarch, the uncontrolled economic power, as indeed in some countries even now a new independent sovereignty of party or race has challenged the Kingdom of God. There is no resting place for Christianity; there is no scheme of social life which realizes the eternal rule of the Father, for every institution is finite and subject therefore to moral as well as natural corruption.

As it is within the nations called democratic and Christian, so it is in the international society. Here not only dictators but democracies also make those claims to absolute national sovereignty which are spurious and invite disaster in a world ruled by the Father of Jesus Christ. Moreover the catastrophes which the pretension to absolute sovereignty brings down on men involve not only transgressors but also the innocent. The crucifixions of the innocent which are taking place in our time leave all nations and religions without excuse before God. Now a faith which sees these things will not be able to defend itself nor divide the nations into sinful and just, Christian and unchristian, democratic and non-democratic. But it will find itself compelled to defend the oppressed, to limit tyranny in the international and interracial society, to participate in international government no matter how disorderly and wicked that government may seem. On this point pacifists, if they put their faith in God and not in pacifism, and coercionists who do not trust in force but in the rule of the Father, must agree. They will make the pacifism or their coercionism part of the larger, inclusive program of action of those who live first of all under the rule of the Father of Jesus Christ.

One thing is plainly evident. The faith which required Christians in America, England, and elsewhere to make their own peculiar contribution to the social structure we call democratic demands of them new ventures in a new time. What the issue is to be we cannot know. We can be certain only that God will do his will despite us if not through us. We and our democracies may be broken if we fail in loyalty to his Kingdom. But his salvation will come nigh to those who seek neither Christianity nor democracy but his Kingdom and its righteousness.

A Christian Interpretation of War

The Conditions for Interpretation

OBJECTIVITY It is imperative for the church when it seeks to interpret war in the light of its faith to be as objective as possible. Objectivity means, first of all, the practice of self-denial, the sacrifice of all undue desire to prove or disprove special positions or to serve special interests. Among the interests or positions which constitute perils to the church in its inquiry the following seem important: the desire to justify participation or non-participation in war in general or in the particular war which gives occasion for this inquiry; the desire of the church to commend itself or to secure its own survival; the desire of men in the church or of those who undertake to speak for the church to eliminate suffering and death from their own lives; the desire of the church to be more righteous in the sight of God than other agencies of his will; the desire to justify the ways of God to men. Self-denial in this sphere also requires that we lay aside any initial value-judgments with which we may come to our inquiry such as the judgment that war is "evil," or "good," that peace is per se better or worse than war.

Objectivity means, in the second place, single-minded attention to an object in a specific context. The specific context in which the church sees and attempts to understand all things is that of God-with-man or man-with-God. Its object of interpretation cannot be war in isolation, which in any case would be unintelligible, nor war as an event in natural history or in human history considered in abstraction from the kingdom of God. The church interprets war as an event in the kingdom or rule of God in which God's action toward man and man's action toward God are to be understood. If it cannot so approach and so interpret war it can have nothing to say as church about war, no matter how much men may use the name of church to give specious authority to their true or false political, economic and psychological interpretations. Stated otherwise, the church, insofar as it is objective, confines its attention to the action of God toward man in war and to the action of man toward God in war. In doing so it follows the example of its prophets and apostles who directed their attention to invasions, deportations, birth and death, especially the death on the cross, as events in the rule of God or to God's action in these events and to man's action in them

159

insofar as it was action toward God. We note also that the church can undertake to discover answers to those questions about war which men ask it to answer only if it practices such objectivity. They are questions about God's presence and goodness and about the ultimate principles of men's action.

It should be remarked further that when the church approaches the subject of war in the context of God-with-man and man-with-God the term "man" is never to be taken abstractly or speculatively. To speak about man in this context is always to speak about ourselves. What we seek to interpret is God's action toward us and our action toward God, not the action of God toward men or mankind with whom we as Christians or as church are not identified.

FAITH   If objectivity in this double sense is imperative it is also possible insofar as the church abides in its faith and so acts on the ground of the conviction that to those who seek the kingdom of God all other needful things will be added—a promise as relevant to mental inquiry as to any other action.

Faith in God not only makes some measure of self-denial or disinterestedness possible but also constitutes the ground and the standpoint of the church's interpretation. As the natural scientist approaches each phenomenon, no matter how distasteful or threatening it may appear to him personally, with the confidence that in it the great regularities of the natural process will be exhibited, so the Christian comes to each event in his or mankind's history with the confidence that he is dealing with something that contains divine meaning, that is intelligible, if not in every detail yet in essence, in terms of the faithful working of God. As the former expects to have his previous understanding of natural process not only verified but also corrected and enlarged, so the latter anticipates that in each new event, loyally accepted and responded to, his understanding of God's way and will, received first in the revelation of Christ, will be corrected, widened and particularized while it is being confirmed.

A distinction needs to be made at this point between the fundamental confidence in God which forms the basis for a Christian's interpretation of any particular event and the special doctrines which he employs in such interpretation. That there is such distinction appears in the fact that many a single-minded man to whom the gift of faith has been given in ways he has not analyzed, is able to deal with war and peace, death and life, victory and defeat in a Christlike spirit without seeking to penetrate intellectually or analytically into what he may be content to call "the mystery of God's ways." He seems to be closer to the heart of the matter than another who brings doctrinal and theological equipment to the task of interpretation but relies more on doctrine and indoctrinated reason than on God for solution of life's problems. Again the distinction between the fundamental faith and the doctrines about the manner of God's working appears in the fact that many men who are confined to what they themselves regard as inadequate views of the manner of his rule yet hold fast to faith in him after the manner of the writers of the 73d Psalm and the Book of Job.

The fundamental faith in Good, which has been given to the church through Jesus Christ and with which it approaches the task of understanding His ways in the events of human warfare, is expressed for the intellect in propositions which constitute the postulates of the mind inquiring in faith. We may attempt to formulate these postulates as follows:

1. God is omnipresent, and the omnipresent is God. God, being the source, sustainer and end of all things, or, the source, sustaining power and end of all things being God, He is no less present in time or place of war than in time or place of peace; his work is being carried on through those who refuse to acknowledge him as well as through those who worship him.

2. God is omni-active, and the omni-active is God. God the omnipresent is active wherever he is at all. Insofar as reality is an activity, and to our minds all reality is activity, God is the activity in all activities.

3. God is good, and the good is God. The source and end of all things, the activity in all things is good as the one object capable of calling forth all love and as all-loving. Conversely the love that operates in all things is the real activity, the omnipresent, the omnipotent power.

4. God is one and the one is God. In moral terms faith in God is the conviction of his faithfulness, of his unity as will. He is always the same; he is not variable in intention or action; he is not one kind of God for us, another for our enemies, one kind for those we judge righteous, another kind for those we judge unrighteous. On the other hand the one purpose which runs through all purposes, the one pattern which combines all patterns, the one reason which operates through all reasons is God or of God.

There may be other ways in which the fundamental faith ought to be expressed and these particular formulations are doubtless subject to challenge, since the verbal and conceptual communication of the fundamental reliance is difficult and always full of ambiguities. Yet the agreement of the Christian church on the fundamental statements of God's oneness, goodness, omnipresence and omnipotence is considerable.

DOCTRINES The church approaches its task of interpretation not only with the fundamental faith that divine action and human response to that divine action are discernible in the midst of war but also with specific doctrines of the manner of God's rule or working and of the manner of man's response. We might call these doctrines statements of the laws of God's and man's action. Such statements have grown out of the church's effort to analyze and formulate its experience of God's rule in other events. While the whole structure of Christian doctrine has relevance to the interpretation of war certain statements are of apparently immediate importance. Among them we may enumerate the doctrines of God's justice, of his love of the sinner, or vicariousness in the divine economy of pleasure and pain, of human solidarity in God's sight, of divine creativity, and, with respect to man's action toward God, the doctrines of original sin and of human responsibility. It must be acknowledged, however, that these doctrines are to a large extent neither wholly clear in themselves nor coherently related to each other whether their formulation in certain great creeds or in the systems of the great teachers of the church be considered. From this point of view the effort of the church to interpret such an event as war in the context of the kingdom of God is as much an effort to gain greater clarity about the manner of God's working as it is an attempt to explain it to others by means of the doctrines.

God's Action in War

Uncritical theology, as expressed in many legal statements, in reports on natural catastrophes, and in other thoughtless utterances makes a distinction between acts of God and the willful acts of men with the assumptions that when an act is the act of God it is not the act of men, and vice versa, and that acts of other finite beings than men are more acts of God than are human acts. Theology proceeding from Christian faith cannot make distinctions in this fashion since God in whom it has faith is not of the order of men, so that their wills are exclusive of his will, their acts of his act. As philosophers may speak of reason active in all the reasoning processes of men without being identical with them and as capable of advancing through the errors as well as the truths of particular reasonings, as natural scientists discern acts of "nature" in the willful and even in so-called unnatural actions of natural men, so, though with a difference, the theologian of monotheistic faith seeks God's action in and through human and all finite action.

Is war then in any sense an act of God, or does the faith in God break down at this point so that war falls outside the universe and indicates that the reality in which we live and move and have our being is plural, unpredictable and irrational in character?

GOD'S "RETRIBUTIVE" JUSTICE IN WAR   It appears that war is an act of God first of all in this sense, that it so belongs to the order of the created universe that given certain acts of men war is the consequence, quite apart from any desire or will on their part for war or for peace. It is, indeed, highly dubious whether any men at any time choose war in the sense that they *will* the labors and sacrifices which war requires of them. They will to extend or maintain their power or possessions and, knowing from past experience that such extension or maintenance involves war, they may be said to consent to war, but it remains their hope that they will be allowed to achieve their desires without war. All nations engaged in conflict today believe that war was forced upon them. The belief is probably correct, though a great fallacy is committed in relating war simply to the will of a human enemy rather than to that whole series of past acts and present desires on the part of the self and others which in the order of creation led to the consequence of war. For this order is one wherein all finite beings are limited by other finite beings and wherein when one transgresses his proper limits he is repelled by another finite agency.

Moreover, the order of creation is such that it is not possible for nations or other groups to carry on spiritual, economic or other types of self-assertion at the expense of fellow-beings in such fashion that the bodies of men and the force of arms will not be involved, for it does not lie within the choice of men who are physical as well as spiritual to draw the lines at which their transgression of the limits of another life, or their willingness to carry on conflict will stop. The order of creation, the rule of God in the world, appears to be such that military war is a necessary consequence of other types of warfare. If war is a consequence of transgression of limits, it is also a consequence of refusal to accept responsibility in a common life, of the effort of men to separate themselves from the fortunes of their neighbors on whom they are really dependent in a common human existence. It appears that the order of life is such that beings who in blinded self-interest refuse to protect their fellow-beings against transgression will themselves be attacked and will then be required by their self-interest to defend their fellow-beings.

In this broad sense war may be said to be act of God, a part of the scheme of divine justice: it is the apparently inevitable consequence of transgression of proper limits on the part of the finite and of the attempt of the finite to live without service of other members of the community of men and nations and creation as a whole.

War, so considered, is seen as part of the "retributive" justice which prevails in the world. It is better, however, to eliminate the word *retribution* from our speech about God, since it suggests many inadequate and inapplicable ideas. The positive element of justice we note here is *the maintenance of order* in the universe and in the human community in particular. There is an order or a rule of divine action which the desires of men cannot change. No matter how much they may wish to escape the suffering and destruction of war, they cannot do the things which lead to war and then evade the consequence. No prayers to God, no repentances change this order; for even God's forgiveness does not eliminate the physical consequences of transgression against the neighbor or of separation from him.

It does not by any means follow that because war belongs to the order of God's justice in this sense men who find themselves "forced" to war can in any way identify their action in warfare with God's action, as though they were in any positive way upholding the order of the universe by going to war. The action and will of God are not identifiable with the action and will of any finite being. Men can accept the justice of God in war as the criminal may accept the justice of the state which upholds an order of society. They cannot claim to be the executors of divine justice when they are evidently the objects of its action.

THE CORRECTIVE JUSTICE OF GOD IN WAR   Though the justice of God which is discerned in some rough fashion in war is often regarded as a vindictive justice in which pain is inflicted as retribution for wrongdoing, two considerations indicate that insofar as any human patterns of justice may be applied to the infinite action the image of *corrective justice* only may be used. The first of these is the consideration that no scheme of vindictive justice fits the experiences of war; that the greater pain and loss come to the greater offenders is not evident in the history of human war or in any particular war. The second consideration is the positive fact that war is indeed a corrective instrument in the internal affairs of the communities which are involved in war. Perhaps this is not always true but it seems largely true and the prophets appear to have understood correctly the relation of war to internal injustice. They were assured that external aggression on Israel, whatever the intention of the finite aggressor, expressed an intention of God to correct and chasten Israel. We note now that under the conditions of warfare the very will of groups to survive requires them to correct those internal injustices which, had they been previously corrected, would have made them so healthy that the temptation to attack them or their temptation to attack others might have been wanting. To be sure, we cannot maintain that external war would not result were internal justice present, but we can see that under the compulsions of war, or for the sake of survival, groups and individuals in the warring nations accept an equality in eating and drinking, in working and suffering, to which in peacetime they render lip-service only. Freedom is given to subject peoples, as to the negroes in America in the time of the Civil War and to the Philippines in the present conflict; rights are recognized, as in the case of India and China and the Jews, which had been previously largely ignored. Respect is accorded to the neighbor who had been held in contempt. Such self-correction is accepted only grudgingly and never to the extent demanded by the conscience, yet war is an instrument of chastening; for in war, as in every other disaster, communities do confront the fundamental conditions for their survival, and find that these conditions include internal justice. The internal justice of wartime is not the product of human wishes but of divine compulsion.

We discern in the present war that the correction demanded of us and grudgingly accepted is not only a correction of practice in our intra-national affairs but in the affairs of other communities, such as the church, which under the threat of war began hesitatingly to move toward unity; such as the inter-national communities, the British empire, the pan-American society, and similar groups which under the same stress began to yield greater rights to the weaker members. So a corrective justice of God operates in war which cannot be equated with the direct intentions of men.

As the previous reflections led us to say that God's action in war is the upholding of an order of the universe, so in the present connection we may say that we discern amid all the darkness of war this gleam of rational pattern—it does tend to restore, though inadequately and incompletely, the true order of health in a society which is engaged in war.

Yet once more it must be pointed out that to discern this relation is not to offer any ground to men for justifying their intentions and actions in war. For war, in human intention and execution, has never aimed and cannot aim at this self-correction of society. The corrective justice which appears in war is not the product of man's will; it is something that compels his will.

VICARIOUS SUFFERING IN WAR   The outstanding fact about war regarded from the point of view of faith in God is the presence of the cross in it. It is Calvary, the place of vicarious suffering and death. Here individuals die for the sake of communities, because of the transgressions of nations. In war the children of the third and fourth generation bear the consequences of their fathers' guilt, for the roots of every war, considered as an event in the order of history or as an example of historic justice, always lie far back. In war the little and the weak peoples, whether we think of racial communities, or of generations, or of economic classes, or of cultural groups, bear the burden of suffering. The maintenance of order in the universe and the internal correction of the justice of groups at war is accomplished, it is apparent, at the cost of individuals and of special people who are not maintained or corrected but slain. And some of them, we must admit, are apparently spiritually maimed even more than physically. They feel forsaken of God and they descend to the abyss. These facts about war are religiously the most difficult. The faith of the church meets its greatest challenge here; here the faith of every Christian is tested.

Yet it is exactly at this point that the action of God, the Father of Jesus Christ, is most apparent in war, for this is the way of his working which was made evident in the cross of Christ. He gives his best-beloved rather than to allow the work of his creation to dissolve into the anarchy of existence which can recognize no order, to decay internally. The intense seriousness of the love of God, as revealed in Jesus Christ's death, is confirmed and recalled and illustrated and reenacted in the vicarious suffering of war.

The apparently objective thing which God is doing in war by means of the vicarious suffering of the relatively innocent is the maintenance of universal order and the correction of internal injustice in human societies. But God does not deal with men simply against their will through compulsion or through the enlistment of their self-interest in the cause of justice. He speaks to them as men of reason and of moral will. There is no appeal that comes to us in wartime for the amendment of our ways, for radical digging down to the roots of our human wrongness, for the enlistment of our best powers against ourselves, than the appeal which comes from the vicarious sufferers. God speaks his word in war through suffering servants. That there are ears which do not hear, or those who hearing will not understand, is true. But the word is spoken and is audible.

The Christian church hearing this word does not maintain that it could understand what is being said by God in war if it had not learned the meaning of his signs through Jesus Christ. It does not maintain that this word spoken in and through the vicarious sufferers is intelligible as a word of God apart from a firm faith in the resurrection. Therefore it must say as it interprets the vicarious suffering of war as divine action that it does so with the conviction and the firm expectation that these physically and spiritually crucified will rise again by the power of God.

Once more it is desirable to append a warning that this interpretation of God's action in war leaves man without any grounds for condoning or excusing his own action in war, since what man intends in war is not to resurrect from the dead but to slay, not to call himself but his enemy to repentance. The discernment of God's way in war can increase confidence in him but not in the self.

Man's Action in War

It is as impossible to say that war is the simple product of human action as it is to interpret peace in this fashion—or culture or life itself. Man's peace is always gift of God, for the bestowing of which he employs other instruments besides the human will; yet it is not given without the active participation of the recipient. War does not come upon men solely by their will, for they do not desire it, but its judgments are not visited upon them or its sacrifices demanded of them by arbitrary power. Human intention and action lead to war and all human conflict is carried on with human will and consent.

As there is something in war that God does to men so there is something in war that men do to God in their action upon each other. It is this aspect of human action that the church seeks to interpret.

OF MAN'S SIN IN WAR 1. The immediate occasion for every war is given by some act of human faithlessness, some breaking of an explicit treaty or of those implicit promises which form the moral basis of the human community and which we undertake to formulate in statements of natural rights and duties. Behind each such act there lies a long series of broken promises; every group of mankind participates in the guilt of this series. Beyond that, the relations between groups are warped and corrupted by the mutual suspicion which past faithlessness and the knowledge of man's tendency not to keep faith have brought about. The temptation to faithless action is given by the faithlessness that others have practiced and which must, on the ground of general experience, be expected of men. Thus war is the exhibition and the consequence of human faithlessness.

Now what is seen to operate in this faithlessness of men in their relations to each other is neither the cunning of animals nor the error of rational intelligences but the will of moral beings whose common life is never merely a natural nor an intellectual but a moral unity, resting on promises and willingly assumed obligations. Yet such is the warping of the moral will that while our common life must rest on the promises we make to each other it must rest also on the expectation that these promises will be broken. This human situation gives to all our social structures a broken and wavering foundation, and apparently makes their eventual collapse in some form of war inevitable.

This human faithlessness of men to men is shot through and through or it is the consequence of a similar broken relationship to God. Men are profoundly distrustful of the goodness of the will which presides over their fortunes, of its faithfulness in carrying out the promises with which they come into life and of fulfilling the expectations which are aroused with life itself. Through their faithless acts toward their fellowmen they seek to gain what they believe themselves to be defrauded of by the universe—the continuance of life, the enjoyment of its fullness, happiness. The distrust of God which forms the background of all human faithlessness has not arisen in the human mind and will apart from acts of faithlessness toward him. Yet, whatever the beginning, the important fact is that the distrust exists.

So men are caught up, as war exhibits, in a vast mesh of suspicion, deceit, promises made and broken, faithlessness in thought and deed.

2. Every war is a religious war in which men attack and defend not simply each other and themselves but their gods, or, as we prefer to say in our officially monotheistic days, their "values"—those more or less invisible realities for the sake of which life is lived and by reference to which it is organized. Though an external analysis seems nothing but a struggle for power in war, it is significant that men do not desire power for its own sake but for the sake of values which power will enable them to serve, realize and enjoy. All wars are religious wars in which men defend the nations, whose history they cherish, for the sake of which they lay down their lives, or civilization, or a church, or ideals such as "Freedom," "Equality," "Unity." Idolatry within Christendom leads to the conception of war as crusade.

It is the great tragedy of human life that for the sake of serving values which are doubtless splendid it must destroy other values which have a glory of their own. Yet it is evident to faith that what is involved in these religious motivations and occasions for war is man's idolatry, the worship of the finite as though it were infinite, the devotion to the relative as though it were absolute, the reliance upon the powerless as though it had power to save. War as religious strife for the defense of values is not the source but the consequence of the idolatry which turns from the one good beyond all goods, and from the one cause on which all causes are dependent, to derivative and created beings. War cannot be analyzed as the simple outcome of idolatry, to be sure, but the idolatry of man in days of peace is a precondition of war and the idolatry of man at war inflames the passions of conflict and lengthens the struggle.

3. No account of man's action in war would be complete without reference to the pride which tempts those who are servants in men's sight to seek mastery and those who are masters in the human view to retain and extend their rule. Here is a human cause of war that is so obvious that almost too much attention is paid to it while the faithlessness and idolatry of human action are ignored. Hence we may be very brief in pointing to this factor. As war begins with some act of faithlessness so it begins with an assertion of mastery. And back of such an assertion there lie the assertions of other members of the human com-

munity, made not in war alone but in so-called peace, made not by military means alone but by economic, intellectual and religious means. Assertion and counter-assertion form an endless series of which the beginning cannot be found. In all such striving after mastery the distrust of God, as the one sovereign of all, and the flight to an idol which will ensure life against the frustration of hopes are evident.

There are other aspects of the sin of man, that is, of his great alienation from God and the accompanying alienation from his fellowmen in groups as well as individually. But the discussion of these three aspects may suffice to indicate the role of man in the causation of war and to make evident that a war does not arise simply out of the transgressions of specific individuals or groups, but rather out of that massive moral and religious wrongness which is the seedbed of all our specific transgressions.

OF MAN'S GOODNESS IN WAR Jesus saw clearly that men, being evil, yet knew how to do good to their children, and used that goodness, reflected in a perverse mirror, as an image of the grace of God. Any interpretation of human action in war which failed to call attention to this goodness of man and stopped with the pointing out of his faithlessness would be inadequate. For this goodness is to us a pointer to the true goodness which redeems us from the tragedy into which sin in the realm of God plunges us. On the other hand without reference to it the description of the true misery of man, as this misery is made dramatically evident in time of war, would be most incomplete.

Men commit those acts which lead to war and go to war not in simple faithlessness but to keep their faith with their fellow-citizens, with allies and with the weaker members of the human community. They go to war to do good to their children to whom they desire to leave a heritage of security. They engage in the acts of war in a comradeship of arms which often excels the comradeship of work or worship. Though the atrocities of a few are called to our attention in wartime we recognize the presence of this goodness of human devotion and this loyal fulfillment of promises as present in the action of all groups. No matter how much we believe the soldiers in the armies of our enemies to be deluded, yet we accord them this respect, that we believe them on the whole to be concerned not for their own lives but for the lives of their children and their comrades and to be obedient to the laws to which they have consented. They are keeping the faith, though not with us. Here then is a common human goodness operative in the midst of war.

Though all human conduct in war is characterized by idolatry, yet in this very idolatry we discern not only a defection from God but a great capacity for devotion, a religious striving and sacrificial living. Though the misdirection of man's loyalties calls for tears, the greatness of his love as exhibited in his sacrifices lifts the heart.

Though striving for mastery in a world where only God can be master is the occasion and a cause of war, yet human conduct in wartime exhibits a human ability for service and self-forgetfulness which is less often or less dramatically shown in time of peace.

So in the dark and broken glass of war there is reflected a universal tendency to faithfulness in promise-keeping, to love of that which is high and beyond the self, to self-sacrifice. Faith interprets these scattered gleams as image of God in man and sees in them an evidence of the faithfulness that will not let man go, and of the fulfillment of the promise that all things will be restored by him to an original, fundamental harmony.

OF MAN'S MISERY War, seen in this context of divine-human relation, is like the cross of Christ the example and illustration of man's misery. It exemplifies and accentuates the moral misery of those who cannot keep their promises to each other without by the same act breaking promises, who cannot give themselves in sacrifice to the highest and best they know without sacrificing others who worship other values, who cannot serve save as through service. They seek to do good to our children and brothers. Our intentions and acts are twisted into deeds which do evil to the children of others and, in the unity of human history, eventually to our own. This twisting and thwarting of our good intentions is not accomplished by wills external to our own, but by our own wills which not only consent to the social habits of our society but which seek our own good in every good of others that they seek. Thus our moral misery is that of men who do not know how to will that which they approve without willing what they disapprove. There is no escape from this dilemma of wartime (which is also the dilemma of peacetime though less evident then). Neither active participation in war for the sake of doing good to our own and other men's children, nor non-participation when these children are being destroyed offers us a way out of the bondage of sin. Thus war is like the cross of Christ which reveals to the righteous and the unrighteous, to fleeing disciples and to aggressive judges, the reality of the prison in which they live.

The moral misery of man is not greater than his religious misery, as he discovers the dilemma in which his loyalties involve him and the manner in which he becomes a crucifier of his brothers as a result of his devotion to his gods, and both moral and religious misery are made poignant and terrible by the physical suffering of war, by the operation of social feeling for sufferers, by the recognition of the anarchy and demonry of which man is capable.

This is what faith, given through the cross, sees when it looks at the human soul in war.

What the Church Does

1. In the light of its understanding of God's action and man's action in war the church will do one thing first and last: carry on in all nations, among all men the ministry of reconciliation, placarding before the eyes of all the image of the Son of God whose body is being broken for our sakes, who can declare to us the love of the one we distrust, and whose sufferings call to continuous, thorough reconstruction of our lives.

2. The church can and must leave us all without excuses but bring us to the acknowledgment of our wrongness. It requires us to measure our faithfulness against the faithfulness of God and not against the faithlessness of our enemies.

3. It directs the minds of all nations to that work of internal social repentance and reorganization which the action of God promotes through war and which when it is done willingly, in cooperation with his demands, goes far beyond the grudging concessions made against our will.

4. In the light of its understanding of war the church calls on all men to refrain from condemnation of each other even while in their will to do good they fight each other. Condemnation like vengeance belongs to God, and he does not exercise it.

5. It seeks by its own action as well as through pressure on the state to limit the power of any finite group and to limit the destructiveness of war, confining it if possible to economic and political action. The church cannot confuse the absence of military warfare with peace, nor

truces in our human political life with reconciliation. The limitation of war to non-military conflict is not the object of its hope. But it is a mundane good which must be sought for the sake of all men.

6. It requires in the name of the one in whom it has faith that the aims in any war be clearly defined, that these aims be for the protection of the weak and that action be directed to these aims.

7. Knowing that war is crucifixion, the church prays for all men, for its enemies, and the enemies of the nation in which it carries on its work, as well as for itself and these nations. It prays in dependence on the God, whose servant it seeks to be, and in relation on his action in chastening and redeeming men in all their communities.

8. The church administers relief to all the sufferers of war, seeing each one as crucified for the sin of all.

9. Where these things are done the church is present; where they are not done religious organizations take the name of church with very doubtful right.

The Idea of Original Sin in American Culture

A theologian who makes the reading of American history one of his avocations is often puzzled by the acceptance on the part of many historians of a pattern of interpretation that seems to him to be logically as well as historically dubious. According to this pattern two tendencies in American life are closely associated with opposing sets of religious ideas. On the one hand conservative, authoritarian and aristocratic tendencies are connected with the doctrine that man is bad, or depraved, or corrupted. On the other hand, it is taken for granted that humanism and humanitarianism, the belief in man's essential goodness and [in] actions directed toward the increase of his liberties or toward the equalization of individual rights and opportunities, are correlated. Sometimes this association of a dark view of human nature with repressive government and of a bright view with liberating activity is set forth in idealistic or rationalistic, sometimes in materialistic or Marxist terms. According to the former the liberating actions follow from the idea about man; according to the latter, the view of man is a rationalization of class interests. In either case the correlation is maintained.

A most consistent presentation of this general pattern of interpretation is to be found in Vernon Louis Parrington's discussion of "The Colonial Mind."[1] Though he discerns in the church polity of New England "a liberal doctrine of natural rights" this was unfortunately "entangled with . . . an absolutist theology that conceived of human nature as inherently evil . . . and projected caste distinctions into eternity—a body of dogmas that it needed two hundred years of experience in America to disintegrate" (p. iv). For this "Puritan conception of human nature as vicious" French romantic theory substituted "the conception of human nature as potentially excellent and capable of infinite development" (p. v). Hence two lines of thought and action may be traced in the Colonial period. The line of liberalism runs through Roger Williams, Benjamin Franklin, and Thomas Jefferson, while the opposing tendency is represented by John Cotton, Jonathan Edwards, and Alexander Hamilton, "men whose grandiose dreams envisaged different ends for America and who followed different paths" from those of the liberals (p. vi). We need not follow the subsequent development of this theme in Parrington but may call attention to the fact that it leads him to associate the doctrine of absolute divine sovereignty with the idea of government by priests, an association that Protestants logically could not make. Further, in the case of John Cotton, for instance, the doctrine of human depravity is explained as providing a basis for the practice of spiritual aristocracy. "Freedom was a prerogative of righteousness; the well-being of society required that the sinner should remain subject to the Saint" (p. 33). It may also be pointed out this scheme of interpretation leaves Parrington completely puzzled by Jonathan Edwards. He can describe him only in paradoxes. "By a curious irony of fate, Jonathan Edwards, reactionary Calvinist and philosophical recluse, became the intellectual leader of the revolutionaries" (p. 161). "It was his fate to devote his noble gifts to the thankless task of re-imprisoning the mind of New England within a system from which his nature and his powers summoned him to unshackle it. He was called to be a transcendental emancipator, but he remained a Calvinist" (p. 163). Had Parrington been less obsessed by his pattern of interpretation he might have suspected that his difficulties were due not to fate's irony, or Edwards' inconsistencies, but to his own faulty logic.

Something like this pattern, though not in developed form, seems to be in A. M. Schlesinger, Jr.'s mind in his description of the *Age of Jackson*.[2] Though he makes a brief reference to the fact that the Jacksonian revolution received strong support from the evangelistic sect, yet he can find no real religious representatives of the movement save a few obscure humanists and late representatives of Republic religion. Professor Ralph Gabriel, in his *The Course of American Democratic Thought*, is far more discerning than Parrington in his understanding of the meaning for democracy of the doctrine of divine sovereignty. Yet he also regards the doctrine of human sinfulness as anti-democratic and associates the emancipating movements of the nineteenth century with the religion of humanity. "Both realistic and romantic democracy," he writes, "were postulated upon the faith in the intelligence and rectitude of the common man. This faith developed slowly at first in the United States; its symbol, universal manhood suffrage, was not generally accepted until the Jacksonian period. Because the Calvinist doctrine of the corrupt individual was an impediment to faith in man, Calvinism declined in its significance."[3] Moreover Gabriel interprets the crusaders for justice, the movements toward new emancipations after the Civil War, as having their religious counterpart in that religion of humanity which was represented by Octavius Brooks Frothingham, Robert Green Ingersoll, and Walt Whitman and which was rooted in Emerson's transcendentalism.[4]

Less critical writers than these repeat the pattern in cruder forms and with less discerning adjustments. Over and over again the stereotype is repeated: the liberal movements which are directed toward equality and liberty are associated with faith in human goodness; the repressive and conservative movements are associated with belief in man's depravity, sinfulness, or corruptness. Humanism and humanitarianism go hand in hand; absolute theism involves both the denigration of man and the exploitation of man by man.

In challenging this pattern of interpretation as a stereotype and in venturing to assert that there is often in history a positive correlation between the doctrine of man's original and universal corruption on the one hand; so-called liberal, emancipating actions on the other, I cannot rely on great familiarity with the details of American history. Such highly competent historians as Perry Miller and William Haller are reconstructing the pattern of interpretation as it applies to the detail of Puritan history in England and America.[5] Much work remains to be done on the greatly neglected movement of revivalism and evangelicalism in America. I suspect that when the relations of these movements to our total culture are made the subject of close inquiry some reinterpretations of the connection between religion and the Jeffersonian, Jacksonian, and Lincolnian movements will be found necessary. Professor Barnes' study of the *Antislavery Impulse* indicates what form some of this interpretation will take.[6] What I wish to do as a theologian and as one interested in the history of theological ideas is to challenge this pattern of interpretation on general grounds.

First of all I should like to point out that there is no evident psychological connection between the idea of human depravity and conservative practice, nor, on the other hand, between the conviction that man is good and the practice of emancipation. Any and every idea man holds may be used defensively or it may be used critically and morally. Conservatism, or the effort to defend established institutions and rights, is not a function of the ideas men hold but a use to which these ideas are put. In the history of Israel the conviction that Israel is a chosen race was used defensively by [one] group of prophets—later called false—and critically by another, the great prophets. The former employed the conviction to prove that Israel was right vis-à-vis neighboring nations; the latter [employed the conviction] to urge upon the nation the necessity of immediate internal reforms. The conviction that God is sovereign was used critically by early Reformers as a basis for their challenge to the church's claim of sovereignty. It could be and was used defensively by many later Protestants to justify the status quo. The idea of human depravity and original sin has been used defensively by defensive religion frequently and effectively—too effectively; but there is nothing in the idea itself which requires or makes inevitable this defensive use. On the other hand, [although] the idea of human goodness has been used critically as a way of challenging established social institutions and practices, there is nothing in the idea itself which compels such use of it, and, indeed, it can be and often is used defensively, that is, for the sake of protecting certain institutions and habits against criticism.

One instance of the defensive use of the idea of original sin and human depravity may be found in the famous witchcraft trials in Massachusetts. Recently a pediatrician deeply interested in psychiatry turned his attention to these trials and called attention to the phenomena of hysteria manifest among the children who accused the men and women brought to trial. His study suggests this to me[:] that the New England pioneers were hard put to it to defend the habits of civilized living in the new environment. In their efforts to preserve their children against the temptations to anarchic freedom which that environment offered they increased, quite unconsciously one may suppose, the emotional overtones of their teachings on sin and hell until they brought the new generation into a situation where the hysteria of panic and frustration was natural. Similar defensive use of the doctrine that man is a sinful and lost creature has been made by generations of Americans in their loving but mistaken zeal to train their children in the way they should go.—Defensive use of the doctrine of original sin has also occurred in connection with government. Doubtless, men have argued with Thomas Hobbes that because man is bad therefore a strict government must be maintained in the whole society as well as in the family. But such defensive use is by no means a necessary consequence of the doctrine. Today our institutions and habits are being defended with the aid of the opposite doctrine. Parents may, as they always have done, exercise discipline over children and require them to behave in accordance with parental habit because they, i.e., the parents, claim that they are good, that they are wise, and enlightened. Our economic institutions are defended by means of the claim that employers are good and can be trusted; that little supervision of the economic practices of citizens is necessary because they are fundamentally honest, enlightened, and free.

To confuse the defensive use of an idea with its meaning is an error of which historians with some knowledge of human psychology should not be guilty. Yet in dealing with the doctrines of man in Western culture they repeatedly fall into this error.

If there is no established psychological connection between conservatism and the doctrine of divine sovereignty and human corruption, neither is there a necessary logical connection. We may take the logic of divine sovereignty as a case in point, first of all. According to Parrington's logic men who begin with the premise of God's absolute sovereignty think as follows: God is absolute sovereign. Therefore the pattern of human government must be monarchical and preferably hierocratic, that is, the priests and preachers as vicegerents of God ought to rule. But such logic is precisely contrary to that of the Puritans and other Protestants. Their thought proceeded rather along the following lines: God is the absolute sovereign. Therefore no prince or church has a right to claim absolute sovereignty over men. Parrington believes that the religious man thinks like this: I must do what God does; if he exercises sovereignty, I ought to exercise sovereignty. But the Protestant and for that matter the Bible-instructed Christian rarely thinks in this fashion. His logic is better illustrated by such statements as: Give not way unto wrath; vengeance is mine, saith the Lord. I will recompense. What God does is what I neither need to do [n]or can do.

So the logic of the religious man, for instance of that John Cotton, whom Parrington so thoroughly misunderstands, is not: men are sinners; therefore we saints must rule them; but all men are sinners, therefore we saints are also sinners, and if we rule [we] must never forget it. Radically and critically used, the conviction that all men are sinners implies logically for the Christian believer that therefore all men are equal. His argument includes, indeed, the idea of creation, that men are equal because they all came from the same source and are made in the same image. But his argument for human equality rests also on the doctrine of sin. There is a radical equalitarianism in that Christian document which above all others influenced the Protestant Reformation, the Puritans in England and America, and had great effect on the continuing revivals in America—Paul's Epistle to the Romans. "Thou art inexcusable, O Man, whosoever thou art that judget: for wherein thou judget another, thou condemnest thyself: for thou that judget doest the same things. . . . There is no respect of persons with God. For as many as have sinned without the law shall also perish without the law; and as many as have sinned in the law shall be judged by the law. . . . What then? Are we better than they? No, in no wise: . . . There is none righteous, no not one. . . . For all have sinned, and come short of the glory of God" (Romans 2 & 3). Logically, that is in accordance with the logic of scriptural and Puritan as well as Edwardsean and Evangelical thinking, the doctrine of original sin and human depravity leads directly to the assertion of human equality. What can have been in Parrington's mind when he connects this doctrine of the Puritans with the projection of "caste distinctions into eternity" and the subjection of the sinners to the saints for the "well-being of society" is difficult for a theologian to fathom.

If in Protestant logic the doctrine of original sin and human depravity implies the assertion of human equality, it also implies the rejection of any human absolutism, of any absolute authoritarianism. It has often been pointed out and recently again underlined that the chief differences between Protestantism and Roman Catholicism are to be found in their respective convictions about sin and authority. Protestantism tends toward a strong view of human corruptness and weak views and practices of authority; Roman Catholicism reverses these interests, tending toward a Christian humanism and strong ideas and practices of authority. Are these accidental connections? Doubtless, Protestant thought and practice in the exercise of human authority has various roots. Its utter rejection of a hierarchical conception of the world is partly responsible for its weakness in exercising authority. But there is also a direct relation between the conviction about the universality and totality of human corruptness and this lack of authoritarianism. If we are such men as this, then it is evident to the Protestant that none of us, individually or collectively, ought to be allowed to exercise anything like absolute authority over the rest of us.

Conversely, since the time of Plato the belief in the fundamental goodness of man has not been found incompatible with aristocratic or monarchic authoritarianism. If men are such beings that they can produce philosopher-kings, if they are naturally inclined not only to wisdom but also to benevolence, [then] patriarchal or aristocratic government, in which the most advanced, the wisest, guide the rest of us, must seem logical and desirable. There is no little indication in our time that this sort of humanism, believing in human goodness and wisdom, leads logically to the diminution rather than the increase of popular liberties. The more I believe in human goodness the less likely will I be, if I am not in a position of authority, to doubt the benevolence of those who are; the more likely will I be, if I am in authority, to question my own disinterestedness.

So much for the psychological and logical connections of the doctrine of original sin with the ideas and practices of equalitarianism and liberalism. We turn now to the historical argument to illustrate, as best we can and in our own one-sided, sinful way, some apparent historical connections between the conviction about sin and the growth of American democratic practice. We must note first just what this idea is, attend then to its prevalence in the American climate of opinion and notice, finally, how it seems to have affected some of our structures and attitudes.

It is not to be supposed that the idea of original sin and human corruption which may have had an effect on political institutions is the idea as it is formulated in a specific systematic theology. As it was the [general] idea of evolution which influenced late nineteenth century thought and not Darwin's special formulation of the theory, nor Spencer's, so it is the general idea of universal and total human corruption which influences political action, not the Westminster formulation of the idea of John Calvin's. In popular use, and for that matter in pulpit use, no great distinction needs to be made between the ideas presented in the Thirty-nine Articles and as set forth in the Westminster Confession. According to the former, original sin is "the fault and corruption of the Nature of every man . . . whereby man is very far again from original righteousness, and is of his own nature inclined to evil."[7] According to the latter: "from this original corruption . . . we are utterly indisposed, disabled, and made opposite to all good, and wholly inclined to all evil."[8] It is doubtful whether many good Calvinists in England or America actually accepted this proposition in the radical fashion in which it was stated by the Westminster divines. Certainly John Calvin did not accept it in this form, for he was well aware that the light of human reason was sufficient to lead men to considerable civil righteousness. The main elements in the general idea were these: [First,] Man's nature is corrupt, not bad; this corruption is universal; it is total. The idea of corruption is to be distinguished from the idea of badness. The bad is that which ought not to be; the corrupt is something good, something that ought to be, turned sour. Since the third century A.D. Christianity had rejected thoroughly the thought that the world consisted of two kingdoms, one of good, the other of evil. Its idea of evil was subordinate to its idea of good; its thought about the fall of man was secondary to its thoughts about creation and redemption. Hence, the affirmation of man's sinfulness never included the affirmation of his badness, his ought-not-to-be-ness. To say that man was corrupt was to say in one brief phrase that he was both a desirable being, highly valued by God, and that he had been twisted, warped, stunted, or misdirected. The doctrine of human corruption in Protestant thinking is always part of a total teaching about man, according to which man is fundamentally valuable in the sight of God and so valued that he is to be redeemed from corruption. To say with Puritans and other Protestants that man is naturally corrupt is equivalent to saying that he is a good being gone wrong, not a wrong being. This doctrine of corruption therefore implies both a high view of man's essential nature and a great respect for fellowmen. The interpretation of Calvinism, that it means that man is to be regarded by his fellowman as a lowly being is prevalent among some late Calvinists and most opponents of Calvinism. It was not Calvin's and not that of the Protestants. Man is a corrupt being, but his corruption is that of a very noble being, not of an animal. Shakespeare's statements about man in *Hamlet,* taken together, are fairly precise statements of the doctrine of corruption:

What a piece of work is a man; how noble in reason, how infinite in faculties; in form and moving, how express and admirable; in action how like an angel; in apprehension how like a god! the beauty of the world; the paragon of animals. And yet, to me, what is this quintessence of dust? Man delights not me.[9]

And why this noble being does not delight Hamlet or Shakespeare is at least partly indicated by another passage:

I am very proud, revengeful, ambitious, with more offenses at my beck than I have thoughts to put them in, imagination to give them shape, or time to act them in. What should such fellows as I do, crawling between heaven and earth? We are arrant knaves all.[10]

Man in the Protestant view is a ruin but he is the ruin of a Coliseum or a Parthenon, not the ruin of a hovel. He is a diseased tree, a warped oak, and not a sick tumbleweed. The doctrine that man was corrupt was part of a view of man which assigned to him an infinitely higher place in the scale of being than was usually associated in later times with the view that man is good or on the way to goodness.

Secondly, the doctrine meant and means that this warping and twisting of human nature is universal. Such interpretations as those which we find in Parrington and others according to which the doctrine meant that some men were corrupt but the others, the redeemed for instance, were no longer so, was expressly rejected by all the great groups. The Anglicans affirmed that "this infection of nature doth remain, yea in them that are regenerated"; while Presbyterians and Congregationalists agreed that "this corruption of nature, during this life, doth remain in those that are regenerated."[11] Whatever else the ascription of the source of this corruption to Adam meant, it always meant and means this, that no one, neither Christian nor saint, had any right to regard himself as exempt from the infection. Universality of original sin always meant to believers that they must think of themselves as equally corrupt with all other men, non-Christians and overt criminals.

Finally the idea of corruption included the affirmation that it was total. By this was evidently meant not only that the totality of mankind was involved but also the total man. Sometimes, of course, when corruption or original sin was equated with badness it was made to mean complete badness, but in the religious and Christian use of the term, total meant involving the whole man. This is evidently John Calvin's idea and that of the American Puritans and Presbyterians. The source of man's inhumanity to man, of his lustfulness and egoism, does not lie, according to this conviction, in some special part of the self. The rationalist affirms that the reason of man is trustworthy, his passions only subject to suspicion; the romanticist suspects the reason but relies on the natural intuition and instincts; the "moral sense" philosopher suspecting speculative reasoning and the animal nature, counts upon the goodness of the conscience. The Protestant affirms that the corruption enters into every action and part of man: reason, conscience, instinct, passion, personal and social affections.

This general idea of a universal and total corruption of mankind has formed a main ingredient in that idea climate of opinion which forms the background of the history of American culture throughout most of its three hundred years of development. One can trace its presence most readily in the preachers and theologians but may discover it no less widely held by statesmen and poets. Beginning with the Colonial period it is unnecessary to prove its presence as a dominant idea, alongside of ideas about divine sovereignty and redemption through Christ in the Puritan preachers of Massachusetts and Connecticut. But it was evidently also a main ingredient in the Reformed or Puritanized Anglicanism of Virginia and New York and in the Presbyterianism of the Middle Colonies. What is most frequently ignored by the Jeffersonian interpreters of American history is that the conviction was held also by Roger Williams in Rhode Island and the Quakers in Pennsylvania and elsewhere. One of Williams' reasons for demanding separation of church and state was that without such separation the church would be infected. Thus he wrote in *The Bloudy Tenent of Persecution*: "The civil state, the world, being in a natural state, dead in sin, whatever be the state-religion into which persons are forced, it is impossible it should be infected. Indeed the living, the believing, the church and spiritual state, that and that only is capable of infection."[12] His letters no less than his argument indicate that one of his premises is that all men are "the children of the first sinful man" and that the Spirit of Christ is "very far from nature." Indeed it is difficult to think of any one in early New England less like Jefferson in his thinking than Roger Williams, however much alike their policies seem to a later age. The Quakers did not reject but affirmed the doctrine of original sin, saying with Robert Barclay that "All Adam's posterity, or mankind . . . or earthly man, is fallen, degenerate, and dead; deprived of the sensation or feeling of this inward testimony or seed of God; and is subject to the power, nature, and seed of the serpent."[13] "All their imaginations are evil perpetually in the sight of God." And "Man, as he is in this state can know nothing aright." The Quakers differed from the rest in believing that something more radical could happen to individual human nature in the way of salvation from sin, [which was more] than Presbyterians, Puritans and Anglicans were willing to concede. But they were a long way from believing in the goodness of man.

In the eighteenth century the leaders of the Revival and Awakening, John Wesley, George Whitefield, Jonathan Edwards, and the Tennents were unanimous not only in conceding but in affirming their conviction of their and all men's corruption. Edwards' *The Great Christian Doctrine of Original Sin Defended* appealed to experience rather than to Scripture.[14] Wesley stated the idea too emphatically:

The fall of man is the very foundation of revealed religion. If this be taken away the Christian religion is subverted nor will it deserve so honorable an appellation as that of a cunningly devised fable.[15]

This, therefore, is the first, grand, distinguishing point between heathenism and Christianity. The one acknowledges that many men are infected with many vices, and are even born with a proneness to them; but supposes withal that in some the natural good much overbalances the evil. The other declares that all men are "conceived in sin, and shapen in wickedness". . . . [A]ll who deny this—call it "original sin" or by any other title—are but heathens still in the fundamental point. . . . [H]ere is the shibboleth: Is man by nature filled with all manner of evil? Is he void of all good? Is he wholly false? Is his soul totally corrupted? . . . [I]s "every imagination of his heart evil continually"? Allow this, and you are so far a Christian. Deny it, and you are but an heathen still.[16]

What the preachers and theologians affirmed poets described in more vivid fashion. How this view of man's corruption, in which state and cosmos were involved, colored Shakespeare's thinking Professor Theodore Spencer has convincingly delineated.[17] We need not do more than mention Milton and Bunyan. Swift, of course, expresses the idea in satire and irony. But it is with the political thinkers in England and America that we are fundamentally concerned. It has often been observed that Hobbes made the fall of man the basis of his whole political philosophy. Certainly his description of human nature as egoistic and aggressive is wholly in line with that of the Puritans, save that they allowed for an original righteousness, which is only slightly recognized by Hobbes. Locke, to be sure, thought of man as naturally social, yet beset by frailty and apt to seize power. Hence his whole scheme of government is based more on man's aptness to defraud and destroy his fellowman than on his fundamentally good nature. Turning to Americans it is, of course, evident that Alexander Hamilton took a very somber view of human nature. In the sixth paper of the *Federalist* he argues that without a strong union frequent and violent quarrels would break out between the states. "To presume a want of motives for such contests," he writes,

would be to forget that men are ambitious, vindictive and rapacious. To look for a continuation of harmony between a number of independent unconnected sovereignties, situated in the same neighborhood, would be to disregard the uniform course of human events, and to set at defiance the accumulated experience of the ages.

He does not accept the idea that evil resides in institutions. Momentary passions and immediate interests, it has invariably been found, "have a more active and imperious control over human conduct than general or remote considerations of policy, utility, or justice. Have republics in practice been less addicted to war than monarchies? Are not the former administered by men as well as the latter? Are there not aversions, predilections, rivalships, and desires of unjust acquisition, that affect nations as well as kings?" Hence the practical maxim which should be adopted for the direction of our political conduct is that "we, as well as other inhabitants of the globe, are yet remote from the happy empire of perfect wisdom and perfect virtue."[18] That John Adams saw eye to eye with Hamilton is, of course, also conceded. "Those who have written on civil government," he asserted, "lay it down as a first principle . . . that whoever found a state, and make proper laws for the government of it, must presume that all men are bad by nature; that they will not fail to show that natural depravity of heart whenever they have fair opportunity."[19] A little later his fellow New Englander, President Dwight, declared that

the fundamental principle of moral and political science, so far as man is concerned, is his Depravity. . . . The corruption of man is not the result of any given form of government nor any given character in rulers, though the rulers of mankind have extensively corrupted them. Republics have been equally corrupt with monarchies. [Hence,] sound and true policy will always consider man as he is. . . . Its measures will be universally calculated for depraved beings.[20]

These are the Federalists but associated with them in the fundamental principle is Jefferson's great and good friend James Madison. With Jefferson he discerned the corruption which comes through religious institutions. "Union of religious sentiments," he wrote, "begets a surprising confidence and ecclesiastical establishments tend to great ignorance and corruption; all of which facilitate the execution of mischievous projects." He was aware too of the evil in governments.

But he reminds Jefferson in a letter that abuse of power by a majority of the people can be as real as abuse by a tyrant. "This is a truth of great importance . . . and is probably more strongly impressed on my mind by facts and reflections suggested by them, than on yours, which has contemplated abuses of power issuing from a very different quarter. Wherever there is an interest and power to do wrong, wrong will generally be done, and not less readily by a powerful and interested party than by a powerful and interested prince."[21] So he also wrote in the *Federalist,* "If the impulse and the opportunity (to carry into effect schemes of oppression) be suffered to coincide, we well know that neither moral nor religious scruples can be relied on as a means of control." Or again, "So strong is this propensity of mankind to fall into mutual animosities that where no substantial occasion presents itself the most frivolous and fanciful distinctions have been sufficient to kindle their unfriendly passions and to excite their most violent conflicts."[22]

How prevalent this presupposition of political action and construction has been among the presidents, the judges, the legislative leaders of the nation in the nineteenth century I am not prepared to state. I can here only call attention to one further point. It is conceded, even by those who see the whole liberal movement in America as a correlate of the romantic view of man that popular support for the Jeffersonian and Jacksonian movements came not so much from the enlightened few but from the more numerous adherents of the sects, in which the belief in human corruption was one of the fundamental points of orientation.

When we survey the three hundred years of American history, it seems at least likely that the Protestant and Evangelical rather than the Renaissance and Enlightenment view of man was the dominant element in our climate of opinion.

It is difficult if not impossible to show direct, especially causal connections between men's fundamental convictions and their practical actions. Verbalized theories and actual theories are often quite different. What a man believes and what he thinks he believes do not always coincide. But certain correlations may be indicated between great ideas in a climate of opinion and the actions and tempers of those who live in that climate.

The most important correlation to which I wish to draw attention is that of the Protestant view of man and the American device of balancing and limiting all powers in the community. I will let Lord Bryce state the idea and then seek to develop it. In *The American Commonwealth* he wrote,

> Someone has said that the American government and constitution are based on the theology of Calvin and the philosophy of Hobbes. This at least is true, that there is a hearty Puritanism in the view of human nature which pervades the instrument of 1787. It is the work of men who believed in original sin, and were resolved to leave open for transgressors no door which they could possibly shut. Compare this spirit with the enthusiastic optimism of the Frenchmen of 1789. It is not merely a difference of race temperaments; it is a difference of fundamental ideas. . . . The aim of the Constitution seems to be not so much to attain great common ends, as to avert the evils which will flow, not merely from a bad government, but from any government strong enough to threaten the pre-existing communities or the individual citizens.[23]

The idea which Bryce discerns as lying back of the American constitution was stated in the very beginning by John Cotton: "Let all the world learn to give mortall men no greater power [than] they are content they shall use, for use it they will. . . . It is necessary . . . that all power that is on earth be limited, Church power or other. . . . It is counted a matter of danger to the State to limit Prerogatives; but it is a further danger, not to have them limited: They will be like a tempest if they be not limited."[24]

The limitation of all power in the American community was provided for, of course, by the constitutional provision for the separation and mutual limitation of the executive, legislative and judicial branches of the government, and the recognition and balancing of states' rights and national rights. It was provided for by the Constitution, the Bill of Rights, and tradition, when the power of individuals and the power of general government were carefully opposed to each other and correlated. Our whole frame and fashion of government rests neither on the principle that the human individual is good and requires little government, nor the principle that government is divinely right, but rather on the principle that individuals with little government will fall into an anarchic war of all against all, and that governments unlimited in their power will become tyrannical. Madison and Lincoln were both deeply concerned with the question how to achieve not simply a proper limitation of governmental power but also a proper limitation by government of the abusive use of power by free individuals. "It has been remarked," said Madison, "that there is a tendency in all governments to an augmentation of power at the expence of liberty. But the remark as usually understood does not appear to me well founded. Power when it has attained a certain degree of energy and independence goes on generally to further degrees. But when below that degree, the direct tendency is toward further degrees of relaxation, until the abuses of liberty beget a sudden transition to an undue degree of power.... It is a melancholy reflection that liberty should be equally exposed to danger whether the Government have too much or too little power, and that the line which divides these extremes should be so inaccurately defined by experience."[25]

A Jeffersonian and romantic philosophy sees the liberties of the individual endangered only by the bad institutions, state and church. The Protestant philosopher sees that the dangers arise from the tendencies of individuals to abuse their powers as well as from such tendencies in the corporations. Hence he restricts and balances all powers, for sin is universal, not particular; total, not confined to one part of life.

What applies to national and local communities, to state and individual, applies also to majorities and minorities. The romantic from Rousseau's day to ours thinks of the good common will represented by the majority, and opposed to the corrupted private will of a faction. The Protestant is bound to suspect anyone who claims to represent the good common will and even if the claim were true that he represents the common will, the Protestant would suspect the goodness of that common will. However that may be, our American, like English and I suppose Scandinavian, democracy may be said to rest, as Sir Ernest Barker somewhere points out, less on the principle of majority rule than on the principle of respect for the rights of minorities. Majority rule we have in common with some totalitarian governments. The limitation of the majority's power not only by internal checks but by external ones is distinctive of our form. Lincoln himself did not interpret, as many later liberals have done, the phrase "government of the people, by the people and for the people" in Rousseau's fashion, as though the people had a common will.[26] I quote Madison once more to underscore my point, that our democracy expects the majority to sin no less than the minority and that it seeks to limit abuses of power wherever they may occur. "Wherever the real power in government lies," he wrote, "there is the danger of oppression. In our Governments the real power lies in the majority of the Community, and the invasion of private rights is *chiefly* to be apprehended, not from acts of Government contrary to the sense of its constituents, but from acts in which the Government is the mere instrument of the major number of its constituents. . . . Where the power is in the few it is natural for them to sacrifice the many to their partialities and corruptions. Where the power, as with us, is in the many, not in the few, the danger can not be great that the few will be thus favored. It is much more to be dreaded that the few will be unnecessarily sacrificed to the many."[27]

The modern romantic regards all this as the rationalization of the defense of property interests. But when we look at Madison's work we have a right to say that he believed what he said and applied the principle impartially.

Another area in which this recognition that because of human corruption all power must be limited has led to balancing and limitation is the area of church state relations. It strikes the theologian as very curious that Roger Williams and the Quakers are mentioned in one breath with Thomas Jefferson by the romantic interpreters of our history. Their reasons for separating church and state were almost opposite to each other. Williams saw in the intermingling of church and state a threat to religion. The corruptions of the natural state were thereby communicated to the spiritual state. And this was one of the reasons why so many of the sectarians supported Jefferson, though of course motives arising out of the rivalry of denominations also played a large part. Jefferson saw the church as corrupt and superstitious and ambitious for power, hence wanted to exclude it from government. The common position which the great middle party took was one which accepted both charges, both church and state are subject to corruption. Hence neither is to be given power over the other. Provision has been made, therefore, for separation and non-interference, but no provision has been made for more active limitation.

The extension of this general principle, that all men in all groups, being corrupted, are inclined to abuse their power and must be limited, has characterized the later practices of our democratic movement. But it has rarely been expressed adequately in theory, and our practice is doubtless suffering from a theory that is not in accord with it. Romantic liberalism which began with the exaltation of the natural man, the savage, moved on, as in Jefferson, to the exaltation of the primitive righteousness of agricultural man. It expressed itself then in popular form in the belief that the employer of free labor, the merchant and businessman represented the good common will. In our time it frequently appears here as well as elsewhere in the world, in faith in the goodness of the proletarian industrial worker. Contrariwise, it discerns evil in a certain layer or institution of society. The romantic abolitionist saw in the slaveholder the concentration of all human wickedness; the prohibitionist in the liquor dealer; the modern romantic finds the root of all evil in Wall Street and the capitalist class. The Protestant follower of John Cotton and James Madison will expect men, no matter what their function in society, no matter what their status, to abuse power so far as they can. All men and movements confuse their relative with an absolute goodness; all want to be gods. Churchmen, farmers, bureaucrats and merchants, experts and practical men, industrial workers and white-collar workers—they all fall under sin and not only fall short of the glory of God, but far short of representing by their desires the desire for the common good.

Hence practice must move from point to point. It will expect that one movement toward absolutism will be followed by another. The absolutist church will be checked by a state which in turn will seek to become a human God; Leviathan will be checked by the propertied classes who will endeavor to make Mammon God; these are checked by the power of organized labor, and this in turn will pretend to represent the good will. The course of American democracy, however, has so far been guided not by the romantic theories of Jefferson and Henry Wallace, but by the Protestant convictions of Cotton, Edwards, Madison, and perhaps Lincoln and Wilson.

There are other correlations between the doctrine of original sin and democratic practice. Reference has been made to the equalitarianism which is logically associated with the radical acceptance of this doctrine. So far as we have used theological terms we have stated our theory of and interest in equality by reference to creation. In practice, however, it might be maintained we have been deeply influenced by the conviction that we are equally under sin. Reference to our origin may lead us to say: I am equal to the best among us; reference to our sin may lead us to confess: I am not better than the worst among us. Perhaps the presence of this conviction at the back of our minds or in the intellectual air which we breathe has contributed something to that spirit of tolerance without which democratic life is impossible, no matter how ingeniously our political structure has been devised, how creatively our statesmen administer our fundamental laws.

In closing I should like to dissociate myself, however, from my fellow New Havener and colleague in Divinity of more than a century ago. I think the conviction of our human wickedness is very important for the wise management of our human affairs, but I cannot believe that President Dwight was near the truth when he wrote: "The fundamental principle of moral and political science, so far as man is concerned, is his Depravity." If we should need to found our moral and political science on a principle about man, then it is doubtful whether we could make any progress, achieve any justice, by beginning with Hobbes. If our moral and political science would need to rest on such foundations of abstract truths about man, then I for one would want to side with the romantics and not with the detractors of man.

In Protestant thought the principle of man's corruption derives its meaning from its context. It stands among convictions about man's creation in the divine image and about his real redemption from his wickedness and from the inhumanity of man to man. The belief in that liberation as an ongoing process, as a possibility relevant to existence in time as well as eternity, as relevant to political as well as to religious life, is for the Protestant even more important than the doctrine of sin. It has had a real effect, I believe, on the struggle for liberty in the democratic countries of the Protestant world. Hence it is a great mistake to dissociate conviction about man's corruption from the conviction about his redemption. But since only one thing can be said at a time, I have had to confine my reflections to the theme of Original Sin and Democracy. I close therefore with the warning that what I have to say is only one chapter in the story. The whole story must be entitled: The Belief in Redemption and the Struggle for Liberty, not Sin and Government.

6

Sermons

Our Reverent Doubt and the Authority of Christ

Now the eleven disciples went to Galilee, to the mountain to which Jesus had directed them. And when they saw him they worshiped him; but some doubted. And Jesus came and said to them, 'All authority in heaven and on earth has been given to me. Go therefore and make disciples of all nations, baptizing them in the name of the Father and of the Son and of the Holy Spirit, teaching them to observe all that I have commanded you; and lo, I am with you always, to the close of the age.' Matthew 28: 16–20 (RSV)

1. Our service today is one of a series of symbolic actions. For many members of the audience it is connected with graduating exercises in Yale University and with ordination. For us of the faculty it is a part of that symbolic ritual with which we celebrate the arrival in port of our ship after another voyage across seas of ignorance and knowledge. Our predecessors and we have made one hundred and twenty-six such crossings. But the joy of arrival does not diminish with repetition. There is no genuine repetition. Every year is new. The seas are always changing. Strange storms mark some of the passages. The crew contains ever new faces. There are always new friends at the dock to welcome the arriving sailors.

2. These are symbolic actions, all of them: anniversary service, or-

dination, graduation. What do they symbolize? If we could put into words what they symbolize there would be no need of the actions. If all the meaning were reducible to ideas there would be no need of gowns and hoods, processions and hymns, of diplomas and seals, of the laying on of hands, of handclasps and smiles, of altars and crosses, of the bread and the wine of Communion. Here we participate in and here we celebrate, here we point to and here we seek to express an unseen and an unmeasured reality. In part what we refer to is a life of sentiment and emotion. There are the sentiments and emotions of parents and sons and daughters, of teachers and students, of friends and companions. Beyond these lie the personal loyalties in which we are bound to another and to the past—to 126 years of the past, to 1,948 years of it, to all the millennia which have gone before. We participate in all these external dramatic actions as a sign and signal of our internal participation in that mostly invisible drama of personal and family and Christian and human history.

3. In that invisible personal and human action to which these outward rites make reference there is one great and towering presence binding together all its diverse scenes and characters. He is not present in any outward form. He wears no gown or hood. You will not feel his hand upon your head in ordination. His voice will pronounce no charge. He will receive no degree. He will not be ordained. He is not here but risen. He is risen and therefore here. In his name we are gathered here. Because of his name, his power, his words, his grace we have come here to study and to teach. In his name and for his cause we now depart. When the president of the University says: By the authority vested in me I admit you to the degree of Bachelor of Divinity and to all the rights and privileges pertaining thereunto, He will be there in no audible tones: All authority has been given me in heaven and on earth. When the clergymen who ordain you lay the charge upon you, he will be there with the mandate: Go into all the world and make disciples of all nations. Now when at our anniversary we recollect the years gone by and look toward the future, he is present: I am with you always, even to the end of the world.

I

Like the disciples on the mountain in Galilee we confront his presence with worship and with doubt. It may be that they were divided into two groups, those who worshipped him and those who doubted, as all our translators have interpreted the passage. But surely the more common, almost the universal attitude of those who are aware of the Lord, is one of mingled doubt and worship.

A. 1. How such a mingling is possible you probably understand from your experience in participating in such rites as these. There is a thrill in anniversary exercises, in graduation ceremonies and ecclesiastical rites of ordination. Some experience the wave of awe against their own will, like pacifists impressed by military parades. But even those who participate with wholly willing minds are not secure against the whisper of doubt which says—"This is all a play; this is unreal. All this world's a stage and all these men and women merely players."

2. What we experience in these external rites and dramas—this combination of awe and doubt—is perhaps even more or at least equally characteristic of that internal, personal and human action in which we participate as we confront our Lord. Here we acknowledge, reverence and worship. We become aware with awe of the strange power of his obedient Sonship to God: we stand amazed by the singular, the mysterious nature of his purity of purpose, by the monolithic character of his faith. We hear words of eternal life. We see the way and the truth. Here there is that which death cannot master. Here there is something that does not belong to this world. Here there is a reality that makes all our schemes and concerns seem tawdry. Here we are reduced to silence or to the simple confession, "My Lord and my God."

And yet amid our worship we hear the voice of doubt. The question arises over and over: Is not this also a play? Are we not dealing here with images and phantoms?

3. There are differences to be sure between the doubtful awe we feel at commencements and ordinations and the awful doubt we know in the presence of the Lord. There are differences of degree. In the one case our more superficial emotions are involved, in the other we are dealing with a worship, awe and doubt that lie at the soul's center. There are differences in kind. When we deal with manifestations of academic and ecclesiastical authority we doubt whether there is a spiritual, personal, moral power commensurate with the external trappings. In the presence of Christ the case is reversed. We do not doubt his spiritual, personal, moral authority. We rather doubt the ability of that power to make itself manifest in the seen and tangible world. And again when we stand before these human authorities our questioning is directed toward them, whether they are not making believe. But in the

presence of the Lord, our doubts are directed toward ourselves, whether we are making believe.

B. It is with this wrestle of worship and doubt that we have been concerned at this Divinity School for a century and a quarter. It is that conflict that you have been carrying on here for three years and more. It is with this that the church has been concerned through all the centuries. In it we shall all continue to the end of our time, until we see him face to face.

1. The conflict takes on many forms: Because we worship we take our doubt seriously and criticize ourselves, seeking to eliminate from our lives what is phantom, dream and fancy. If we did not worship we would turn over the task of the criticism of religion to anthropologists, psychologists and historians. Because we worship, because the supernal Christ is there, therefore we examine the Scriptures, the records of his revelation in the past; therefore we criticize our religious experience; therefore we seek to find the faults in the structure of our church and of its teaching. It is the worship which, in part at least, drives our doubt of ourselves to examine our reasoning, our moralizing, our living. If what we worshipped were a matter of slight importance, then our doubts of ourselves would soon turn into a new kind of self-confidence. We would be able to say: we have discovered the flaw, and go about our business in this world. But our worship drives us to discover the roots of our doubt. So it has always been and so doubtless it will always be with those who stand before the risen Christ. We will carry on our criticism here—our criticism of the Scriptures, of the creeds and dogmas, of the schools and movements, for more years in the future than we have in the past, God willing. You will not stop the pursuit of your self-doubtings in the ministry. And all this not because we doubt but because we worship in our doubting.

2. There is another way in which the wrestle of worship with doubt makes itself manifest. Because we doubt what we worship we forever seek to make manifest by means of our own power this reality which we worship. We engaged in the conflict with ourselves in order that we may mold this rough and chaotic stuff of our lives into something that may make evident the reality of the Spirit of Christ. We reform and divide and reunite the churches; we form call-groups and engage in various spiritual exercises in order to make visible and tangible in the world the presence of a Lord whom we worship but whom it cannot see as we cannot see him. We engage in social action of one sort or

another that His spirit may put on flesh and blood and that the kingdoms of this world may make evident his authority. In all of this we manifest our worship—We believe that He is supreme. And we make known our doubt—We do not believe Him to be real until we make Him so, nor powerful until He is upheld by our own strong right arms.

This is our dilemma and this is our fate. If this were all that could be said about our lives as Christians in this school, in the church, in the ministry, it would be enough in many ways. Better to be a doubtful worshipper of Jesus Christ than not a worshipper at all. Better to have met him once in some movement forever subject to question, than never to have had his hand placed upon us.

II

But it is not all that is to be said, and even this could not be said were there not more. Or if it is all that we can say, it is not all that is being said. For in this awful and doubtful meeting we hear from him, in one form or another, the words he spoke to his disciples in Galilee: "All authority in heaven and on earth has been given me. Go therefore and make disciples of all nations, baptizing them in the name of the Father and of the Son and of the Holy Spirit. And lo, I am with you always, to the close of the ages."

A. We are not dealing with the conflict of authorities within ourselves. It is not simply so that the authority of our religious experience of Christ wrestles with the authority of our reason or of our caution. There is one over against us who exercises his authority over our experience and our reason, our desires and our doubts.

As we reflect upon our lives we are aware that it was his authority which brought us here. He has been and is our fate. We thought that it was in our freedom that we came to our hill in Galilee. But we see now that it was his appointment. We thought that we had chosen him; but now we understand that he has chosen us. We thought we came as volunteers. Now we know that we have been drafted. We look upon the tortuous way of our lives, on all the decisions we made in our freedom, on all the decisions others have made for us in their freedom. We regard the history of this school. We look upon the way the Christian church has come to this day and hour of meeting with him. And we are made aware of his authority. He has not worked in the way of compulsion. But neither has he waited on our consent. He has exercised authority over the spiritual universe in which we live, but even the winds and waves have been his servants. There has been no escape from him. In our freedom we have said: Lord, to whom shall we go? He has challenged us in our freedom asking, Will you also go away? But amidst all this there has been the simple voice of his authority: "Follow me!" And we have come.

B. If he has manifested his authority by bringing us to this meeting with him through the compulsion of his simple word, he manifests it again in the way in which he takes command.

Whether we have come as volunteers or as drafted, whether we worship more or doubt more does not affect him. He issues his command to us: Teach and baptize the nations. And we obey and shall obey. We twist and turn, we evade and seek to escape. The history of the church is also a history of the evasion of this commandment. But he exercises his authority in securing our obedience. So far as it is up to us in our freedom we see to it that some of his commandments are taught in some parts of this world. We made our selections of those commandments which we will teach. We each select some part of the world to which we will teach them. We elect to baptize this part of the world or that. But by his authority he sees to it that all his commandments are taught and that all the nations are baptized.

Some of us will want to teach his moral commandment: Love thy neighbor as thyself. Some will want to teach his religious commandment: Love the Lord thy God. Some of us will want to baptize rather than teach. We will want to bring men into the mystical union with him; we will say everything depends on regeneration. And others of us will teach the commandments rather than baptize. Some of us will want to teach and baptize the nations in their social unity. Some will attend to individuals in the nations. And we will quarrel with one another. We will do many different things. But by his authority all these things are done. If we were the masters some things would be done. He manifests his authority in the way he secures complete obedience from our diversity, in our diversity, through our diversity.

C. He manifests his authority by being with us always.

The statement "I am with you always" is usually taken as a consoling and merciful promise. Surely, it is that. It is the promise on which we count in our worship and our doubt. No matter where we go and what our future holds, He will be there. The extent to which he keeps that promise has been attested again in our time by all the martyrs of our day who have confessed that he has been present in the midst of torture and in the darkness when they had nothing and no one to count upon. We rely upon that promise now. Though we take the wings of the morning and work in Oriental lands, he will be there. Though we lie down in hell, he will be there.

But the statement is something besides a promise. It is the statement of his authority. His kingship, his rule, his claim upon us is something that we cannot escape. Genuine authority is the authority which is not limited by space or time. We can escape the authority of the home. We may escape the authority of the nation. We may renounce our loyalty to the sovereign state. There is no such escape for us from the Kingship of Christ. What Judas discovered and Peter discovered we discover and shall discover. Though we deny him, he will not deny us. He is faithful and true and claims us in our unwillingness as well as in our willingness.

His government is not external. It permeates our being and the being of this world. He is with us always so that when we deny him his glance finds us and arrests us, so that when we transgress his commandments, we cannot forget him.

Sometimes it may seem as though we had escaped his Lordship. A whole generation of Christians may seem to be able to get along with some substitute for him. An individual may, like a famous Yale professor, put his faith into a desk drawer and find after a lapse of years that nothing is left. But that man spoke too soon. There is no emancipation from Jesus Christ. I will be with you always.

D. He manifests his authority in the end.

1. In our freedom we travel toward many ends. The goals of this age are various. Your goals and hopes are as many as there are individuals present. Our ends are the ends of hopes. There are also the ends of our fears.

We have our social hopes for a warless world where bear and eagle will lie down together, where the star of Israel and the moon of Islam will wave together in a harmony of the spheres. We have our social fears, of destruction, anarchy and barbarism. We have our personal hopes and our personal fears.

The authority of Christ manifests itself in his presence in all these ends of our hopes and fears. We can imagine no kingdom of God on earth in which he will not be present, nor any crucifixion of mankind where he will not be, lending significance and meaning, forgiving and redeeming. Whatever be the ends in our minds, by his authority he is present in them. He exercises authority over all our hopes and fears, directing them toward himself.

2. He manifests his authority by transforming all our fears into the hope of his coming. Our fears of the future are real. Each individual looking into himself questions his ability to meet the tasks required of him. Our society knows once more that the day of the Lord is darkness and not light. Yet an authority has taken hold of us. It is not the authority of commandment anymore, but the authority of truth and revelation. And by it we know, beyond all our worship and our doubt, that this Lord is reality, that to him belongs the victory and the power, that he is King and will be King, over our lives and over the world.

At his name every knee shall bow, including our own stubborn knees, and all tongues shall confess, including our halting, stammering tongues, that Jesus Christ is Lord, to the glory of God the Father.

Amen and amen.

The Logic of the Cross

The doctrine of the cross is sheer folly to those on their way to ruin, but to us who are on the way to salvation it is the power of God. I Corinthians 1:18 (NEB)

I

The problem of the lost and the saved is a difficult one for believers as well as nonbelievers. Many of those who today are rediscovering the Gospel are bothered by the distinction. A young Indian Christian confessed his difficulties not long ago when he asked about the fate of his mother, who had not been converted. But many of us who have been raised in the Christian tradition continue to be bothered by this question. Some light on the problem came to me not long ago when I was asked to consider the situation of a woman who had been bedfast for fifteen years or more and who would not do the one thing she needed to do to get well. To be sure, she often prayed for health, took many medicines, and thought that she was taking excellent care of herself. But she did not believe that she could get well. Some light also came from stories of the French Resistance movement. There were evidently two sorts of people in France in the days of the German Occupation, both of whom wanted to be free of the oppressor. But one group did not believe that any liberation was possible. The other group passionately believed that liberation was coming to them. They believed that in due time the armies of the Allies would be victorious. Hence they reacted to oppression in a wholly different way from that which the members of the first group took. With this experience and these stories in mind, I returned to the passage about the perishing and the saved and discovered that it could legitimately be translated like this. The Logos—that is, the logic of the Cross—is folly to those who *are perishing* but to us who *are being saved* it is the power of God.

We can understand very well what this means, that the Logic of the Cross of Christ is said to be folly to those who are perishing. We have all understood what sort of thinking we do when we believe that we are perishing. Against the background of that conviction, we develop a wisdom and a strategy of life into which the logic of the Cross does not fit. It becomes a sheer nonsense, something that does not make sense and which must, therefore, be dealt with as superstition or myth or insignificant historical fact, or an emotional symbol that does not need to be taken into account.

The conviction that we are perishing is sometimes expressed in more personal, sometimes in more social terms. Sometimes it is stated in ethical, sometimes in scientific terms. It may appear in the certainty that there is nothing to our existence as persons except this physical life and that the death of our body is our annihilation, that as living persons we are suspended for a moment between two great abysses, the nothing out of which we came and the nothing to which we go. When we think socially the background conviction may be that it is by our own efforts that we have created our civilization out of nothingness, but that it must also pass away as all other civilizations have gone; and that unless we exert ourselves fully, it will perish very soon. The conviction that we are perishing is accompanied by the certainty that we are surrounded by enemies, human and natural, by a world of powers as well as of political empires, that are intent in one way or another on our extinction.

Perhaps we do not acknowledge that the first principle of our thinking is this premise: we are perishing. We often start at a slightly lower point, saying that self-preservation is the first law of life. This is a way of saying that we believe that if we do not preserve ourselves we will not be preserved. What is back of this idea is evidently another one, namely, the conviction that our frustration, our annihilation, our death is a law of the behavior of all that surrounds us. When we feel strong and are full of zest, we seem to be saying, in effect, that this self-preservation, which is the first law of our life, is also a possibility. We will be able to preserve ourselves against all antagonists of mind and body, self and society. But even this optimism is surrounded by an aura of pessimism. The sense that nature is stronger than we never quite forsakes us. The knowledge that "all lovely things must have an ending, all lovely things must fade and die" is at the back of our minds.

In this situation, believing that we are perishing, we develop the wisdom of survival. This is a very practical wisdom, first of all. It is the animal wisdom of protective coloration, of defensive claws and jaws. It is the practical human wisdom of learning how to get along in the world without inviting attack. It has cruder and more refined forms. It is the wisdom of "look younger and live longer" and "how to survive bomb attacks." But we use this wisdom not only in this practical way. We also develop it in scientific fashion.

The great evolutionary science of Darwin undertook to understand the vast variety of nature by means first of the idea of evolution and then also by means of the Hobbesian idea that life is the war of all against all and that selection occurs through the survival of the fittest. There is much political science which not only studies the structure and dynamics of social life but also accepts among its first principles the theory of power as the essence of political existence and the theory of universal war. The wisdom of survival appears in economics and politics as well as in science. It is used to guide the strategies of power politics and of free enterprise. With the aid of the wisdom of survival, we seek to answer in its various forms the question: how shall we defend ourselves against perishing too soon in a world of enemies? How shall we be able to live a little longer? How shall we handle with care those precious packages of personal and social life which are marked in red letters "Fragile" and "Perishable"?

The wisdom of survival is not the wisdom of a world of life but of a world of death. Its basic idea is that of outliving foes and friends. To survive is not to live but to outlive. The specter of perishing, of the nothingness that surrounds us, is not banished by the wisdom of survival. This is true of that strategy of the perishing which appears in the desire for social immortality as well as of the strategy which appears in the effort to maintain biological life. What a great skill men employ in order to create some work in politics, in science, in art, in family life, by means of which they will be remembered a little while longer! The knowledge that even this will pass away is never far from us.

The wisdom of the perishing appears also in our careful calculation of measures for filling with meaning these passing years of life. We want to put as much joyful experience into the vanishing moment as is possible. Youth is as conscious of its evanescence as age of the briefness of its threescore years and ten. And if it were not, it would be reminded by the aged that one is only young once. Hence our Stoic and our Epicurean systems of conduct are concerned with the question, how to get the most out of life. The debate is always going on among the advocates of the different systems. Some recommend that we gather rosebuds while we may, since time is still flying, and some affirm that above all else we must "to our own selves be true," that virtue is a great joy. Some recommend that we fill up our passing life with religion. Some substitute scientific investigation, and others, art. But on one thing they are all agreed, that our sickness is a fatal illness and that we must labor mightily to put as much meaning as is possible into the moments that are rapidly slipping away.

The wisdom of the perishing is a temporal wisdom. It is a wisdom which concentrates intensely on the present. It admonishes us always that it is later than we think, that the past is gone beyond the possibility of being retrieved, that the future is uncertain, or that the hour of crisis is at hand.

From the point of view of the wisdom of the perishing the cross is evident nonsense. When we are asking the question, What must we do to survive? and with it confront the cross, we find no answer there. It is something that does not fit into our pattern. We who live in Christendom have become so accustomed to this socially accepted symbol of the cross that we will not express ourselves boldly upon the subject as the old Greeks did or as modern Marxists do, yet we must confess that we find its meaning so impenetrable that we must either ignore it or interpret it in a manner that makes nonsense out of it. It is nonsense to us who are perishing, who are surrounded by enemies, to be asked to take our eyes off of these living enemies waiting to destroy us and to look with concentration on the One whom we mistakenly killed as our enemy. Does not such concentration on the cross enervate us, deprive us of vigilance, fill us with feelings of guilt, all of which instead of contributing to our ability to survive puts us at a disadvantage in the struggle for existence?

It is nonsense that we who need to survive should direct all our thought toward One who was not a survivor. The wisdom of survival can study the strategy of an Augustus Caesar, the genius of the Roman Empire, the shrewdness of Caiaphas, all of whom were able to outlive Jesus. But what can it learn from One who was not able to maintain himself in life against Roman, Jewish, and ordinary human wisdom of survival?

It is nonsense that we who must devote so much time to the discovery of our enemies and to the study of their strategy—whether these enemies be bacilli or empires—should try to find help in One who forgave his enemies and readily yielded himself up to them. It is nonsense that we should accept as the Christ, as the great world statesman, the great leader of the human cause, One who was unable to enlist the support of his own people, who was rejected not only by his nation's enemies but by his own kindred. In all of our wisdom of survival we look for leadership to those who are able to engage the enthusiasm and even fanatical support of men. The cross is the symbol of One who was forsaken by friends as well as by foes.

To be sure, it is not usually in this way that we reject the cross as having no logical meaning for us. What we do instead is to twist and reinterpret and modify that cross so as to make of it something that will fit into our wisdom of survival. We make ourselves believe that holy splinters from its wood will cure our diseases. We try to find a way of translating it into an effective weapon of soul-force by means of which we may defeat our enemies and so survive. We use historical criticism and say that it was not really necessary for Jesus to die, that it was only because he misinterpreted history that he went to the cross. Or we try in other ways to make out of the uncrucified Jesus an effective leader. We paint the cross on our battle flags and carry it before us in our crusades, trying to make it in some way a rallying point for nations and churches afraid of perishing. In these and in other devious ways we make nonsense out of it by domesticating it and making it a part of the wisdom of survival. In honesty, ought we not to translate Paul's words into contemporary terms, saying, "To the Russians the word of the cross is a trap, an opiate for the people; and to the Americans it is folly. For the Russians demand a visible sign of class victory in an economic world, and the Americans demand the know-how of success in a material universe."

II

When we have said this and made our confession of unbelief, we know the cross remains. Stumbling block and nonsense that it is to us who are perishing, it stands untouched by our rejection of it. The reality that does not fit into our wisdom remains in history. This offense to our desire to survive survives. It survives in its very negation. The communism which fights against it affirms its power in the denial— and re-enacts crucifixions. The Christendom which undertakes to twist the meaning of the cross into something that will fit into its wisdom confesses to its presence and power by its uneasy, guilty conscience. The cross survives in our society and in our history against all the efforts of its foes to eradicate it and of its apparent friends to hide it behind lilies. In our own lives it survives the questionings and rebellions of our youth and the cynicisms and accommodations of our aged. It survives not only through the churches but also despite them, not only through the colleges and universities but in contradiction to them. It survives in our historical memory as the memory of a murder must survive in the mind of a criminal. It survives as the memory of the death of a beloved brother remains in the mind of a man who witnesses it. Indeed, it was both a murder and a brother's death. It is built into our history more solidly than the Copernican, the French, and Russian revolutions.

This cross of Christ which is in our history is not an argument. It is not a hypothesis with which we come to history. It is not a philosophy or theology or any set of beliefs. Philosophies and theologies cluster around it, but it itself is a simple, stark event. To be sure it does not stand alone but is the focusing point of the life of a man, of the story of a people, of the faith of a new community, and yet it is a simple event. The cross in history may be compared to the kind of an event which an astronomer means when, having computed the positions of the planets with the aid of his excellent Ptolemaean wisdom he discovers a planet in a position that does not fit into the scheme. His whole wisdom is called into question, and eventually the Copernican or Einsteinian revolution of his science may result. So the cross as a simple event calls into question the foundations of our worldly wisdom. It raises the question whether our principal assumption is not fallacious. This ultimate assumption is that we *are perishing*. On this we build the practical and theoretic wisdom of our time. This gives us our orientation. When the cross raises the question about the truth of that first assumption it does not lead us to the opposite, to the affirmation that we are not perishing. It does not deny the wisdom completely, any more than Copernican astronomy denies Ptolemaean astronomy. The cross rather raises the question whether we do not need a presupposition beyond the one we have adopted. Not whether we come from nothing and go to nothing but whether beyond that nothing there is not Being. The new hypothesis: We are being saved. We are indeed coming through disaster, but we will not be lost. The cross does not deny the reality of death. It reinforces it. It denies its finality. In various ways by means of our theology we may ask how it is that from the cross we come to raise this question and make this great assumption: "We are perishing" to this other one, "We are being saved"? However we explain the transition, this remains the fact, that in our history the *cross has been and is that demonstration of the power of God whereby that conversion of the first principle of our thought is accomplished.* However we may explain it, the cross of Christ in human history is a challenge to that second formulation of the wisdom of the perishing which is made when we say that self-preservation is the first law of life. Again the cross of Christ does not lead us to make the opposite assumption, that self-crucifixion is the first law of life. But it does raise before us the immeasurable possibility that we could begin our thinking with the statement "God's preservation of ourselves is the first law of our history."

When we believe that we are perishing we see ourselves in a world surrounded by foes. We interpret the presence of the foes with the suspicious attitude of those who see death, in the whole environment. When the cross rises into view the scene is changed. It does not make our enemies into friends, to be sure, but it does bring us at least dimly to the realization that foes and friends in our environment are all under the control of the final prevailing love of God. We learn somehow to say, "I am persuaded that neither life nor death, nor the heedlessness of nature, nor the blind operation of natural laws, nor the fateful forces of history, nor the cruelty of men, nor the strange forces within me, nor any other awful thing can separate us from the love of God which is in Christ Jesus our Lord." Here is a new beginning for a wisdom which is not the strategy of survival but the strategy of salvation, reconciliation, resurrection. It is the kind of wisdom which we see exemplified in the struggles of sick people who believe they are getting well and in the bravery under opposition which folk in occupied countries manifest when they are assured that they are being liberated.

On the basis of this new beginning we struggle toward new wisdom in every field. We are required to do [a] new kind of thinking about history and nature as well as to develop a new kind of practical, ethical wisdom. We must seek to work it out in all the strategies of life, in our education, our political obedience, our religious worship, in our whole cultural life. The wisdom of the cross does not lead us to the kind of thinking that removes us from the world of active duties. On the contrary, it asks us to deal with all of these active needs from the point of view of men who believe that they are being saved instead of believing that they are perishing. This is indeed the wisdom and the power of God with which we are dealing here. It is not a wisdom and a power which we can acquire in any ready-made fashion for ourselves. The cross is a challenge to think, not to substitute dogma for thinking. It is a challenge to interpret experience, not substitute the experience of ancient men for our own. The wisdom of being saved, however, is not only one which we must appropriate intellectually. It is something that needs to reach deep into our emotional and unconscious life. For all the wisdom of the perishing is not a purely intellectual wisdom. It is based on deep, dark affairs which lie beyond the reach of our conceptual thinking. And so must the wisdom of the cross enter into the deepest parts of our personal life where it can and does bring about the change in the affairs and lives and hopes of the living, dying, rising self.

Man's Work and God's

Lord, thou hast been our dwelling place in all generations.
Before the mountains were brought forth,
    or ever thou hadst formed the earth and the world,
    from everlasting to everlasting thou art God.
The days of our years are threescore years and ten,
Or even by reason of strength fourscore years;
Yet is their pride but labor and sorrow;
For it is soon gone and we fly away. . . .
Return, O Lord; how long?
And let it repent thee concerning thy servants.
O satisfy us in the morning with thy lovingkindness,
That we may rejoice and be glad all our days.
Let they work appear unto thy servants,
And thy glory upon their children.
And let the favor of the Lord our God be upon us;
And establish thou the work of our hands upon us;
Yea, the work of our hands establish thou it. Psalm 90: 1–2, 10, 13–17[1]

I

The Ninetieth Psalm is one of the world's great poems. It sings with the melody and harmony of music. The thought of God's eternity and the idea of human transiency are interwoven in its verses like theme and counter-theme in a symphonic movement. As in so much music there is in it the "sense of regret and melancholy for the impermanence of human things, of sorrow for the loveliness that was and is no longer."[2] Yet the Psalm is no "Symphony Pathetique." It does not end upon a note of melancholy resignation, but rather with a kind of trumpet call of passionate hope and assertion: Let the favor of the Lord our God be upon us, and establish thou the work of our hands; yea! The work of our hands, establish thou it!

If at first glance or as a result of liturgical associations the poem seems to us to be a dirge, fit to be sung at funerals, or pored over by the aged in their declining years, better acquaintance leads us to understand it as a song of work, a prayer to be said as we go about our business in school and church and nation. It speaks of our condition as workers and intertwines the themes of human and divine labor.

It culminates in the prayer that arises out of reflection on the impermanence of human existence. We know that we are passing; that we are such stuff as dreams are made of, that in the ceaseless march of the generations we shall pass away like waves of the sea. But in this transient life we like to think that our work will abide and that our lives will have been made meaningful by their contributions to structures that endure. So the scholar thinks of science, the grand structure of knowledge to which he is allowed to add some refinement of method, some new understanding of the real. So the citizen thinks of his nation; the churchman of his church. All of us in past decades have been taught to think like this of our civilization, the work of our hands which will outlast us and to which we are permitted to add some valuable addition.

But when we have taken comfort from the fact that our transient personal life is given a kind of immortality by its participation in the construction of enduring works, we are again made disconsolate by the realization that this too must pass away. We are reminded by history that "all our pomp of yesterday is one with Nineveh and Tyre."[3] We look on ruined statues and read on broken stone the vain inscription, "My name is Ozymandias, king of kings, look on my works ye mighty, and despair."[4] We see upon the horizon of the impending future the storm-clouds of destruction and gaze upon the skyscrapers of our cities, the granite halls of our capitols, with the prophecy ringing in our ears: "Not one stone will be left upon another" [Mark 13:2; Luke 21:6].

Our sense of the impermanence of our work arises not only out of our view of history, out of our participation in the work of civilization and our knowledge of the transiency of culture in its great aspects. It becomes more personal and more poignant as we repeat over and over again the same chores we did yesterday and which we know must be done again tomorrow. There is a great frustration in the work of the householder. There is no cleansing of linen or of dishes which must not be done over again tomorrow or within a few hours; no satisfaction of the human appetites which must not give way to hunger. John Masefield speaks for all the suppliers of our perennial needs: "To get the whole world out of bed / And washed, and dressed, and warmed, and fed, / To work, and back to bed again, / Believe me, Saul, costs worlds of pain."[5] The endless repetition of work which adds nothing permanent is the lot of teacher and doctor and statesman, of preacher and lawyer, of farmer and store-keeper, and banker. Where is the slum-clearance project which provides for the prevention of all new slums?

When can the statesman make an enduring peace which will not need to be remade tomorrow in the presence of new issues? What curing of diseases contains within it a guarantee that no new illness will undo the work that has been done? What consolation and forgiveness offered by the Gospel, will not need to be repeated tomorrow as new stains and new griefs come to men?

Again we are made disconsolate in the midst of work which should give enduring meaning to our lives by the reflection that the labors we expend may be used, and probably will be used, not only constructively but destructively. The mother who "did not raise her boy to be a soldier" finds that he has indeed become a soldier, subject to destruction and required to be a destroyer. The scientist who seeks to add to the structure of welfare and peace, finds that he has created or made possible the creation of new instruments of destruction. The statesman who has made peace between nations, discovers that he has forged a new alliance thereby, which may be potent for the destruction of peace. The reformer of the church finds that he has sown the seeds for a new deformation. The preacher discovers that with his preaching of the Gospel he has increased the fears of men and contributed to internal division in the soul.

II

In this situation in the midst of our impermanent and destructive works, which yet give meaning to our existence, we pray as the Psalmist did. The prayer of the Ninetieth Psalm is a universal and ever human prayer. It asks for two things for which we all ask, though we are not always conscious of doing so: Let thy work appear unto thy servants; and establish thou the work of our hands.

Let thy work appear unto thy servants. Sometimes we feel in the midst of these many tasks in our vast world as though we were laborers in a gigantic factory where something is being made that we can never see. We are being required to stamp out this piece of sheet metal, to make this handle, to tighten this bolt—and to do all this over and over again without knowing what the whole process is all about. Occasionally we may be attacked by doubt in the midst of the vast confusion, the noises and the apparently random movements going on about us. Then we are inclined to say—"nothing is being accomplished, nothing is going on. We are being driven to meaningless chores by blind, chanceful or willful taskmasters." But for the most part we fundamentally believe that something is going on, something is being accomplished; that a mighty work is being accomplished; that this transient history of our seventy or so years and of our human centuries and millennia amounts to something. Yet we desperately desire to know what it is. So we make our silent or our public prayers to the transcendent One beyond all these many works and workers. Let thy work appear unto thy servants. Show us what you are doing with all the things that we are doing. Show us what it is that we are working on. Let the beauty of the Lord our God be upon us. We dimly see and hope that this is something glorious on which we are engaged. Something which, if we knew what it was, we could take pride in acknowledging as a work we had been allowed to serve.

And then we add to that prayer for the revelation of the whole purpose and meaning of history this second petition: Establish thou the work of our hands. Build this particular thing that we are doing into the permanent structure. Establish it, not for our glory, but as a part of something in which we can rejoice because it is truly good. This is the prayer of every parent for his child. He has labored and suffered for its training, its health and well-being. He knows that he has made grievous errors, but here is his work—not something he has made but a being on which he has expended his labor and for the sake of whom he exists. O God, he cannot but pray, establish thou my work; make my child a citizen of thy kingdom; establish it, glorify it; use it; preserve it. It is the prayer of the pastor for his people. Of the teacher for his students. Of the statesman for his nation. It is the prayer which we all make consciously or unconsciously for our culture, for this whole work of our hands on which we labor all our lives and which is forever threatened with destruction or decay.

III

Is this prayer, this universal human prayer, ever answered? One might offer many illustrations of its partial answer from personal and from social history. But we shall do well to concentrate on one demonstration of answer to such a prayer. It is the demonstration which is before us in this Ninetieth Psalm. Here is the prayer but here also is the answer.

Here is a poem—the work of a man's hand and of his brain and doubtless of his whole mind and body. It endures. Here it is on the printed page of the Bible. There it is in the hymnals and the anthologies. But much more than that, it is engraved, partly as a whole, upon the memories of millions of men. It is built into the emotions and affections of generations. Here are the enduring words echoing in this unsubstantial air: "Lord, thou hast been our dwelling place in all generations. Before the mountains were brought forth, or ever thou hadst formed the earth and the world, from everlasting to everlasting thou art God." If anything is established among us, this work is established. It is more ancient than the Forum and it is whole. It is older than the cathedrals and far more widely used. It is no historic ruin, artificially preserved to remind men of old forgotten things but a house that people dwell in, where they find nourishment and rest.

How was this work established? How was this prayer answered? Evidently it was not established without the labor of the poet who passed away after his threescore years and ten, or who like many another singer died in this youth. The worker had something to do with the endurance of his work.

For one thing he was a good craftsman. There may be flaws in the poem from the point of view of craftsmanship which a critic could point out. But it is nevertheless the work of a master artist who spared no pains. Perhaps only those who have tried to write poems will understand how this apparently effortless music represents years of struggle to master the art, how much revision was necessary for the polishing of these gems of phrase, how long was the period of reflection before inspiration came, how difficult was the transition from inspiration to accomplishment.

For another thing this workman used good materials, honest stuff. He used the most permanent though apparently most transitory material—human emotions, the long, long thoughts of men, the longings of their souls, their wonder in the presence of the eternal mystery, their reverence before the Creator of heaven and earth, their tendency toward despair, their reviving hopes.

The editor of the *Oxford Book of Christian Verse* asks in his preface why his collection must be so thin.[6] An anthology of love poetry, he points out, would be a fat volume but good religious verse is scarce. He gives a number of reasons why this is so. For one thing, religious emotions are not felt so profoundly by so many people as the emotions of human love. But a chief reason for the dearth of first-rate religious verse, the writer points out, is that men appearing before the Almighty pretend to be more respectable than they are. And good poetry cannot be constructed out of pretended emotion, or out of anything but the honest stuff of life itself. The Psalmists, he goes on to say, like John Donne, were honest men. They appeared before God and in their art, as they were—full of doubt and love and anger and every human emotion. They did not come to their art in Sunday dress but in workday garments; with no piously composed faces but with all their sins and virtues equally, honestly written on their brows and in their eyes. Again this workman contributed something of importance by the manner in which he did his work. He did not labor for his own glory. His name is not recorded. He did not provide by means of a bold signature at the head of the poem for his own remembrance. The Psalm is now ascribed to Moses, but Moses is not made famous by it. Whoever wrote it, tried only to work carefully and honestly without reference to his own fame, fortune or endurance. All that, he left to the one to whom he prayed.

Yet none of these contributions made by the craftsman and the artist established his work. More was needed than he could supply if his work was to be established, his prayer answered. And, indeed, much over which he had no control happened to his product.

His work was established by deeds not his own. It was given endurance in part by its inclusion in a large structure that built into unity the labors of many. It was included in the hymn-book of the synagogue along with the Psalms of many other poets, good artists also who had worked without reference to their own glory, had spared no pains, had used good material. It was included in the Bible, together with the books of evangelists and apostles. It was included in the Scriptures of the Jewish people along with the works of prophets, lawgivers, and chroniclers of history. It was included in the mighty epic, the great history, the magnificent proclamation of God's care for the world manifest and to be manifest finally in Jesus Christ.

The human work was established by being made a part of the showing forth of that great artistry and statesmanship of God for which the Psalmist prayed: "Let thy work appear unto thy servants, and thy glory upon their children." Show us, Almighty and Transcendent Being, what you are doing. And the Transcendent One made that very petition a part of the revelation of his work. For by this poem, too, in its setting, with its companion pieces, we are enabled to see, though dimly still, and more by faith than sight, that this whole story of our human life is the story of a supernal, everlasting creation and a cosmic redemption, of God's own artistry and God's own liberation of his world from dull-ness and shame, from immorality and brutality, from destruction and decay.

Our own prayers for the establishment of our work and for the mak-ing known to us of the meaning of all existence will not be answered, surely, in any other way than was the Psalmist's. They will not be an-swered without our efforts. Our shabby work, our faithless cutting of corners, our efforts to get by, these will but furnish fuel for the world's Gehennas where all the trash we men produce and accumulate must be destroyed if there is to be any glory. Yet even our best work cannot endure unless the transcendent power in being that presides over and works in all our working includes what we do in its deed, a deed not of final destruction but of final recreation. Not of enslavement to fu-tility but of liberation to action, not of death dealing but of life-giving.

Notes

FOREWORD

1. All quotations included in this foreword, save that from a letter, come from personal journals kept by H. Richard Niebuhr. These journals are not available to the public.

INTRODUCTION

1. For biographical information, see Jon Diefenthaler, *H. Richard Niebuhr: A Lifetime of Reflections on the Church and the World* (Macon, Ga.: Mercer University Press, 1986); and James W. Fowler, *To See the Kingdom: The Theological Vision of H. Richard Niebuhr* (Nashville and New York: Abingdon Press, 1974). For Niebuhr's writings, see the bibliographies compiled by Fowler (277–283) and by William G. Chrystal, "The Young H. Richard Niebuhr," *Theology Today* 38 (1981): 231–35. For helpful background data, though with questionable psychohistorical judgments about HRN, see Richard Wightman Fox, *Reinhold Niebuhr: A Biography* (San Francisco: Harper & Row, 1985). Also illuminating is William G. Chrystal, *A Father's Mantle: The Legacy of Gustav Niebuhr*, fwd. by Richard R. Niebuhr (New York: Pilgrim Press, 1982). For interpretations of Niebuhr's theology, see the essays collected in Paul Ramsey, ed., *Faith and Ethics: The Theology of H. Richard Niebuhr* (New York: Harper & Row, 1957; rev. ed., 1965); and Ronald F. Thiemann, ed., *The Legacy of H. Richard Niebuhr*, Harvard Theological Studies, no. 36 (Minneapolis: Fortress Press, 1991).

2. One essay survives from HRN's time at Union: "Kingdom, Gospel, and Otherworldliness" (1919), Archives, Andover-Harvard Theological Library. In the midst of the despair following the First World War, already in this essay Niebuhr is critical of the optimistic "Kingdom" theology of the nineteenth

century, and he finds himself wondering whether the church will seek and find a new otherworldliness. See HRN, "Towards a New Other-Worldliness," *Theology Today* 1 (1944): 78–87.

3. Niebuhr himself acknowledged this indebtedness in the prefaces to two of his books: HRN, *The Meaning of Revelation* (New York: Macmillan, 1941), x [1967 pbk., xi]; idem, *Christ and Culture* (New York: Harper & Brothers, 1951), xii. In 1962 he listed Troeltsch's *Social Teaching of the Christian Churches* as one of the ten most influential books in his life. HRN, "Ex Libris," *Christian Century* 79 (June 13, 1962): 754.

4. On the "church" and "sect" types, see Ernst Troeltsch, *Die Soziallehren der christlichen Kirchen und Gruppe* (Tübingen: J. C. B. Mohr [Paul Siebeck], 1912) [ET:*The Social Teaching of the Christian Churches*, trans. Olive Wyon, 2 vols. (London: George Allen & Unwin, 1931)].

5. See HRN, "Can German and American Christians Understand Each Other?" *Christian Century* 47 (July 23, 1930): 914–16; and HRN's letters, entitled "Some Observations on Life in Germany," published from time to time in *Evangelical Herald* 29 (July 1930): 556–57, 575; 29 (August 1930): 676–77, 695–96. See also idem, "German-American Relations," *Evangelical Herald* 29 (September 1930): 713, 715; idem, "Germany After the Election," *Evangelical Herald* 29 (November 1930): 911, 915; idem, "Some Observations on Russia, I," and "Some Observations on Russia, II," *Evangelical Herald* 29 (October 1930): 795–96, 815–16.

6. The label "neo-orthodoxy" became attached to a celebrated list of twentieth-century Protestant theologians who mounted a radical rethinking of the heritage of nineteenth-century liberalism. United more by common themes than by any substantive consensus, the list included Karl Barth, Eduard Thurneyson, and Emil Brunner in Switzerland; Rudolph Bultmann and Friedrich Gogarten in Germany; Paul Tillich, and the Niebuhrs in the United States; Anders Nygren and Gustav Aulén in Sweden; John Baillie, Donald M. Baillie, and T. F. Torrance in Scotland; and (to some extent) William Temple in England. In addition to the writings of these authors, consult the discussion and bibliographies in Alasdair I. C. Herron, *A Century of Protestant Theology* (Philadelphia: Westminster, 1980), chs. 3–6; and James C. Livingston, *Modern Christian Thought: From the Enlightenment to Vatican II* (New York: Macmillan, 1971), chs. 11, 12, and 15.

7. HRN, "From the Religion of Humanity to the Religion of God," *Theological Magazine of the Evangelical Synod of North America* 57 (November 1929): 401–9. Idem, "Toward the Independence of the Church," in H. Richard Niebuhr, Wilhelm Pauck, and Francis P. Miller, *The Church Against the World* (Chicago and New York: Willett, Clark, 1935), 123–24.

8. Karl Barth, *Der Römerbrief,* Erste Fassung (Bern: G. A. Bäschlin, 1919); Zweite Fassung (Munich: Chr. Kaiser Verlag, 1922). Niebuhr's personal copy of *Der Römerbrief* was presented by Richard R. Niebuhr as a gift to HRN's former student, Hans Frei, of the Yale University faculty.

9. HRN, "Ex Libris," 754. Idem, "Reformation: Continuing Imperative," *Christian Century* 77 (March 2, 1960): 248–51; reprinted in *How My Mind Has*

Changed, ed. Harold E. Fey (Cleveland and New York: World Publishing, Meridian Books, 1961), 69–80.

10. See HRN, "Translator's Preface," in Paul Tillich, *The Religious Situation*, trans. H. Richard Niebuhr (New York: Henry Holt, 1932), vii–xxii.

11. Paul Tillich to HRN, October 25, 1957, in Manuscript Collection, Andover-Harvard Theological Library.

12. HRN, *The Responsible Self: An Essay in Christian Moral Philosophy* (New York: Harper & Row, 1963), 126.

13. HRN, *The Kingdom of God in America* (New York: Harper & Row, 1937).

14. Ibid., 193.

15. HRN, *The Meaning of Revelation*, x [pbk., xi].

16. Ibid., 68 [pbk., 69].

17. Albert C. Outler to Charles E. Raynall III, April 24, 1986, letter courtesy of Charles E. Raynall III.

18. For an excellent study of Niebuhr's work as viewed through the lens of *Christ and Culture*, see Douglas F. Ottati, *Meaning and Method in H. Richard Niebuhr's Theology* (Washington, D.C.: University Press of America, 1982).

19. See *The Meaning of Revelation*, 185–86 [pbk., 134–35].

20. HRN, *Radical Monotheism and Western Culture* (Lincoln: University of Nebraska Press, 1960); reprinted and revised: *Radical Monotheism and Western Culture, with Supplementary Essays* (New York: Harper & Row, 1960).

21. HRN, *Faith on Earth: An Inquiry into the Structure of Human Faith*, ed. Richard R. Niebuhr (New Haven: Yale University Press, 1989).

22. HRN, *The Purpose of the Church and Its Ministry: Reflections on the Aims of Theological Education* (New York: Harper & Brothers, 1956); *The Ministry in Historical Perspectives*, ed. H. Richard Niebuhr and Daniel Day Williams (New York: Harper & Brothers, 1956); *The Advancement of Theological Education*, H. Richard Niebuhr, Daniel Day Williams, and James M. Gustafson (New York: Harper & Brothers, 1957).

23. For a helpful account of how Niebuhr's ethics might have unfolded, see James M. Gustafson, "Introduction," to *The Responsible Self*, 1–41.

24. For the abbreviated version, see HRN, "On the Meaning of Responsibility," lecture delivered at Cambridge University, May 25, 1960, Archives, Andover-Harvard Theological Library.

25. Three essays from the unpublished corpus have been published in journals and for that reason have not been included: HRN, "Reflections on Faith, Hope, and Love," *Journal of Religious Ethics* 2:1 (1974): 151–56; idem, "The Social Gospel and the Mind of Jesus," ed. D. Yeager, *Journal of Religious Ethics* 16:1 (1988): 109–27; idem, "The Limitation of Power and Religious Liberty," ed. W. S. Johnson, *Religion and Values in Public Life* 3:2 (1995): 1–4.

26. For a partial bibliography of the unpublished papers, see Fowler, *To See the Kingdom*, 281–83.

27. See Dorothy Ruth Parks, "The Cole Lectures: A History of Distinction," *The Spire*, Vanderbilt University Divinity School and Oberlin Graduate School of Theology, Commemorative Issue, 15:2 (1993): 10–14.

28. Among Schleiermacher studies, see Richard R. Niebuhr, *Schleiermacher on*

Christ and Religion: A New Introduction (New York: Scribner, 1964); Martin Redeker, *Friedrich Schleiermacher: Leben und Werk* (Berlin: Walter de Gruyter, 1968); Brian Gerrish, *Tradition and the Modern World: Reformed Theology in the Nineteenth Century* (Chicago: University of Chicago Press, 1978); idem, *The Old Protestantism and the New: Essays on the Reformation Heritage* (Chicago: University of Chicago Press, 1982). The classic work from the eschatological theologians is Jürgen Moltmann, *Theologie der Hoffnung* (Munich: Chr. Kaiser Verlag, 1965) [ET: *The Theology of Hope*, trans. J. W. Leitch (New York: Harper & Row, 1967)].

29. HRN, "The Old-Time Religion Isn't Good Enough," handwritten sermon preached at Connecticut College on October 25, 1959, and at Guilford Congregational Church on December 4, 1959, Archives, Andover-Harvard Theological Library.

30. See HRN's early article, "Theology and Psychology: A Sterile Union," *Christian Century* 44 (January 13, 1927): 47–48, in which he speaks of Schleiermacher's emphasis on feeling as a "blind alley."

31. HRN, *Faith on Earth*, 117.

32. HRN, "The Disorder of Man in the Church of God," in *Man's Disorder and God's Design*, Amsterdam Assembly Series, 4 vols., vol. 1, *The Universal Church in God's Design* (New York: Harper & Brothers, 1949), 78–88; idem, "Who are the Unbelievers and What Do They Believe?" report submitted to the Secretariat for Evangelism, World Council of Churches, in *The Christian Hope and the Task of the Church: Six Ecumenical Surveys and the Report of the Assembly Prepared by the Advisory Commission on the Main Theme, 1954* (New York, 1954), 35–37. A copy of this report is among the unpublished HRN papers at Harvard.

33. HRN, *The Social Sources of Denominationalism* (New York: Henry Holt, 1929); idem, "The Gift of Catholic Vision," *Theology Today* 4 (1948): 507–21.

34. Niebuhr's papers include a set of student notes from the fall term, 1950, entitled "The Christian Interpretation of History." Archives, Andover-Harvard Theological Library. In his opening lecture, Niebuhr spoke of that interpretation as an "experimental" and "relatively new" discipline.

35. HRN, *The Kingdom of God in America*, xiii.

36. HRN, "A Communication: The Only Way Into the Kingdom of God" *Christian Century* 49 (April 6, 1932): 447.

37. See HRN, *Radical Monotheism and Western Culture with Supplementary Essays*, 38, 112. See HRN, Class Lecture in Christian Ethics, March 28, 1952, Student Lecture Notes, Archives, Andover-Harvard Theological Library.

38. See *The Meaning of Revelation*, pref. and ch. 1.

39. Cf. HRN, "Living Tradition in Theology," handwritten lecture outline, delivered at Hartford Theological Seminary, October 1956, and at Illif School of Theology, January 22, 1957, in Archives, Andover-Harvard Theological Library.

40. *The Meaning of Revelation*, ch. 2.

41. Other essays in this volume prepared for the "Theological Discussion Group" include "Reinhold Niebuhr's Interpretation of History" and "The Kingdom of God and Eschatology in the Social Gospel and in Barthianism." Another paper HRN prepared for the group was published posthumously in

1974: "Reflections on Faith, Hope, and Love," *Journal of Religious Ethics* 2:1 (1974): 151–56.

42. For more on the group, see Samuel McCrea Cavert, "The Younger Theologians," *Religion in Life* 5 (1936): 520–31. For HRN's participation, see Diefenthaler, *A Lifetime of Reflections*, 32–33.

43. See HRN, *The Meaning of Revelation*, pref.

44. Reinhold Niebuhr, *Faith and History: A Comparison of Christian and Modern Views of History* (New York: Scribner, 1949). Diefenthaler believes HRN's paper was presented in 1949 (*A Lifetime of Reflections*, 65 n. 36).

45. Richard B. Miller, ed., *War in the Twentieth Century: Sources in Theological Ethics*, Library of Theological Ethics (Louisville, Ky.: Westminster/John Knox Press, 1992), 3–5.

46. HRN, "The Grace of Doing Nothing," *Christian Century* 49 (March 23, 1932): 378–80.

47. Reinhold Niebuhr, "Must We Do Nothing?" *Christian Century* 49 (March 30, 1932): 415–17.

48. HRN, "A Communication: The Only Way Into the Kingdom of God," 447.

49. HRN, "From the Religion of Humanity to the Religion of God." 401–9.

50. HRN, "Between Barth and Schleiermacher," unpublished fragment, Archives, Andover-Harvard Theological Library: "Between Barth, the great objectivist in theology . . . and Schleiermacher, the great subjectivist . . . I cannot judge so as to say that the one is right and the other wrong. Nor do I know of a human court which can make the judgment"(2).

51. The title originally was "Kingdom of God and Eschatology (Social Gospel and Barthianism)," a topic assigned to HRN by the "Theological Discussion Group."

52. In addition to *The Kingdom of God in America*, important published essays on these themes include HRN, "From the Religion of Humanity to the Religion of God," 401–9; idem, "The Social Gospel and the Liberal Theology," *The Keryx* 22 (May 1931): 12–13, 18; idem, "Faith, Works, and Social Salvation," *Religion in Life* 1 (1932): 426–30; and idem, "The Attack Upon the Social Gospel," *Religion in Life* 5 (1936): 176–81. See also the posthumously published piece, dating from 1933: "The Social Gospel and the Mind of Jesus," ed. Yeager, 109–27.

53. HRN, "The Social Gospel and the Liberal Theology" 18. [available from the Archives of Eden Theological Seminary].

54. See HRN, "The Social Gospel and the Mind of Jesus," 126. This was an address before the American Theological Society on April 21, 1933, which HRN did not publish during his lifetime. The term "revolutionary strategy" appears in idem, "The Attack Upon the Social Gospel," 181.

55. Karl Barth, *Die Kirchliche Dogmatik*, Zweiter Band, *Die Lehre von Gott*, Zweiter Halbband (Zurich: Evangelischer Verlag Zollikon, 1942). Niebuhr's assessment of Barth's statements about ethics in the earlier part-volume, *Die Kirchliche Dogmatik* 1:2, had been largely negative. See HRN, "Theology and the Critique

of the Christian Life," handwritten manuscript, n.d., Archives, Andover-Harvard Theological Library.

56. See Leo Sandon, "Jonathan Edwards and H. Richard Niebuhr," *Religious Studies* 12 (1976): 101–15; idem, "H. Richard Niebuhr's Interpretation of the American Tradition" (Ph.D. diss., Boston University, 1985); and Thomas A. Byrnes, "H. Richard Niebuhr's Reconstruction of Jonathan Edwards' Moral Theology," in *Annual of the Society of Christian Ethics*, 1985, ed., Alan B. Anderson (Washington, D.C.: Georgetown University Press), 19–32.

57. HRN, "Ex Libris," 754.

58. Jonathan Edwards, *Ethical Writings*, ed. Paul Ramsey, vol. 8 of *The Works of Jonathan Edwards*, ed. Harry S. Stout (New Haven: Yale University Press, 1989).

59. Martin Buber, *Ich und Du* (1923), in *Werke*, vol. 1, *Schriften zur Philosophie* (Munich: Kösel, 1962) [ET: *I and Thou*, trans. Ronald Gregor Smith, 2nd ed. (New York: Scribner, 1958)].

60. HRN, "Reformation: Continuing Imperative," 248–51.

61. See HRN, "Radical Faith in Political Community," in *Radical Monotheism and Western Culture with Supplementary Essays*, ch. 5, esp. p. 70.

62. HRN put this point with exceptional clarity in an address to the Fellowship of Christian Socialists: HRN, "The Christian Church in the World's Crisis," *Christianity and Society* 6:3 (1941): 11–17. See Diefenthaler, "World War and Democracy," in *A Lifetime of Reflections*, ch. 3.

63. Niebuhr had made a similar point in *The Kingdom of God in America*, 75–87, and in an unpublished lecture from 1939. See HRN, "The Limitation of Power and Religious Liberty," typescript of an address delivered at the Institution of Human Relations, Williamstown, Massachusetts, on August 27, 1939, Archives, Andover-Harvard Theological Library. See also HRN, "The Protestant Movement and Democracy in the United States," in *The Shaping of American Religion*, ed. James W. Smith and Leland Jamison (Princeton: Princeton University Press, 1961), 20–71.

64. HRN planned a comprehensive treatise on Christian ethics, to be completed in his retirement; judging from his courses on the subject at Yale, it would have included more sustained reflection on concrete moral problems than has survived in his published works. See, e.g., HRN, Christian Ethics Lectures, 1960–61; idem, Miscellaneous Lecture Notes, 1958–59; idem, Christian Ethics Course, 1952, Student Lecture Notes, all in Archives, Andover-Harvard Theological Library.

65. HRN, "War as the Judgment of God," *Christian Century* 59 (May 3, 1942): 630–33; idem, "Is God in the War?" 59 (August 5, 1942): 953–55; idem, "War as Crucifixion," 60 (April 28, 1943): 513–15. For an analysis of these and the earlier articles from the 1930s, see Richard B. Miller, *Interpretations in Conflict: Ethics, Pacifism and the Just-War Tradition* (Chicago: University of Chicago Press, 1991), ch. 5; idem, "H. Richard Niebuhr's War Articles: A Transvaluation of Value," *Journal of Religion* 68 (April 1988): 242–62. All Niebuhr's war articles are reprinted in Miller, *War in the Twentieth Century*.

66. HRN, "War as Crucifixion," 515.

67. See R. L. Calhoun et al., "The Relation of the Church to the War in the

Light of the Christian Faith," *Social Action* 10 (December 15, 1944): 3–79. Partial, edited versions are reproduced in John H. Leith, ed., *Creeds of the Churches: A Reader in Christian Doctrine from the Bible to the Present*, 3d ed. (Atlanta: John Knox Press, 1982), 522–54; and in Miller, *War in the Twentieth Century*, 71–124.

68. Robert L. Calhoun to Reinhold Niebuhr, November 27, 1944, in possession of Albert C. Outler, courtesy of Charles E. Raynall III. Said Calhoun: "Since Richard has been so miserable during the past two months I have been unwilling to bother him. . . . Since he had so fundamental a share in preparing the material on which the [commission's report] is based, and since I checked with him on certain intermediate stages of revision and have tried to take into account his reactions. . . . it has seemed to me quite intolerable that Dick's name should not be included."

69. For HRN, vicarious suffering demonstrates the tragedy of human existence and hence suggests that the "analogy of war and crucifixion . . . [is] more than an analogy" ("War as Crucifixion," 514). The Calhoun Commission, on the other hand, stated, "War is in a general sense a crucifixion of both man and God, but it is not the crucifixion of Jesus Christ, and it is not a chief source of man's salvation. What made the tragedy on Calvary uniquely redemptive was the Man on the middle cross, and the unmixed revelation of love and power that was in him" (Calhoun et al., "The Relation of the Church to the War," 38–39).

70. See HRN, "The Idea of Covenant and American Democracy," *Church History* 23 (1954): 126–35.

71. HRN to Reinhold Niebuhr, n.d. [1937], Reinhold Niebuhr Papers, Library of Congress, quoted in Fox, *Reinhold Niebuhr*, 183.

72. Reinhold Niebuhr, *Leaves From the Notebook of a Tamed Cynic*, fwd. by Martin Marty (New York: Harper & Row, 1929, 1957), 15.

73. See also HRN, "The Ethics of Survival," outline of a sermon preached at The College Church of the Claremont Colleges, March 4, 1962; and idem, "The Wisdom of Survival and the Logic of the Cross," sermon outline, n.d., Archives, Andover-Harvard Theological Library.

THE POSITION OF THEOLOGY TODAY

From "Next Steps in Theology," The Cole Lectures, Vanderbilt University, April 1961. HRN began the lecture with these brief remarks: "Dean Martin, Colleagues of the Faculty of the Divinity School of Vanderbilt University, Students and Friends. I have looked forward to this occasion with considerable trepidation knowing about the reputation of the Cole Lectureship as one of the distinguished theological lectureships in the country. I did not expect as I was looking toward this future that my anxiety would be so much increased by having the names of all the distinguished men named again and have before me one of those distinguished Cole lecturers of the past. But my anxiety is somewhat assuaged by the cordiality of your welcome and by the knowledge that we are all friends in this Christian theological community." The manuscript of the lecture begins with the following comments, which HRN deleted from his oral presentation, since he had changed the title of the lectures after the manuscript had been typed: "I have given to the course of lectures you have asked me to deliver the general title 'Theological Frontiers.' [HRN has crossed through this title in the manuscript and has written in by hand, 'Next Steps in Theology.'] In an important sense that title is a misnomer, for theology is never on the frontier. The front line in religion is always taken by priests and prophets, by evangelists and apostles. These are the ministers who live in direct encounter with human beings in all their concrete actuality, who must work in the truly new situations that arise every day. Theology is related to those task forces of the militant church as war colleges and military institutes located far back from the front, are related to fighting armies. Yet it is part of the duty of such institutes to look toward the future, to assess the probable movements of enemies and allies, to plan ahead. And so it is with the theology that we carry on in our schools, our training and research centers. No small part of our business in such seminaries as this is to think ten or twenty or thirty years ahead, to assess what opportunities and dilemmas our churches with their ministers will encounter, and so to make preparation for future battles. In this sense we can speak of theological frontiers."

1. P. T. Forsyth, *The Work of Christ* (London: Hodder & Stoughton, 1910), 144.

2. HRN is referring to the theological movement labeled, somewhat inaptly, "neo-orthodoxy," dating in Europe from the first edition of Karl Barth's *Römerbrief* (Bern: G. A. Bäschlin, 1919) and in the United States from Reinhold Niebuhr's *Moral Man and Immoral Society* (New York: Scribner, 1932).

3. If you want a scientific account of how a man rides a bicycle, read Michael Polanyi's *Personal Knowledge*; he knows something about a bicycle rider the bicycle rider himself does not know. [HRN's aside, referring to Michael Polanyi, *Personal Knowledge: Towards a Post-Critical Philosophy* (Chicago: University of Chicago Press, 1958), ch. 4.]

4. Think of Oscar Cullmann's *Christ and Time.* The big battle has been won, there are only mopping-up operations—what mopping-up operations! [HRN's aside, referring to Oscar Cullmann, *Christ and Time: The Primitive Conception of Time and History*, trans. Floyd V. Filson (Philadelphia: Westminster Press, 1962).]

5. See Johannes Weiss, *Die Predigt Jesu vom Reich Gottes*, 2d ed. (Gütersloh, 1900); idem, *Die Idee des Reiches Gottes in der Theologie* (Giessen, 1901); and Albert Schweitzer, *Vom Reimarus zu Wrede: Eine Geschichte der Leben-Jesu-Forschung* (Tübingen, 1906) [ET: *The Quest of the Historical Jesus: A Critical Study of its Progress from Reimarus to Wrede*, trans. W. Montgomery (New York: Macmillan, 1961)].

6. John Calvin, *Institutes of the Christian Religion*, 2 vols., trans. John Allen (Philadelphia: Presbyterian Board of Publication, 1932), 1:46.

7. This particular word is an interpolation from the voice recording. The sentence was an extemporaneous remark.

8. *Institutes,* 47.

9. Karl Barth, *Knowledge of God and the Service of God According to the Teaching of the Reformation: Recalling The Scottish Confession of 1560*, The Gifford Lectures

Delivered in the University of Aberdeen in 1937 and 1938, trans. J. L. M. Haire and Ian Henderson (London: Hodder & Stoughton, 1938), 26.

TOWARD NEW SYMBOLS

From "Next Steps in Theology," The Cole Lectures, Vanderbilt University, April, 1961. Typescript augmented by voice recording.

1. Joseph Lortz, *Die Reformation in Deutschland,* 2 vols., 3d ed. (Freiburg, 1949) [ET: *The Reformation in Germany,* trans. Ronald Walls, 2 vols. (New York: Herder & Herder, 1968)]. In an aside, HRN remarked, "Professor Sellers just informs me that he is bishop now." James Earl Sellers taught Christian ethics at Vanderbilt. HRN made similar references to the fresh quality of Luther's work in an unpublished paper, "Martin Luther and the Renewal of Human Confidence," typescript (21 pp.) of an address delivered at Valparaiso University, 1959, Archives, Andover-Harvard Theological Library.

2. Lortz, *The Reformation,* 1:483, 485. HRN is offering his own translation from the German text, *Die Reformation.*

3. Horace Bushnell, "Preliminary Dissertation on the Nature of Language As Related to Thought and Spirit," in *God in Christ: Three Discourses Delivered at New Haven, Cambridge, and Andover, with a Preliminary Dissertation on Language* (Hartford: Brown & Parsons, 1849); Jonathan Edwards, *Images or Shadows of Divine Things,* in Wallace E. Anderson, Mason I. Lowance Jr., and David H. Watters, eds., *The Typological Writings,* vol. 2 of *The Works of Jonathan Edwards,* ed. Harry Stout (New Haven: Yale University Press, 1957).

4. Ernst Cassirer, *The Philosophy of Symbolic Forms,* trans. Ralph Manheim, 3 vols. (New Haven: Yale University Press, 1953–57); Benjamin Lee Whorf, *Language, Thought, and Reality: Selected Writings,* ed. John B. Carroll (Cambridge: MIT Press, 1956); E. H. Gombrich, *Art and Illusion: A Study in the Psychology of Pictorial Representation* (New York: Pantheon, 1960). See also Philip Ellis Wheelwright, *The Burning Fountain: A Study in the Language of Symbolism* (Bloomington: Indiana University Press, 1954).

TOWARD THE RECOVERY OF FEELING

From "Next Steps in Theology," The Cole Lectures, Vanderbilt University, April 1961. Transcribed from voice recording.

1. The Russian cosmonaut Yuri Gagarin, who was the first human being to fly in space, on April 12, 1961.

2. See, e.g., A. J. Ayer, *Language, Truth and Logic* (New York: Dover, 1936; 2d ed., 1946).

3. Archibald MacLeish, *Poetry and Experience* (Cambridge: Riverside Press, 1961), 66.

4. R. G. Collingwood, *Principles of Art* (Oxford: Clarendon Press, 1938), 78–79.

5. HRN quotes from the RSV but changes "fornication" (*porneía*) to "immorality."

6. Editor's interpolation from a brief gap in the tape recording.

7. Jonathan Edwards, *Religious Affections*, ed. John E. Smith, vol. 2 of *The Works of Jonathan Edwards*, ed. Harry Stout (New Haven: Yale University Press, 1959).

8. Sermon preached July 8, 1741, in Enfield, Connecticut, "Sinners in the Hands of an Angry God," in Jonathan Edwards, *Works of President Edwards*, ed. Sereno E. Dwight, 10 vols. (New York: S. Converse, 1829–30) 7:163–177.

9. Erik H. Erikson, *Childhood and Society* (New York: Norton, 1950).

10. Jonathan Edwards, *Religious Affections*, 99 (cf. 95).

THE DOCTRINE OF THE TRINITY AND THE UNITY OF THE CHURCH

Originally published in *Theology Today* (1946): 371–84.

1. D. C. Macintosh, *The Reasonableness of Christianity* (New York: Scribner, 1928), 155.

2. McGiffert, *The God of the Early Christians* (New York: Scribner, 1924), esp. ch. 2.

3. Nathan Söderblom, *Vater, Sohn und Geist* (Tübingen, 1909), 63f.

4. Emanuel Swedenborg, *The True Christian Religion*, Everyman's Library (London: J. M. Dent, 1900), 5, 3.

5. George A. Gordon, *My Education and Religion. An Autobiography* (Boston, 1925), 55–56.

6. Söderblom, *The True Christian Religion*, 44–45, 69ff.

7. Channing, *Unitarian Christianity and Other Essays* (New York: Liberal Arts Press, 1957), 23, 22.

THE CHURCH DEFINES ITSELF IN THE WORLD

Undated typescript, ca. 1957.

1. Paul Weiss, *Modes of Being* (Carbondale: Southern Illinois University, 1958), ch. 1.

2. "Being simply considered," a term of art, was used by Jonathan Edwards to indicate all of reality with God at its head. See Jonathan Edwards, *The Nature of True Virtue*, in *Ethical Writings*, ed. Paul Ramsey, vol. 8 of *The Works of Jonathan Edwards*, ed. Harry Stout (New Haven: Yale University Press, 1989).

A THEOLOGIAN'S APPROACH TO HISTORY

Handwritten manuscript of an address to the American History Association in Washington, D.C., December 30, 1955. A two-page typescript of introductory remarks is included at the beginning. The typescript contains the subtitle "History's Role in Theology."

1. R. G. Collingwood, *The Idea of History*, ed. T. M. Knox (New York: Oxford University Press, 1946).

2. René Descartes, *Discourse on Method*, in *Discourse on Method and Meditations*, trans. F. E. Suttcliffe (New York: Penguin, 1968), part 1.

3. At this point, HRN wrote "Illustration" in the margin.

REFLECTIONS ON THE CHRISTIAN THEORY OF HISTORY

Undated typescript prepared for the "Theological Discussion Group."

1. Editorial interpolation. See this comment from HRN's course at Yale entitled "The Christian Interpretation of History": "The eschatological problem is still a burr under the saddle. Sometimes we think the eschatological problem has been solved. Here is the Jesus of history, and the Jesus of history has a certain view of history, and he acts in history because he has a certain view of history, because he is a historical being. Or, making it more paradoxical, the problem is that there is a history in the Jesus of history, a view of history; and so the history in the Jesus of history comes into conflict with the history in the believer in Jesus. This Jesus believed that history ended in a kind of disaster, God bringing down new heaven and new earth; but this believer believes in progress. Can he really believe in the Jesus of history while rejecting the history of the Jesus of history? This was Schweitzer's problem." [Albert Schweitzer, *The Quest of the Historical Jesus: A Critical Study of Its Progress from Reimarus to Wrede*, trans. W. Montgomery (New York: Macmillan, 1961)].

2. Giuseppe Mazzini, *Life and Writings of Joseph Mazzini*, vol. 2, *Critical and Literary* (London: Smith, Elder, 1890), 23; Ludwig Feuerbach, *The Essence of Christianity*, trans. George Eliot, intro. by Karl Barth, fwd. by H. Richard Niebuhr (New York: Harper Torchbook, 1957), 7ff.; see idem, *Principles of the Philosophy of the Future*, trans. Manfred H. Vogel (Indianapolis: Hackett, 1986).

3. [HRN's note:] I am thinking here of Nicolai Hartmann's discussion of teleology and causality.

4. [HRN's note:] I speak vaguely about this rule of God as revealed in Jesus Christ because I only see it vaguely. I am only wanting to point to "something there," and that something there is the only source of meaning for life.

REINHOLD NIEBUHR'S INTREPRETATION OF HISTORY

Paper prepared for the "Theological Discussion Group in 1949."

1. *The Nature and Destiny of Man: A Christian Interpretation*, vol. 2, *Human Destiny* (New York: Scribner, 1943); *Faith and History: A Comparison of Christian and Modern Views of History* (New York: Scribner, 1949).

2. *Faith and History*, 18–20, 22ff.

3. *Human Destiny*, 36ff., 308.

4. Ibid., 1.

5. Ibid., 300; *Faith and History*, passim.

6. *Human Destiny*, 7ff.

7. Ibid., 257; *Faith and History*, ch. 12.

8. *Human Destiny*, 258–59.

9. *Faith and History*, 27.

10. Ibid.

11. Ibid., 229, 33.

12. Ibid., 48. Reinhold Niebuhr is quoting Erich Frank, *Philosophical Understanding and Religious Truth* (Oxford: Oxford University Press, 1945), 58.

13. See esp. *Human Destiny*, chs. 2 and 3.

14. *Faith and History*, 214ff.
15. *Human Destiny*, 76ff.
16. *The Nature and Destiny of Man*, vol. 1, *Human Nature* (New York: Scribner, 1941), ch. 10.
17. *Human Destiny*, ch. 10.
18. See *Faith and History*, 33 and passim.
19. Ibid., 129, 131, 132.

THEOLOGY IN A TIME OF DISILLUSIONMENT

Handwritten manuscript, Alumni Lecture, Yale Divinity School, 1931.
1. Theodore Dreiser, *An American Tragedy*, 2 vols. (New York: Boni & Liveright, 1925); Sinclair Lewis, *Main Street: The story of Carol Kennicott* (New York: Harcourt, Brace & Howe, 1920).
2. Lytton Strachey, *Eminent Victorians: Cardinal Manning, Florence Nightingale, Dr. Arnold, General Gordon* (New York, 1918); Edgar Lee Masters, *Lincoln: The Man* (New York: Dodd, Mead, 1931).
3. John Fiske, *Through Nature to God* (New York: Houghton, Mifflin, 1899), 53.
4. George A. Gordon, *Through Man to God* (Boston and New York: Houghton Mifflin, 1906), 140–41.
5. Source unknown.
6. Bertrand Russell, "The Free Man's Worship," in *Philosophical Essays* (London: Longmans Green, 1910). Originally published in 1903 in the *Independent Review*.
7. Vernon Louis Parrington, *Main Currents in American Thought: An Interpretation of American Literature from the Beginnings to 1920*, vol. 3, *The Beginnings of Critical Realism in America* (New York: Harcourt, Brace, 1930), xxviii.
8. Rudolf Otto, *The Idea of the Holy*, trans. John W. Harvey (London: Oxford University Press, 1923); Emil Brunner, *Philosophy of Religion*, trans. A. J. D. Farrer and Bertram Lee Woolf (New York: Scribner, 1937), 132.

THE KINGDOM OF GOD AND ESCHATOLOGY IN THE SOCIAL GOSPEL AND IN BARTHIANISM

Undated mimeograph prepared for the "Theological Discussion Group."
1. Walter Rauschenbusch, *A Theology for the Social Gospel* (New York: Macmillan, 1917), 131.
2. Ibid., 140, 142.
3. Ibid., 144.

THE ANACHRONISM OF JONATHAN EDWARDS

Handwritten manuscript of an address delivered in Northampton, Massachusetts, on March 9, 1958, to commemorate the bicentennial of the death of Jonathan Edwards.

1. Phyllis McGinley, "The Theology of Jonathan Edwards," *Harpers Magazine* (October 1957), 73. The rhyme runs on for five more verses.

2. Vernon Louis Parrington, *Main Currents in American Thought: An Interpretation of American Literature from the Beginnings to 1920*, vol. 1, *The Colonial Mind, 1620–1800*, (New York: Harcourt, Brace, 1927), 162, 152.

3. Ibid., 162–63.

4. Sermon preached July 8, 1741, in Enfield, Connecticut, "Sinners in the Hands of an Angry God," in Jonathan Edwards, *Works of President Edwards*, ed. Sereno E. Dwight, 10 vols. (New York: S. Converse, 1829–30), 7:163–77.

5. *Hamlet* II.ii. The passage concludes: "And yet, to me, what is this quintessence of dust? Man delights not me; no, nor woman neither, though by your smiling you seem to say so."

6. See "The will is always determined by the strongest motive"; "The will always is as the greatest apparent good is." Jonathan Edwards, *Freedom of the Will*, ed. Paul Ramsey, vol. 1 of *The Works of Jonathan Edwards*, ed. Harry Stout (New Haven: Yale University Press, 1957), 142.

7. The text of the sermon is in fact Deuteronomy 32:35, "Their foot shall slide in due time." However, Edwards immediately cites and also employs Psalm 73:18, "Surely thou didst set them in slippery places; thou castedst them down into destruction." HRN conflates the actual text and the first part of Psalm 73:18.

ADDRESS ON MARTIN BUBER'S EIGHTIETH BIRTHDAY

Transcription of an address delivered before American Friends of the Hebrew University on April 17, 1958, in New York.

THE RELATION OF CHRISTIANITY AND DEMOCRACY

Typescript of the Earl Lecture, Berkeley Divinity School, Berkeley, California, October 1940.

1. *Webster's Collegiate Dictionary*, 4th ed., Merriam Series (London: G. Bell & Sons,; Springfield, Mass.: G. & C. Merriam, 1932), 178.

2. [HRN's note:] The phrase "faith in the Father of Jesus Christ" is, of course, very inclusive, requiring considerable elaboration to make explicit its implicit meanings. In our connection it may be taken in one of two senses, as meaning either that a fatherly power is at work in all events and may be relied upon, or that the actual power, the determiner of destiny, evident in all events, is neither an inimical nor an indifferent but a saving force. When the latter approach is made our phrase may be taken to include the idea that reconciliation to the ruling power is accomplished by Jesus Christ.

3. Abraham Lincoln, Address at Gettysburg, November 19, 1863, *Collected Works of Abraham Lincoln*, ed. Roy P. Basler (New Brunswick, N.J.: Rutgers University Press, 1953), 7:21.

4. [HRN's note:] Faith and reason are related in politics as elsewhere: they are neither substitutes for each other nor partners co-operating on the same plane. Faith in the Father of Jesus Christ frees reason from its worship of idols,

including itself; reason acknowledge but does not supply faith in God. A faith that does not liberate is not trust in God but a belief about him; and a reason that does not rest in faith in God rests, explicitly or implicitly, on some other pre-rational confidence.

5. [HRN's note:] In the Christian church we often seek to trace directly to religious roots such elements in American political life as the separation of church and state, the Bill of Rights, etc. These doubtless have religious sources, but they are also the product of many other interests and forces. Perhaps we ought to think more of the empirical and rational sources of our Constitution and say that if it is wisely constructed, that is largely due to the disinterestedness and objectivity of the founders. They knew how limited a thing government is and were free to adopt reasonable measures appropriate to limited ends. Though religion often decries such objectivity, faith in God is its necessary presupposition. Disinterestedness is possible only where there is a great confidence in the universe or in its ruling principle.

6. James Madison, *A Memorial and Remonstrance* (1785), in *Sources of the Political Thought of James Madison*, rev. ed., ed. Marvin Meyers (Hanover, N.H.: University Press of New England, 1981), 7.

A CHRISTIAN INTERPRETATION OF WAR

Mimeographed document prepared by HRN for a commission of twenty-six scholars appointed during World War II by the Federal Council of the Churches of Christ in America. The commission, chaired by Professor Robert Lowry Calhoun of Yale University, was to report on the church in wartime. The commission's report appeared in *Social Action* in December 1944. HRN's mimeograph bears the handwritten date, "1943."

THE IDEA OF ORIGINAL SIN IN AMERICAN CULTURE

Handwritten manuscript, identified with the notation "Princeton University/ Program of Studies in American Civilization, February 24, 1949."

1. See Parrington, *Main Currents in American Thought: An Interpretation of American Literature from the Beginnings to 1920*, vol. 1, *The Colonial Mind, 1620–1800* (New York: Harcourt, Brace, 1927).

2. Arthur M. Schlesinger Jr., *Age of Jackson* (Boston: Little, Brown, 1945).

3. Ralph H. Gabriel, *The Course of American Democratic Thought* (New York: Ronald Press, 1940), 37f.

4. Ibid., chs. 15, 16.

5. See, e.g., Perry Miller and Thomas Johnson, *The Puritans*, ed. George McCandlish (New York: Harper & Row, 1963); and William Haller, *The Rise of Puritanism, or The way to the new Jerusalem as set forth in pulpit and press from Thomas Cartwright to John Lilburne and John Milton, 1570–1643* (New York: Columbia University Press, 1938).

6. Gilbert H. Barnes, *The Antislavery Impulse, 1830–1844* (New York: D. Appleton-Century, 1933).

7. The Thirty-nine Articles of the Church of England, Art. IX, "Of Original

or Birth-Sin." The language used here is taken from the American Revision of 1801. See *The Creeds of Christendom with a History and Critical Notes*, ed. Philip Schaff, 3 vols. (New York: Harper & Brothers, 1919), 3:492–93.

8. The Westminster Confession of Faith, Chapter VI, par. IV. See Schaff, *Creeds*, 3:615.

9. *Hamlet*, II.ii. 304–10.

10. Ibid., III.i. 125–30.

11. Thirty-nine Articles, Art. IX; Westminster Confession, Chapter VI, par. V. The Savoy Declaration, no. 1658 ("A Declaration of the Faith and Order Owned and practised in the Congregational Churches in England"), uses the same language as the Westminster Confession.

12. Roger Williams, *The Bloudy Tenent of Persecution, For Cause of Conscience Discussed: And Mr. Cotton's Letter Examined and Answered*, ed. Edward Bean Underhill (London: J. Haddon, 1848), 97.

13. Robert Barclay, *An Apology for The True Christian Divinity Being an Explanation and Vindication of the Principles and Doctrines of the People Called Quakers* (Philadelphia: Friends' Book-Store, 1908), Prop. IV, 97.

14. Jonathan Edwards, *Original Sin*, ed. Clyde A. Holbrook, vol. 3 of *The Works of Jonathan Edwards*, ed. Harry Stout (New Haven: Yale University Press, 1970).

15. John Wesley, *The Doctrine of Original Sin According to Scripture, Reason, and Experience* (1757), in *The Works of John Wesley*, ed. Thomas Watson, 14 vols., 3d ed. (London, 1872), 9:194.

16. John Wesley, sermon, "Original Sin" (1759), in *The Works of John Wesley*, vol. 2, *Sermons II*, ed. Albert C. Outler (Nashville: Abingdon Press, 1985), 183–84.

17. See Theodore Spencer, *Shakespeare and the Nature of Man*, Lowell Lectures (1942), 2d ed. (New York: Collier, 1949), esp. ch. 4.

18. Alexander Hamilton, John Jay, and James Madison, *The Federalist or The New Constitution*, Everyman's Library (London: J. M. Dent; New York: E. P. Dutton, 1929), No. 6, pp. 20, 22, 25.

19. John Adams, *The Works of John Adams, second president of the United States: With a life of the author, notes and illustrations by his grandson Charles Francis Adams*, 10 vols. (Boston: Little, Brown, 1850–1856), 4:408.

20. Timothy Dwight, *Theology Explained and Defended: A Series of Sermons, with a Memoir of the Life of the Author*, 5 vols. (London: William Baynes, 1822), Sermon 33, 2:16–35.

21. Madison to Jefferson, from New York, October 17, 1788, in *The Papers of James Madison*, vol. 11, *7 March 1788–1 March 1789*, ed. Robert A. Rutland, Charles F. Hobson, et al. (Charlottesville: University Press of Virginia, 1977), 298.

22. *The Federalist*, 44–45, 55.

23. James Bryce, *The American Commonwealth*, vol. 1, *The National Government—The State Governments* (New York: Macmillan, 1913), 306–7.

24. John Cotton, *The End of the World*, A Library of American Puritan Writings, ed. Sacvan Bercovitch, vol. 14 (New York: AMS Press, 1982), chs. 13, 71, 72.

25. Madison to Jefferson, October 17, 1788, in *The Papers of James Madison,* 11: 299.

26. Abraham Lincoln, Address at Gettysburg, November 19, 1863, *Collected Works of Abraham Lincoln,* ed. Roy P. Basler (New Brunswick, N.J.: Rutgers University Press, 1953), 7:21.

27. Madison to Jefferson, October 17, 1788, in *The Papers of James Madison,* 11: 298, 300.

OUR REVERENT DOUBT AND THE AUTHORITY OF CHRIST

Typescript, anniversary sermon, Yale Divinity School, June 6, 1948.

THE LOGIC OF THE CROSS

Undated typescript of a sermon.

MAN'S WORK AND GOD'S

Undated typescript of a sermon.

1. The translation is HRN's own, apparently working from the RSV as a starting point.

2. C. Gray, *A Survey of Contemporary Music* (London: Oxford University Press, 1938).

3. Rudyard Kipling, "Recessional," in *Best Loved Religious Poems: Gleaned from Many Sources,* ed. James Gilchrist Lawson (New York: Fleming H. Revell, 1963), 37.

4. Percy Bysshe Shelley, "Ozymandias," in *Norton Anthology of Poetry,* ed. Arthur M. Eastman (New York: Norton, 1970), 287.

5. John Masefield, *The Everlasting Mercy* (New York: Macmillan, 1917), 54.

6. Lord David Cecil, ed., *The Oxford Book of Christian Verse* (Oxford: Clarendon Press, 1940), xi–xiii.

Index

Index